Polpop

Polpop:

Politics and Popular Culture in America

James Combs

Bowling Green University Popular Press
Bowling Green, Ohio 43403

Contents

To Two Fathers
Cecil Combs
and
Bert Rasnick

Preface

In his preface to *The Discourses,* Machiavelli admitted that his study was "as dangerous almost as the exploration of unknown seas and continents" but that he had nevertheless "resolved to open a new route" for the "common benefit of all". Now I know how he felt. For this book attempts to navigate a rather misty sea and chart a tangled jungle of a continent. It tries to explore, and make some sense out of, the relationship between popular culture and politics. The author has studied popular culture for several years now, and has concluded that popular culture is a pervasive influence in American life, even though this influence is often subtle and unrecognized. This conviction determined the exploration, but did not make the voyage any easier.

In any case, the book tries to utilize some concepts which will give the reader a map of the new continent. The point of the book is to educate, to alert the reader as to the extent to which he or she is a creature of popular culture too. It ranges over different aspects of popular culture, pointing to the political messages overtly or covertly contained therein. Mass experience with popular culture then translates into something with political consequences. Armed with our rough map of this new continent, the reader—and the researcher—may be able to identify in more detail the contours of this new terrain.

The points on the map may also be new to the reader—play, myth, the American Dream. But these ideas are really quite simple. The book takes the position that popular culture is important politically because we play with it, and by doing so, learn from it. Popular culture involves playing with myths, cultural stories which give symbolic "flesh" to what we believe and how we act. The central myth of American culture is what is called the American Dream, a complex set of symbols and stories about what America

1

means and what her destiny is. Professor Walter R. Fisher of the University of Southern California has made a useful distinction between the "moralistic" and "materialistic" components of the American Dream, and we utilize that distinction herein. The use of such concepts is to interpret popular culture, to classify and explain the popular flora and fauna we encounter on our quest.

The book is by necessity interdisciplinary, and may be of use to readers interested in not only politics, but also mass communication, sociology, American culture and history, and of course popular culture. It is written in a style that tries to be clear and simple for the undergraduate reader, yet deal with fairly complex interpretations. The book also includes extensive bibliography for the reader's use and an appendix recommending research topics and class projects. Popular culture is, after all, easily available, and is convenient for students to analyze. Instructors will find, I believe, that many students enjoy studying popular culture, and quickly become critically aware of the popular sea in which they swim.

Thanks are due to several people who contributed to this project. Mickey Sego of King's Court was a cooperative editor who didn't harass or interfere in any way, and that contributed much to my peace of mind, disposition, and probably the quality of the book. Thanks are due Vice-President Baepler of Valparaiso University, who came up with funds at the right moments. Indeed, this project began on a University Research Professorship at VU in 1979-80, and so the school had much to do with the genesis and the completion of the work. Carol Lewis did an admirable job of typing the manuscript under difficult circumstances, and indeed made many needed corrections of tense, syntax, and the like. Patty Giannis did an excellent job of proofing the rough copy, and gave her delicate grasp of English prose to the book. Debbie Stride aided helpfully in researching different topics treated in the book. Other colleagues, such as Dan Nimmo and Al Trost, provided suggestions that helped. The help of all these people is much appreciated. For those whose contribution was negative, I will simply maintain a disrespectful and eternal silence.

Chapter One
Popular Culture and American Politics

It is the aim of education to make people self-aware. Thus, a book used for educational purposes should in some sense contribute to making the reader a bit more aware of himself. If you take away from this book a larger view of how modern culture and politics affects our lives, the book will have succeeded. What I want to do — as entertainingly as possible — is to direct your attention to popular culture, and to point out to you the extent that the modern cultural phenomenon relates to politics. Popular culture is something we take for granted, and rarely do we think of it as "political." I contend that popular culture is quite political in some deep and "subtle" ways. Simply put, I think popular culture both shapes and reflects our ideas, therefore affecting our perceptions and actions about politics. But this contention will take a bit of proving. To that end, let me ask the reader some questions that will help our inquiry.

What do you know?
You may think this is a silly question. (Don't I know what I know?) But, as professors are always telling you, things are not that simple. Knowing is a complicated process. Where we get and how we use the jumble of thoughts that run through our heads remains difficult to pin down. We get ideas and images about the world from various experiences throughout our lives. We are conscious. We have our own personal biography, our own life. We "identify" ourselves by name, affiliation, and experience. We have values, beliefs, attitudes, opinions, and images of the world. We think — although we are never totally sure — that all these ideas have some validity. We all believe we are "right" somehow. Yet, has it ever occurred to you that most of what you know you got from the world *outside* of your head? Somebody else gave you your ideas and images about the

3

world. Thus, what you know is dependent on what you pick up from the world *outside* your head.

There is something else you might reflect on. Since we are limited by being human, we have to use our imagination to extend our knowledge of the world. That is, you and I imagine what the world of economics or politics or Soviet Russia is like by using the ideas and images we have of those worlds. This we might term "psycho-logic." We want to make sense out of the world beyond our senses, so we use the fund of ideas and images in our head to imagine what those worlds "out there" are like. We do not directly experience the world of international politics; we "know" about it through using the pictures in our heads to imagine what it is like, what is going on.

Since it is possible that the knowledge other people provide us might be wrong, and our imagined worlds may not correspond with the real world, this should then remind us that our sure and certain knowledge may not be so accurate. And that's not all.

What do you know about yourself?

Reflect on this. You think you "know yourself." I exist; I occupy a point in time and space; I know who I am, what I think. In other words, you have an identity. Yet, this identity is hard to pin down. Are you the same self you were when you started reading this book, or as you were ten years ago? The same problems mentioned above apply. For one thing, a good bit of our self is social; that is, we are what we are because of what other people have told us we are. We must also remember that our identity changes over time. What we know about ourselves now is not what we knew ten years ago. Not only do we learn about the world, we also learn about ourselves. Such learning changes us. And, of course, we not only imagine what the world is like, we imagine what ourselves are like. Using the ideas and images we have acquired, we give ourselves definition. Our "self-image" is what we think about ourselves. We "identify" ourselves, using the fund of knowledge we have acquired. Thus, an identity is formed and changed through the dynamic process of what the world has told us about us, combined with how we use that knowledge to think about ourselves.

What do you know about the world?

It follows that our knowledge about the world outside is personal. Simply, what we know is mediated by the fact that we are what we are. We have a changing self, seek to cope in the world, use knowledge for a variety of psychological purposes, relate to other people, and attempt to figure out what's going on. Yet, for a variety of reasons, the knowledge we seek and use about the world is not systematic. We do not have the time to gather enough knowledge about the world, for the world is too big and complicated for that anyway. So we just try to use the most convenient sources of learning we can — past experience, scraps of information, and imagery. In other words, we use whatever sources we trust. These sources are various — family, friends, co-workers, and the mass media to cite a few examples. But remember: their image of the world suffers from the same limitations as ours. They might tell us that such-and-such is so when in fact it isn't!

What do you know about the political world?

What, indeed? The political world is one of those worlds outside of our immediate experience. But we still seek and use knowledge about it. We talk about it, are taught about it in school, and see television news about it. But politics is complicated, changing, and confusing. Even political scientists who study it all their lives do not fully understand it. So we seek out "reliable sources." We rely on a mish-mash of ideas and images which give the political world form, and political situations meaning. As we face each new political event, we put it into the context of those ideas and images, imagining the new event to conform to our expectations about the political world as a whole. Thus, what we think about the political world does not necessarily reflect reality. Instead, it often reflects the past and present ideas and images that have helped to create our personal and political identity.

What do you know about yourself as a citizen?

Our self-image includes knowledge about the social roles we play, or would like to play. We all play roles such as student, son, daughter, basketball player, husband, or wife. But our society also has created a political role called "citizen." Most of us do not reflect much on this role. We tend to play it only infrequently. We vote, follow election campaigns, and perhaps feel some slight obligation to "take an interest" in public affairs. Yet, most people's political identity probably remains ill defined. What is your political self-image? In any case, remember that whatever we think about ourselves as citizens derives from cues we pick up from others and how we define the importance of the citizen role in our lives.

Where do you learn all this?

We learn — and unlearn — throughout our lives. We begin

learning about ourselves and the world in childhood and keep trying to understand it until death. Much of learning is consciously sought and taught, but a lot more is unconsciously picked up. We learn much about ourselves and the world as kids from our parents and other significant people in our lives. Our parents help define our political identity, and how important politics and the citizen role is for our lives. We also learn quite a bit at school about the world from teachers, books, maps, and so on. We learn about the world from our friends and co-workers.

But we also learn in lots of other ways from lots of other sources. And that is the point of this exercise. As cultural beings, we acquire and use knowledge from many sources and in a wide variety of ways. "Culture" does not only include family, school, work life, and friends. It includes a vast world, remote from our immediate experience, in which we participate every day in one way or another. This is the world of social *play*. It is our basic contention here that you and I learn a great deal about ourselves and the world from the play-worlds in which we participate.

What do we mean by play-worlds? Well, not all of life is formal work. We learn a lot directly through our families and are taught things in school. We learn how to do a job and learn something of the responsibilities of adulthood and the world of work. But not all of life is work, nor is it serious. We have leisure time in which we engage in play — sports, television, music, casual talk, reading, dating, and so on. We participate in these activities for the pure hell of it, just for fun. In such activities, be they something as stressful and dangerous as mountain climbing or something as quiet as reading poetry, we "play around," not for its work-value but for its play-value. We enjoy it. We have chosen it. It gives us pleasure. It is play.

Now the reader, being smart, knows what the author is getting at. We are "surrounded" by play-worlds, and the sum of these arenas of play is what we loosely term as American "popular culture." Popular culture has been given many definitions, but we are most familiar with it as an activity of play — the movies, television, sports, popular music, newspapers — in which significant segments of the popular takes part. It is "popular" to play or watch sports; television shows are part of popular "culture" of the country. But popular culture is even more inclusive than that, including things that were popular in the past, other things which are popular to groups of people you do not know, and things that will become popular in the future. People always have and always will play with popular creations. Their past play as well as their present play affects them as does the play of the groups they identify with. In short, folks are constantly attracted to new popular objects that affect their perspectives.

Many believe that because play is "frivolous," it has no impact on us. Such a belief is wrong. Popular culture is so much a part of our lives that we cannot deny its developmental powers. Since we spend so much time and energy on it, we cannot escape its socializing and politicizing effects. Like formal education or family rearing, popular culture is part of our "learning environment." Hence, popular culture stands as a major tool that molds our ideas and images about the world. Though our pop culture education is informal — we usually do not attend to pop culture for its "educational" value — it nevertheless provides us with information and images upon which we develop our opinions and attitudes. We would not be quite what we are, nor would our society be quite the same, without the impact of popular culture. Nor, for that matter, would American politics.

What do you learn from popular culture?

Now we get to the hard part. It is one thing to assert that we learn from popular culture; it is another to pin down exactly what we learn. For such learning is subtle, complex, mostly "unconscious," and longterm. Though we are exposed to enormous amounts of popular materials, it is difficult to ascertain which or how much influences us. Statistics state that the average American child has witnessed 13,000 murders on television by the time he is fourteen, but this does not mean that every child will become a murderer because of this exposure. There are simply too many other sources of learning that influence us. Furthermore, we forget much of the popular culture we experience. Yet, the large amount we do not forget remains part of the fund of knowledge that we bring to the world in our efforts to understand it and cope with it. This fund, whether we are conscious of it or not, helps us to form our identities and choose our actions in both our personal lives and politics.

What do you do with this popular learning?

Thus, popular culture is a resource, something present in our lives from which we can learn things that help us to make sense out of ourselves and the world. In the broadest terms, popular culture helps to give form and content to our *images*. We imagine what we are like and what the world is like. We see ourselves in roles, we make plans to act, and we give structure to the world beyond our immediate environment. Our imagination is enriched — given form and content — from a variety of sources, not the least of which is popular culture. We use popular culture as a source of imaginative ideas — cues, if you will — that help us to understand and act. Consider a typical situation. Thinking and acting are not separate processes, but occur together as part of our daily coping strategies. Consider how we commonly face the day. We get up imagining what the day will be like and what we will have to do to get through it. You have a test, have to give an oral presentation, have a date, must write home. We imagine what it will be like, make plans to deal with it, and then actually go out and act in it. At night, we drift off to sleep reflecting on how well we did, or what we might have done differently.

In other words, we all "script" our lives, seeing ourselves as if we were in a social drama. Through the use of our self-image, we imagine ourselves in roles, rehearse for them, actually perform them, and critique our own performance. We see others in their roles, and communicate with them in the drama of everyday life. We use our fund of knowledge to inform our actions in this drama. What we have learned from popular culture is part of that fund. Since we constantly live in the "presence" of popular culture, we cannot help but use popular culture to help us know and act in the social drama. We have to "play" in the world of real action, and we use the "play" of popular culture to help us "play" in our everyday dramas.

An example

Still not convinced? Think again on how much popular culture is a part of our lives. We hum the tunes of popular music, read the comics, or talk about the news or last night's episode of a popular television program. We can identify a wide variety of celebrities, remember many movies, and so on. This wide exposure affects not only our consciousness, but also our actions. When we play softball, we take on the mannerisms of famous major leaguers. We take up fads — dress, dances, games, speech, products, etc. — that incorporate popular creations into our everyday lives.

We must realize, however, that the significance of popular culture goes beyond the "surface manifestations" of popular play. Our imaginative pictures of our world, our plans, our role-playing — indeed, our whole lives — are deeply affected by popular culture. Simply, we are arguing a variation of the old saw that life imitates art. More specifically, we are contending that life uses art and makes it a part of our lives that serves as a resource for coping with everyday existence.

Take the soap opera. Many millions of Americans watch the daytime soaps. Nighttime variants — such as *Dallas* — have a mass worldwide following. The appeal of soaps has been variously explained — that they are "filler" in the mundane life of the housewife, student, and lunchtime crowd; that they are diverting fantasy for a lot of lonely and frustrated people; that they reassure people that things they believe in still win out and evil is punished. It is likely that people "get out" of soaps a wide variety of messages. Let us remember that the soaps are a classic example of popular play. People converge on the soaps as an audience for a range of reasons, not the least of which is they are just plain fun to watch! But the diversity of reasons as to why people are drawn to the soaps does not lessen their effect, however dimly conscious we may be of it.

The soaps are what we might call a *symbolic reality,* an imaginary world that we "occupy" only in our minds. The social drama in the soap is a "heightened" world, wherein we can identify the characters and conflicts that in one way or another we see, or expect to see, in ordinary life. In this sense, the soaps provide us with a source of learning. By playing with the soap play, we learn something about how people act, how we can act, and what we can do when we are faced with similar situations. As a pop-dramatic form, the soap helps us to understand our own dramas. The soaps in subtle ways help us "identify" ourselves and the nature of the world we must act in.

Let us take one of the best understood ways in which this process works: role modeling. Since we are looking for cues as to how to play roles in the world, and what to expect from other people playing roles that we identify, we seek our role models that help us to "flesh out" what it is like to play a certain role. We may model our own behavior in the role of say, student by emulating "significant others" who give us cues as to how we should act. For instance, our parents, an uncle, a senior student, or perhaps some mythical conception of a "good offspring." When we act, we have in mind people, real or imagined, who give us cues as to how to act in that particular role. Such emulation most probably is as old as man himself. In the contemporary world, role models spring from the world of popular culture. We gain "advice" on what to do from such figures and include it in our "script." We get ideas of what might be done to us by role models other than those with which we identify. From the soaps, we might identify a conflict in our lives with our parents, and sympathize much with a son or daughter as a positive role model, and also see a domineering father as a negative role model. In any case, the dramatized conflict may impress us as relevant to our lives, and in subtle ways affect both our perception of our own real conflict and our conduct in it. As we employ these role models in our own behavior patterns, the symbolic reality of the soaps finds use in the "real" reality of our lives.

The quest for competence

Our argument, then, is really quite simple and unmysterious. We all are trying to cope in a complex and changing world, and seek ways in which to understand ourselves and the world. To give it a word, we all more or less seek to be *competent* — in work, friendships, love, or whatever involves acting in a role. "Self-competence" means that we can deal with ourselves; "social competence" means that we can act effectively in our relations with the world. We use the stock of images we have, part of which are drawn from our pop culture fund, in our coping strategies with ourselves and the world. What we learn in the playing with popular culture contributes to our attempt to identify ourselves as competent. A role model is used by us as a way of self-identity and identifying how to act. Such "lessons" gained from popular culture mean that it is not just fun, diversion, or harmless escapism, but rather something that has pragmatic uses in our efforts to get along with ourselves and the world. Consequently, the "lessons" learned from popular culture are used in our quest for political competence.

What do you learn about politics from popular culture?

Since that is what this book is about, clearly we are going to say: Many things! But in general — sticking to our guns here — what we learn from popular culture about politics is knowledge about our political selves and the world. The play-worlds of popular culture give us ideas and images about politics that we find use for in our effort to understand something of our "political selves" and the nature of the political world "out there." We try to imagine ourselves as possessing a self-created political identity. We want to believe that our political self has enough form and content to allow us to competently play the political role of "citizen" and at least understand political roles such as Senator or President. We want to understand with competence the characteristics of the political world beyond our own lives, and use sources of knowledge to try to imagine what it is like.

Thus, the play-world of popular culture is part of what political scientists call our *political socialization,* the process by which we acquire ideas and images about our political selves and the political world. We may have learned many things about politics while we grew up from our parents, teachers, and friends. But this was supplemented, even supplanted, by what we learned from seeing popular news accounts, watching television shows, hearing music, reading pop books and comics, and so on. What we come to think about our American political past, present, and future derives from the totality of the jumble of messages that have impressed us and which we use. We do not pretend to understand exactly how this process works, but we do assert that the importance of popular culture in our socialization to politics is increasingly growing in power and importance.

The power of popular culture to teach us rests only partially in its omnipresence and constant call for attention. Most of the power and effectiveness of popular culture lies in its ability to dramatize so impressively messages that we can retain and use in our lives. For this reason, it comes as no shock to contemporary parents or teachers that popular culture has a powerful and sometimes pervasive effect over the attitudes and actions of young people today. And actually, why should we expect anything else? Popular culture is usually more interesting than the forms of school or parental socialization. Popular culture has drama — color, characters, plots, and excitement; it transports us into an imaginative world beyond the mundane. In short, it gives us a sense of participation in a world beyond parents and school and helps us to identify with that world beyond with a power that rivals even the primal bonds of family or the repetitious grind of school lessons.

Let us pursue this a bit. Think of what we learn about politics from our family — very early and primitive messages about what politics and government are, who the leading actors are (the President as the leading role), who we identify with (Republicans, Democrats, or whatever), what goes on in that mysterious world out there, who the Good Guys and Bad Guys are. School has us salute the flag and say the pledge of allegiance; teaches us American history, usually from our side of things; and introduces us to patriotic pageants and rituals. We also pick up bits and pieces about politics from other sources, such as friends.

But popular culture is always there, and there are presentations of or allusions to politics. The news shows us a dramatic world of action and conflict, of Big People doing Big Things in remote places. We recognize show biz personalities such as rock singers at rallies for candidates. We see the dramatization of politics on a favorite television show. We read political thrillers. And so on. All these play-activities give us ideas and images about the political world and our own role — active or passive — in it. They enrich our fantastic image of politics through the dramatization of a symbolic reality that we can imagine through the media of popular culture.

However, popular culture is not necessarily in conflict with other agencies of socialization. Indeed, it may be quite supportive of what we have learned about politics from family and teacher. There are, of course, great pressures on popular culture creators to support valued political symbols. For example, many people want popular culture to depict their country's past as heroic and in the right in wars. Too, we may seek out or only retain those messages from popular culture that support what we have already learned from family and school. We often want to believe what we already believe, and tend to ignore or forget messages that threaten these held beliefs. If we have a choice of going to the movies, we might go to the movie we think will reinforce that which we already believe. If we watch a news show, we may only remember — and later use — those stories which dramatize what we want to believe about the world.

On the other hand, our political learning might be quite incomplete or inadequate from school and family. In that case, other sources come into play, for we desire to discover something about the political world which makes us at least understand it so that we can achieve a bit of self-competence about it. How much time did your family spend on political learning? Probably not much. How much time did you spend learning to be a "citizen" in the grades and high school? Most probably, very little. Since many Americans do not receive much overt political socialization, they seek out cues from other sources about what it means to me and what it's like. Since popular culture is an ubiquitous and powerful source of all sorts of messages about the world, it seems to follow that all of us ill-socialized people, desiring to understand an important part of our lives, seek out and use messages from popular culture that tell us something about politics.

The soaps are a good example again. The soaps are not primarily political, but they do employ political elements in their story lines. On election day or the 4th of July, some trusted figure on the show might talk about the "citizen's responsibility," in a manner that might reinforce things we have heard before. Soaps might depict a story that gives us two conflicting messages about politics: on the one hand, a handsome and "good guy" lawyer may run for D.A.; on the other, he may be opposed by a crooked and sinister "bad guy" opponent. If we prefer to believe that politics is generally good and reformable, we would rather watch — and identify with — the good guy; if we believe that politics is inherently corrupt, then we may at least understand the role of the bad guy, and think the good guy crazy for getting into such a mess. Depending upon whatever belief we bring to the show, we may later "remember" only those images from the story that reinforce our belief. But if our beliefs about politics are relatively unformed — and uninformed — then popular culture might serve as *primary* socialization, making an impression on us because of the dramatic quality of the story or image we have seen. The soap is obviously not designed for that purpose, but rather to entertain a mass audience. But through the play of entertainment, people pick up messages that they use for coping strategies in many areas of everyday life, including politics.

Let us state the negative to illustrate. Suppose that all you had learned about politics and government (or for that matter, any other area of life, such as economics or religion) was from family and school. You were shut off from any exposure to popular culture all your life — no television, radio, movies, newspapers, popular magazines, records, advertising, sports, pop religion. You heard nothing about the American past through popular culture. Indeed, you heard nothing about the American present or future. Remember: that means no news broadcasts, no morning paper, no *Time* magazine, no political ads, no rock 'n roll, no nothin'. Do you have any doubts that you would be a very different person? Do you doubt that your knowledge of, and attitude toward, politics and government is likely to be very different?

Such a "thought experiment" should convince us that popular culture is indeed central to our lives. It does help shape our social identities. It does help us learn to play roles. It does tell us much of what we come to believe the world is like. It does help to define our likes and dislikes, cultural preferences, and social prejudices. And without doubt, it does help us to construct a "political self." It does aid us in our desire to be self-competent, and at some minimal level, politically self-confident. Much of what we know about the political world, and how we act toward it, is influenced — sometimes heavily so — by what we have learned from popular culture.

What are the political consequences of such a phenomenon?

That, dear reader, we shall return to in the last chapter. You cannot expect me to give away all my good lines at the start! But we can say this: If popular culture is a major source of political learning, then it does suggest several Good Questions, indeed the kind of questions that inspired this book. Perhaps the most obvious question is this: If popular culture is such an important part of our lives, and such a big source of our political knowledge, then why haven't political scientists studied it? That one is tough to answer. In a review of a major and massive study of American political communication and public opinion, the reviewers noted this shortcoming in the text:

> One of the curious omissions in this otherwise comprehensive text involves political implications of mass media "entertainment." Despite the existence of relevant theory and research and growing interest in this area, Nimmo [the author] fails to cover movies, comic books, sound recordings, prime time television drama, and other aspects of informal political culture . . .[1]

It is those "aspects of informal political culture" that are the subject matter of this book. In an effort to explore the politicizing power of American pop culture, we shall explore the many consequences of popular culture on our attitudes and identities. The reader should have already gotten the idea that one of the reasons we are what we are — including our political being — is because of popular culture. In other words, we are exploring the linkages between popular culture and political culture.

What, pray, is political culture?

When we speak of "the culture" of a people, we include about everything, noting the distinctive way they think and act as opposed to other peoples. The Japanese, the Russians, the Germans, and so on, simply do things differently than we. The sum of the distinctive things they — or we — do is usually termed "culture." Culture is both in our heads and observable in society. Our distinctive way of doing things is manifest in both what we think and how we act. This means that culture includes our "psychological orientations" toward things and the way things are organized and done. Thus, our distinctive attitudes toward religion, economics, and politics transacts with the organized way religion, economics, and politics are conducted in society. The way Americans worship, work, and politick is their cultural way of doing things, however strange it may seem to people from other countries.

We acquire culture through socialization, including, of course, our ideas about popular culture. We "carry" culture and use it our entire lives; indeed, we are the "mediators" of culture. By using it to adapt to changing circumstances, we change it in the process, although often in very subtle ways. By adapting to and using new forms of popular culture, we have in effect helped to change culture. New dances, new music, new movie and book formulas, the entire congeries of popular culture both reflect change in culture and help to shape it. When, for example, women became more prominent in rock music after the 1960s, it reflected cultural changes in the status of women, and, by women singing of their new status, helped to further the change (and the reaction to it). But culture both changes and does not change — it is like a seamless loom of interconnected strands in which the past, present, and the future are all connected by meshed cultural connections.

The various parts of a culture are connected in subtle ways. The "subcultures" of a culture participate in the larger culture, but yet are distinguishable from it. Popular culture is distinguishable from high culture. One can tell the difference in atmosphere between a first-night opening of a metropolitan opera and a rock concert in a ballpark. Similarly, the economic culture or religious culture is distinguishable from the political culture. One may study these subcultures and the relationships between them. American religion, for example, both affects and is affected by the ideology and the practice of capitalism. Change in one subculture brings conflict, reaction, and change from another. Changes in popular culture, for example, often upset religious institutions. The various forms of popular music that have succeeded each other in this century — ragtime, jazz, swing, bebop, the various kinds of rock — have all inspired reactions from those concerned with the morals of the young.

It is, of course, the relationship between popular culture and political culture with which this book is concerned. Popular culture is a pervasive, changing, and complex force in American culture, and its relationship to American political culture has not been explored sufficiently. Popular culture includes the distinctive ways we Americans play, that is, how we think and act toward popular objects — sports, religion, show biz, and other forms of popular entertainment. Political culture also includes the distinctive ways we Americans play with politics, that is, how we think and act toward political objects. If politics is play for most people, as we shall argue it is, then this may mean that the way we think and act toward popular culture in general may have powerful, if covert, effects on the way we think and act toward our political culture.

Political culture involves the widely shared orientations of people toward themselves as a political self and the politics and government of their country. These orientations are developed via socialization, but are used, retained, and changed as we live our lives. We play with politics as it unfolds for us through the mass media and popular talk about it. Our play with it helps give political culture both its continuity and changeability. We play with it in our daily "civic lives" when politics crosses our minds. Since it is play, then it seems logical to assume that we may use it and evaluate it in the same terms that we do other areas of popular culture. If that is the case, then the relationship between political culture and popular culture may be more powerful than has hitherto been thought.

As Americans, we are all both popular creatures and political creatures. We have to come to terms with — to cope with — these worlds. If, as we claim, much of our political identity and our image of the political world is drawn from popular culture, then it behooves us to understand this influence. Understanding this will include understanding both politics *in* popular culture and politics *as* popular culture. In the former case, we will look at how politics is treated in popular culture — in the news, in shows, in sports, and so on. We will also, however, look at politics as a popular phenomenon, at what it means for politics to be conducted in a popular culture. Our argument will be that politics in such a society is a part of popular culture, and is subject to the "logic" of popular culture.

A mirror and a lamp

To use a mixed metaphor, popular culture is for us both a mirror and a lamp. If our aim here is self-education — to make the reader more aware of himself — then clearly we want to teach the reader how to "read" popular culture as a mirror, albeit an ambiguous one. What does popular culture reflect about society and politics? What do we see in popular culture that tells us about popular images of politics? To understand the popular culture we use to understand politics gives us an idea as to what masses of people might well believe about politics. In that way, popular culture is a major source of evidence as to the popular mind, since it in some sense reflects what people think about politics at a particular time. And since we are all part of that popular mind, then it may tell us something about our own picture of politics.

But popular culture is also a lamp. It not only reflects something of the American popular mind, it also illuminates our picture of political reality, and by doing so, enriches and changes it. The popular imagery of popular culture gives us clues as to how to think and act toward the world, including politics. Popular culture is not only created, it is played with by audiences. Their use of it includes their interpretations of politics. We do not just see ourselves in a social mirror after the fact; popular culture is not just an archeological artifact of what another time and place were like. Rather, by learning from popular culture, we are provided with a light to use in understanding and acting in the future. Popular culture may distort the future as much as the past, but it is nevertheless one of the signposts we use to guide us into the future. We utilize popular culture to understand the past, the present, and the future.[2]

What is to follow

In this introductory chapter, we have tried to show how that popular culture is related to politics through what individuals — you and I — do with the popular objects that we encounter in everyday life. When we ask, what is going on when we play with popular culture, we must answer that play is quite consequential. Play has not only cultural meanings, it has cultural consequences — including political cultural meanings and consequences. We will point to this theme again and again in the substantive chapters that follow.

To that end, this is how we will proceed. Part One will deal with American Popular Dramas and their relationship to Politics. We will look at arenas of popular play in which we participate — either actively or passively — and from which we learn something about politics. These are:

First, the political uses of the popular past myths, legends, and heroes for the present and future.

Second, the Western myth in particular and its consequences for American politics.

Third, the relationship between popular sports and politics.

Fourth, popular religion and politics.

Part Two will look at the various aspects of Popular Media in America and its relation to the Drama of American Politics. Here we will in turn look at:

First, the depiction and reporting of American politics by the popular media.

Second, the uses of the popular art of American political propaganda.

Third, the relationship between Show Business and politics.

Fourth, the vision of the political future in Popular Culture, especially Science Fiction.

Finally, we want to draw some conclusions about the role and impact of popular culture on American politics, returning to some of the themes we introduced in this chapter.

The thrust of this chapter has been to get the reader to see himself both as a popular and political being. If, by the end of the book, the reader is more self-aware of these aspects of his or her American identity, the book will have succeeded. After all, the book is about us, since we are the people who make American popular culture and politics.

Notes

[1] Dennis Davis and Marilyn Jackson-Beeck, "Review of *Political Communication and Public Opinion in America* by Dan Nimmo," *Political Communication Review,* Vol. 3, no. 2 (Fall 1978), pp. 22-24.

[2] This introductory chapter has been informed by ideas from a wide variety of sources. I will point to works that were influential in the argument made in Chapter One, and also works that the interested students might want to use to extend and deepen their knowledge of popular culture.

If one wants to look at some works for a general knowledge of popular culture, I recommend: Robert Jewett and John Shelton Lawrence, *The American Monomyth* (Doubleday Anchor, 1977); Frank McConnell, *Storytelling and Mythmaking: Images from Film and Literature* (Oxford U.P., 1979); David Altheide and Robert P. Snow, *Media Logic* (Sage, 1979); Michael R. Real, *Mass-Mediated Culture* (Prentice-Hall, 1977); and John Cawelti, *Adventure, Mystery, and Romance* (University of Chicago P., 1976). See also two illuminating collections, Jack Nachbar, et. al., *The Popular Culture Reader* (Bowling Green U. Popular Press, 1978) and John E. O'Connor and Martin A. Jackson (eds.), *American History/American Film* (Frederick Ungar, 1979).

The philosophical roots of the perspective adopted in this book is drawn from such seminal modern thinkers and Kenneth Burke, George Herbert Mead, and Ernst Cassirer. For Burke, see the interpretation of his work by Hugh D. Duncan, *Communications and Social Order* (Bedminster Press, 1962) and *Symbols in Society* (Oxford U.P., 1968). See also the collection in James Combs and Michael Mansfield (eds.) *Drama in Life* (Hastings House, 1976), and James Combs, *Dimensions of Political Drama* (Goodyear, 1980). For Mead, see his *Mind, Self, and Society* (University of Chicago P., 1934), Herbert Blumer, *Symbolic Interactionism* (Prentice-Hall, 1969), and David L. Miller, *George H. Mead: Self, Language, and the World* (University of Texas P., 1973). For Cassirer, see his *An Essay on Man* (Yale U.P., 1944), and the treatment of modern mythmaking in Dan Nimmo and James Combs, *Subliminal Politics: Myths & Mythmakers in America* (Prentice-Hall, 1980).

The book's argument turns on the idea that our knowledge is imaginative, symbolic, and communicated to us from external sources such as popular culture. This notion was influenced by such works as Kenneth Boulding, *The Image: Knowledge in Life and Society* (Ann Arbor Paperbacks, 1961); Karl Mannheim, *Ideology and Utopia* (Harcourt, Brace, and World. n.d.); Peter L. Berger and Thomas Luckmann, *The Social Construction of Reality* (Doubleday, 1966); George N. Gordon, *The Languages of Communication* (Hastings House, 1969); Dan D. Nimmo, *Popular Images of Politics* (Prentice-Hall, 1974); Walter Lippmann, *Public Opinion* (Free Press, 1965); Marshall McLuhan, *Understanding Media: The Extensions of Man* (Signet, 1966); Paul Watzlawick, *How Real is Real?* (Vintage Books, 1977); Ernest G. Bormann, "Fantasy and Rhetorical Vision: The Rhetorical Criticism of Social Reality," *Quarterly Journal of Speech,* Vol. 58 (1972), pp. 396-407.

The emergence of our identity through play is an idea derived from much work. See, chiefly, Allen Wheelis, *The Quest for Identity* (Norton, 1958); Orrin E. Klapp, *The Collective Search for Identity* (Holt, Rinehart, and Winston, 1969); Jean Piaget, *Play, Dreams, and Imitation in Childhood* (Norton, 1951); Eric Erikson, *Toys and Reasons: Stages in the Ritualization of*

Experience (Norton, 1977); Northrop Frye, *Fables of Identity* (Harcourt, Brace, and World, 1963). The concept of play is explored by Johan Huizinga, *Homo Ludens* (Beacon, 1956); David L. Miller, *Gods and Games* (World, 1970); Gregory Bateson, "A Theory of Play and Fantasy," *Psychiatric Research Reports,* Vol. 2 (1955), pp. 39-51; M. Csikszentmihalyi, *Beyond Boredom and Anxiety: The Experience of Play in Work and Games* (Jossey-Bass, 1975), and with Stith Bennett, "An Exploratory Model of Play," *American Anthropologist,* Vol. 73 (February 1971), pp. 45-57; William Stephenson, *The Play Theory of Mass Communication* (University of Chicago P., 1967) and "Applications of Communication Theory: V. Play-Theoretical Aspects of Science," *Operant Subjectivity,* Vol. 4 (1980), pp. 2-16; Eric Berne, *Games People Play* (Grove Press, 1965); Clifford Geertz, "Deep Play: Notes on the Balinese Cockfight," in *The Interpretation of Cultures* (Basic Books, 1973); D.E. Berlyne, "Laughter, Humor, and Play," *The Handbook of Social Psychology,* 2nd, ed., edited by G. Lindzey and Elliot Aronson, Vol. 3 (Addison-Wesley, 1969), pp. 795-852; W. Lance Bennett, "When Politics Becomes Play," *Political Behavior,* Vol. 1 (1979), pp. 331-359; S. Miller, "Ends, Means, and Galumphing: Some Leitmotifs of Play," *American Anthropologist* (1973), Vol. 75, pp. 87-98; Jerome S. Bruner, et. al. (eds.), *Play: Its Role in Development and Evolution* (Basic Books, 1976), and is implicit in the remarkable book by Douglas Hofstadter, *Godel, Escher, Bach: An Eternal Golden Braid* (Basic Books, 1979).

The ideas about culture, political culture, and popular culture derives largely from the following. First, from some of the classic critiques of modern American culture: Louis Hartz, *The Liberal Tradition in America* (Harcourt, Brace, and World, 1955); C. Wright Mills, *The Power Elite* (Oxford U.P., 1956); Jules Henry, *Culture Against Man* (Random House, 1963); William Kornhauser, *The Politics of Mass Society* (Free Press, 1959); David Riesman, et. al., *The Lonely Crowd* (Yale U.P., 1950); Herbert Marcuse, *One-Dimensional Man* (Beacon, 1964); Phillip Slater, *The Pursuit of Loneliness* (Beacon, 1970); Daniel Boorstin, *The Image* (Harper & Row, 1964); H.L. Nieburg, *Culture Storm* (St. Martin's, 1973); Daniel Bell, *The Cultural Contradictions of Capitalism* (Basic Books, 1976); Bernard Rosenberg (ed.), *Analyses of Contemporary Society* (Thomas Y. Crowell, 1966). For the idea of political culture, see Gabriel Almond and Sidney Verba, *The Civic Culture* (Princeton U.P., 1963); Almond and G. Bingham Powell, *Comparative Politics: A Developmental Approach* (Little, Brown, 1966); Walter A. Rosenbaum, *Political Culture* (Praeger, 1975); Almond and Verba (eds.), *The Civic Culture Revisited* (Little, Brown, 1980); Donald J. Devine, *The Political Culture of the United States* (Little, Brown, 1972); *Publius: The Journal of Federalism,* Vol. 10, no. 2 (Spring 1980). Ideas about popular culture were influenced by such works as Bernard Rosenberg and David Manning White (eds.) *Mass Culture* (The Free Press, 1957) and *Mass Culture Revisited* (Van Nostrand Reinholt, 1971); Marshall McLuhan, *The Mechanical Bride* (Vanguard, 1951); Bernard Berelson and Morris Janowitz (eds.), *Reader in Public Opinion and Communication* (The Free Press, 1953); Alan Casty (ed.), *Mass Media and Mass Man* (Holt, Rinehart & Winston, 1968); William Hammel (ed.), *The Popular Arts in America* (Harcourt, Brace, Jovanovich, 1977); David Manning White and John Pendleton (eds.), *Popular Culture: Mirror of American Life* (Regents of University of California, 1977); Arthur Asa Berger, *Pop Culture* (Pflaum/Standard, 1980); Fredric Rissover and David C. Birch (eds.), *Mass Media and the Popular Arts* (McGraw-Hill, 1977); Edward Jay Whetmore, *Media America* (Wadsworth, 1979); Francis and Ludmilla Boelker (eds.), *Mass Media: Forces in Our Society* (Harcourt, Brace, Jovanovich, 1978); David Burner, Robert D. Marcus, and Jorj Tilson (eds.) *American Through the Looking Glass* (Prentice-Hall, 1974); George H. Lewis, *Side Saddle on the Golden Calf: Social Structure and Popular Culture in America* (Goodyear, 1972); Harold Schechter and Jonna Gormely Semeiks (eds.), *Patterns in Popular Culture* (Harper & Row, 1980); C.W.E. Bibsby (ed.), *Approaches to Popular Culture* (Bowling Green University Popular Press, 1976); Donald McQuade and Robert Atwan (eds.), *Popular Writing in America* (Oxford University P., 1974). I also utilized the major bibliographic essays in M. Thomas Inge (ed.), *Handbook of American Popular Culture,* Vols. I, II, III (Greenwood Press, 1979, 1980, 1981) and Peter Davidson/Rolf Meyerson/Edward Ehils (eds.), *Literary Taste, Culture & Mass Communication,* 14 vols. (Somerset House, 1979). The many interpretive and polemical books on popular culture includes John Wiley Nelson, *Your God is Alive and Well and Appearing in Popular Culture* (Westminster, 1976); Arthur Asa Berger, *The TV-Guided American* (Walker & Co., 1976); George Nelly, *Revolt into Style: The Pop Arts* (Doubleday Anchor, 1971); Jeffrey Schrank, *Snap, Crackle, and Popular Taste* (Delta, 1977); Marshall Fishwick, *Parameters Man-Media Mosaic* (Bowling Green University Popular Press, 1978); Jeff Nuttall, *Bomb Culture* (Delacorte Press, 1968). See also the many collections published by the Bowling Green University Popular Press, such as *Heroes of Popular Culture* (1970), *Icons of America* (1977), and their journals, the *Journal of Popular Culture,* the *Journal of Cultural Geography,* the *Journal of American Culture,* and others. Harold Schechter's *The New Gods,* published by them (1980), is perhaps the best psychological treatment of popular culture to date.

Two studies of leisure I also found useful: Eric Larrabee and Rolf Meyerson (eds.) *Mass Leisure* The Free Press, 1958), and Thomas M. Kando, *Leisure and Popular Culture in Transition* (C.V. Mosby Co., 1975). The former volume includes an interesting piece by Martha Wolfenstein, "The Emergency of Fun Morality," also in the *Journal of Social Issues,* Vol. 7 (1951), pp. 10-15.

There are a wide variety of approaches to popular culture — Marxist, Freudian, and Jungian, structural, critical, aesthetic, you name it. The issue is far from settled: see John G. Cawelti, "Notes Toward an Aesthetic of Popular Culture," *Journal of Popular Culture,* Vol. 4 (Fall 1971), pp. 255-268; David Madden, "The Necessity for an Aesthetics of Popular Culture," *Journal of Popular Culture* (Summer 1973), pp. 1-13; Paul M. Hirsch, "Social Science Approaches to Popular Culture: A Review and Critique," *Journal of Popular Culture,* Vol. XI (Fall 1977), pp. 401-413; Albert Kreiling, "Toward a Cultural Studies Approach for the Sociology of Popular Culture," *Communication Research,* Vol. 5 (July 1978), pp. 240-263; Rolf Meyerson, "The Sociology of Popular Culture," same journal and number, pp. 330-338; Stuart Levine, "Art, Values, Institutions and Culture: An Essay in American Studies Methodology and Relevance," *American Quarterly,* Vol. XXIV (May 1972), pp. 131-165; Bruce Kuklick, "Myth and Symbol in American Studies," *American Quarterly;* Leslie Fiedler, "Giving the Devil His Due," *Journal of Popular Culture,* Vol. XII (Fall 1979), pp. 204-205; Arnold Rose, "Popular Logic in the Study of Covert Culture," in his *Theory and Method in the Social Sciences* (University of Minnesota, 1954), pp. 320-326; Bernard Bowron, Leo Marx, and Arnold Rose, "Literature and Covert Culture," *American Quarterly,* Vol. IX (Winter 1957), pp. 377-386; Umberto Eco, The Role of the Reader (Indiana University P., 1979).

The idea about competence is taken from M. Brewster Smith, "Competence and Socialization," in John A. Clausen (ed.), *Socialization and Society* (Little, Brown, 1968), pp. 270-320.

The literature on the effects of popular culture is now beginning to demonstrate some clues about its importance on learning and action. Just as a sample, the reader might like to look at some attempts to link popular culture to behavior: S.J. Baran, "How TV and Film Portrayals Affect Sexual Satisfaction in College Students," *Journalism Quarterly,* Vol. 53 (1976), pp. 468-473; Baran, "Sex on TV and Adolescent Sexual Self-Image," *Journal of Broadcasting,* Vol. 20 (1976), pp. 61-68; Baran and J.A Courtright, "Factors in the Acquisition of Sexual Information by Young People," *Journalism Quarterly,* Vol. 24 (1980); Baran and D.K. Davis, *Mass Communication and Everyday Life* (Wadsworth, 1981); George Gerbner and Larry Gross, "The Scary World of TV's Heavy Viewer," *Psychology Today* (April 1976); George Comstock, et. al., (eds.), *Television and Human Behavior* (Columbia University P., 1978); Marie Winn, *The Plug-In Drug* (Bantam, 1978); Marilyn Jackson-Beeck and Jeff Sobal, "The Social World of Heavy Television Viewers," *Journal of Broadcasting,* Vol. 24 (Winter 1980), pp. 5-11; John L. Caughey, "Artificial Social Relations in Modern America," *American Quarterly,* Vol. 30 (1978), pp. 70-89; Neil Vidmar and Milton Rokeach, "Archie Bunker's Bigotry: A Study in Selective Perception and Exposure," *Journal of Communication,* Vol. 24 (Winter 1974), pp. 36-47.

In the chapters to come, we will list bibliographic references which pertain to subjects discussed there. After the last chapter, we will point the reader to literature which he or she may be able to use in further research into popular culture. Bibliographies on popular culture are available from the National American Studies Faculty of the American Studies Association, University of Pennsylvania, Philadelphia, PA, 19104. See too *Abstracts of Popular Culture,* available from Bowling Green University Popular Press.

Part I

American Popular Dramas and Politics

An Introductory Note

In the opening chapter, we tried to state what seems to be the "essence" of the relationship between popular culture and politics. The reader will be happy to know that most of the rest of the book will not be so abstract. We will not get down to cases. We will continue to insist that, when one looks at the larger scheme of things, popular culture is a powerful influence in our lives, and that one cannot fully understand American society and politics without grasping it a bit.

In this first part of the book, we want to look at the major popular dramas in which many Americans participate, one way or another. Why do we call them popular *dramas?* Because, you will recall, play-forms such as the Western, sports, and religion are symbolic realities which take on dramatic overtones for the participant. We distinguish this from the dramas explicitly created by the media treated in the second part of the book simply for the reason that these dramas, at least in origin, were created by, and are sustained by, us the people. We created in folk tradition play historical myths, including the Western; created the sports that we still enjoy; took part in popular religious dramas; and so on. True, these play-forms became big business and were taken over by media organizations, but their dramatic origin and appeal remains intact. They were and are popular dramas, with their roots firmly in the consciousness of the American people.

Now it is the political significance of these popular play-forms with which we are concerned here. We will focus on the dramas specifically originating in the popular media in the second part.

Obviously, this division is not iron-clad, nor is it meant to be. Popular sports, for example, is something created by the people in play, but it is also something that is now a mediated drama. But the distinction is more than merely arbitrary. This first part focuses on aspects of popular culture that are key parts of the American *mythic legacy,* by which we mean they are play-forms with a history, a lore, and a symbolic significance they bring to the present from the past. Cultural myths are a part of the consciousness of Americans, expressed in play-forms, but bearing on how we come to think and act toward the world, including politics. The popular dramas we will treat here are popular because they are a part of our legacy.

This is not to say that the second part of the book will not be about mythmaking. The first part is simply distinguishable because the popular play in question is created among the people, while the second half is more about how popular play is created by media elites and then directed at the people. But wherever the symbolic dramas of popular culture originate, and whomever perpetuates them, they are a part of a larger cultural mass consciousness which has political consequences. So let us, in turn, first look at some of these very American pop dramas to glean their political import.

Chapter Two
Popular Folk Heritage And American Politics

In the first chapter, we emphasized that many of our notions about politics come from popular culture. All our lives, we "pick up" notions about the political world from the movies, television, magazines, newspapers, music, and so on. Indeed, many ideas and images which inform our picture of politics may have an origin and significance quite remote from application to politics. Yet, through indirect ways, we apply them to politics. In this first part of the book, we want to point to four sources of political knowledge which most of us pick up in the course of our lives: popular notions of the political past; the Western myth; popular sports; and popular religion. Even though the sources and intentions of these popular activities are for the most part not directly political, the consequences of the knowledge we gain from them — as we will try to show — are quite political.

The Political Uses of the Past

We all live in a society that has a past, and that past is both valued and remembered. Professional historians attempt to reconstruct and interpret the course of the past, but more generally our culture celebrates the memory of events, personages, and values which it receives from the past. Parents, schoolteachers, politicians, and journalists tell us about that past we are supposed to appreciate and carry forward. We learn from a variety of sources about that past, and are told that our generation is the latest carrier of values and examples from the past that should guide our conduct in the future. Our image of the past — what happened in our country's history and what it means — helps to stir in us that emotion known as *patriotism,* those positive feelings and identifications with our own country. Knowing about our country's past makes us feel a part

24

of it, and helps to give us an identity as a cultural being. This is a normal process in most nations: Iranians, Russians, and Japanese young people learn ideas and images about their past which help them to define themselves, too.

But this past we learn about is a symbolic reality. We did not experience ours directly; what we know about it somebody else told us. Past events are attributed qualities in succeeding presents for the purposes of the present. The past is dramatized, used as an example, glorified, and so forth. Its transformation into a symbolic reality makes it more interesting, more glorious, and politically useful. A founding revolution — such as the American Revolution — comes to be a dramatic clash of heroic good guys against villainous bad guys whose outcome was foreordained and which still instructs us, the inheritors. The "historical truth" of the matter becomes lost in the course of time, but what Lincoln called "the mystic chords of memory" elevates that past into something quite different.[1]

We have referred to this process as the creation of a *mythic legacy*. Making the past into a symbolic reality is mythmaking, but this mythmaking comes to be part of the cultural and political legacy we inherit and act upon. Our image of the past is something we have learned as "true." We don't think of it as mythical. But its importance for us is that we *use* it — the mythic past gives us reference points, a sense of the symbolic significance of the culture of which we are a part, a place in time, in short, a feeling of identity. The events and figures of The Revolution — Washington, Valley Forge, the Declaration of Independence — help define our political identity.[2]

Folklore and Heroism

Now every political culture socializes young people by communicating to them such a mythic legacy. This legacy has an impact on our political identity in the present we live in in two basic forms: by giving us a political *folklore,* and by giving us a legacy of political *heroism,* both drawn from the mythic past.

Folklore refers to a mythic legacy of cultural traditions which create a symbolic reality. Such traditions emerge in complex ways. They may be spontaneous traditions that arise among "the folk" over time (proverbs, for example); they may be the product of an "official" tradition preserved by religion or government; as we shall see, they may be created or re-created from original folk materials; or they may be a combination of all of these. Thus, our political folklore may have a variety of sources.[3]

Indeed, we may speak usefully of many folklores, and many political folklores. A pluralistic country such as the United States breaks down into many subcultures and groups — religious, ethnic, work, racial, regional, and so on. American political culture is distinguished by identifiable groups, each with a folklore — the Democratic and Republican parties, interest groups such as the AFL-CIO, and movements such as the civil rights movement.

Folk heroism refers to a mythic legacy of cultural traditions which create a symbolic personage. Heroic figures are the most evident of such personages, but it is also the case that such traditions include villains, fools, and other role-types in symbolic form. Heroic qualities reside in some larger-than-life figure who committed great deeds in a mythical past, usually a so-called *heroic time* — some past period that is exalted into a time and place in which cultural dramas of symbolic significance were enacted, and from which we can learn. Certainly most cultures have exemplars of political heroism, as well as other roles. If George Washington was our first hero, then Benedict Arnold was our first villain. Since then we have added a rich array of qualities — some conflicting — which we identify as characteristic of American heroes. We recognize heroism because we are familiar with the folk tradition that tells us what a hero is like.[4]

The popularization of the past

It is one of the constant themes of this book that American society and politics have been transformed by popular culture. It is the case that the United States from the very start of the republic was in some sense a "popular society" and that there existed a popular culture. The mythic legacy that emerged from the American experience began to appear in popular books, stage shows, written songs, prepared speeches, and newspaper articles. In the spirit of free enterprise, it was thought quite all right to celebrate the heroes of the Revolution and patriotic myth in stage shows, popular books, icons, and other media. Ever since, popular culture has used, transformed, and re-created our past as a mythic setting to tell popular stories for a particular present. By doing so, our consciousness of the past — and its political relevance for our lives — has been constantly reshaped.

Our folk tradition, then, has become the province of the purveyors of popular culture. This is not to say that we do not pick up and remember ideas and images of our political heritage from family, friends, and school. But it is to assert that we learn a great deal of what we know about the political past from popular culture. Think of the American Revolution. What comes to mind? Undoubtedly, a jumble of things. But the most vivid dimensions of the kaleidoscope may well be drawn from popular culture — Walt Disney, movie depictions, Bicentennial re-enactments, John Jakes-type historical novels, "kidvid" television programs, pop figurines of General Washington at prayer, and so on. Such things help to form the "stuff" of what we know about the political folk story of The Revolution. Our knowledge of other past events and figures, such as The Civil War and Lincoln, are similarly shaped.

Knowledge of the past and political expectations

Our inheritance of a political folklore from popular culture as well as other sources, affects much our expectations as to how contemporary politics does or should work. In a broader sense, the depiction of the past, the present, and the future in popular culture may have impact on what we think should be done politically. For example, the depiction of a nuclear future may want us to wish for disarmament. The depiction of present "conspiracies" may make us suspicious of the motives and actions of political elites. In considering social and political questions involving such matters, the past is always a reference point, a mythic standard against which the present can be judged. Whatever myths about the past one accepts, we cannot avoid judging the present by reference to that standard. Whether one buys the heroic myth that the story of America has been a glorious march to world leadership, or the negative myth that the story has been one of bloody imperial conquest and exploitation, one certainly cannot avoid interpreting what's happening now in that light.

Popular culture provides us both positive and negative images of the past, and it is a matter of personal preference as to which ones we are drawn. Our preferences are often influenced by what other folk tales we have heard tell us about the past, our own life experiences, and what we *want* to believe about the world in general. As members of a political culture with a mythic story it is enacting, we may assume that most people want to believe it, and that the culture is in great trouble if large numbers of people don't believe it. The existence of many negative treatments of the past in popular culture is a signal that popular opinion may be turning to doubt, and is attracted to popular creations which dramatize the worst.

War movies may serve as an example. War movies may depict us clearly as heroic good guys, and the enemy as inhuman and lawless; our war motives are noble and defensive, theirs are ignoble and aggressive. During the height of war fever (as in the early days of World War II), the stories possess these polar values. But in periods of disillusionment and doubt (as after World War I and Vietnam), war movies are more negative, focusing on the ambiguity and horror of the conflict rather than on its heroic and patriotic qualities. Such movies may reflect — and in some cases, shape — our image of war, and the wisdom of our country's involvement in them. People at a particular time are seeking ways of understanding just what happened in their immediate past, and a war movie may dramatize their own dimly understood feelings. And, of course, this may break down into those groups that want to believe the myth of our heroic intent, and those who want to disbelieve it. In the case of Vietnam, John Wayne's *The Green Berets,* or *Patton* (although about World War II, *Patton* reaffirmed for many our "noble cause" by depicting an undoubting hero in another heroic time) attracted the former; *The Deer Hunter* and *Apocalypse Now* the latter.

Thus, popular culture may offer us different versions of the past from which we may "select." They all may be mythic, but our will to believe some version of the past is great. But whatever popular image of the American past we believe in, it will color our responses to events and figures in the political present. If the heroic past of war movies moves a person, perhaps he will be attracted to politicians in a present who articulate that popular belief, and believe politics should include an aggressive military stance. If not, a person may prefer peace candidates. If the present does not "live out" the folk story we believe from the past, then we may believe that the tale has gone awry or has been delayed, but will someday aright itself through the correct political leader and action. We are part of the American story we believe in; it is no wonder, then, that we are attracted to popular versions of the story which reassure us that the logic of the story will work itself out.

The popular folklore of the American dream

But what are the major versions of the American story? What does the American past, present, and future "mean"? The search for this meaning has been central to our attempts at self-identity as a people. The "American Dream" is that central folktale, the cultural story which links together past, present, and future. We realize the dream either by restoring the past in the future, or be realizing what was promised in the past in the future. The former is a "conservative" myth, the latter a "liberal" myth. But in both cases popular culture treats in story form versions of the Dream for our elucidation as to what the world looks like when the Dream was either realized and lost, or when it will be realized.

Both versions of the story stem from the course of American history — the Puritan belief in establishing a "City on a Hill," the Jeffersonian rights of "life, liberty, and the pursuit of happiness," the image of conquering and taming the frontier, creating the cornucopia of plenty out of a rich continent, and the adventure of industry and invention. American history is so short that we created a folklore almost overnight, using such play-creations to give mythic flesh to developing cultural feelings about ourselves and what we as a people "mean." At the risk of oversimplification, let us point to two major dimensions of the American dream, how they are treated in popular culture, and what relevance they have for politics.

America has developed a folktale about itself as the "carrier" of a historic mission to create something new in the world, a unique community destined to be "the last best hope of mankind." But from the start there has been conflict over the nature and outcome of the cultural quest. The folktale has us pursuing two values that often conflict: on the one hand, the creation of a *materialistic community,* based on the value of achievement and the realization of prosperity for all; on the other, the creation of a *moral community,* based on the value of equality and the realization of ideals for all. These two aspects of the American Dream have been formulated in various ways, have clashed and blended, and have been represented in both popular culture and politics. Let us point to representations of them first in popular culture and then point to their relevance in politics.[5]

The folklore of the materialistic community

The materialistic dimension of the American Dream stems from the ideology of capitalism and the myth of unlimited abundance. Prosperity was the product of individual initiative in a competitive marketplace, creating social abundance in a forever expanding system of economic growth. Legends grew about "self-made men," great overnight fortunes, the world that beat a path to someone's doorstep because he built a better mousetrap. The myth developed a dark side: "robber barons" exploited masses of laborers living in poverty and squalor; the rich were seen as selfish and living in opulent excess; the many did not share in the bounty. Both the promise and the failure of the materialistic community pervaded popular culture.

In particular, popular culture dramatized both the positive and negative sides of the myth through *heroes,* mythical figures who represented some widely held attitude about the myth. The logic of such folktales was that they dramatized how the myth either worked or did not work, was either redeeming or corrupting. Such folktales are *morality plays,* which in this case illustrate the moral of materialism as a lesson for the rest of us. Typically, the virtues of the myth are tested by the hero and found either worthwhile or wanting.

The most famous positive tale of the materialistic myth is the Horatio Alger tradition. Horatio Alger was a pop novelist during the heroic age of material growth in the late nineteenth century. Drawing on the "gospel of wealth," Alger's boy heroes are poor but upright, but achievement-oriented and self-reliant. Through a variety of adventures, their virtue is rewarded, and in the end they become successful and wealthy. The moral was simply that anyone with ambition and initiative could realize the American Dream of material achievement.

The materialistic myth goes back at least to Benjamin Franklin's *Poor Richard's Almanac,* but it is as current as the novels of Ayn Rand and the "success" industry, including self-help books such as *Restoring the American Dream.* The myth is evident in famous "self-improvement" classics such as Dale Carnegie's *How to Win Friends and Influence People,* Norman Vincent Peale's *Power of Positive Thinking,* and W. Clement Stone's *Success Through a Positive Mental Attitude.* The "moral" of this myth is that of rugged individualism and private enterprise, which overcomes obstacles in our paths. Some of the philistine features of business boosterism was satirized in Sinclair Lewis's novel *Babbitt.*

The materialistic myth has been transformed in recent decades by popular celebration of achievement in areas other than business. Lindbergh's flight was one of the key events in this change. While he did not make a fortune or invent something, nevertheless through hard work and endurance, he achieved something heroic. Similarly, athletes and astronauts were to become popular heroes. The *Rocky* movies were an old-fashioned celebration of the achievement ethic. But too, the astronomical earnings of athletes, entertainers, and other pop figures, plus hedonistic and outrageous life styles, have seemed to many a perversion of the myth. In any event, the spirit of material acquisition as a fulfillment of the American Dream is still both exemplified by the careers of pop figures and extolled in popular creations.[6]

The folklore of the moral community

The moral dimension of the American dream stems from both the political values of the Founding and the heritage of religious idealism. Popular culture has long celebrated the myth by depicting moral communities or heroes that exemplify the myth. Rather than extolling the virtues of material acquisition, here virtue is in seeking some moral value — love, community peace and harmony, human dignity, and equality. Soap operas, romantic novels, even popular music are pervaded with the theme of the problematic nature of, but ideal value of, moral relations. Rather than businessmen or inventors, social role-types such as doctors and lawyers are often portrayed as moral leaders whose idealism and altruism fulfills values such as justice and family solidarity. The "kindly country doctor" who heals both physical and spiritual ailments is a recurrent role-type in our folklore — Doc Adams of *Gunsmoke,* Marcus Welby, even Bones of *Star Trek.*

Perhaps the most pervasive popular motif for the celebration of the moral community is the family drama. Family life has long been thought crucial to the realization of morality, and popular culture has explored the ideal. In the 1970s, when the family was thought to be in trouble, television shows such as *The Waltons* and *Little House on the Prairie* celebrated family life in mythical past times, both having the recurrent theme that family love and loyalty were the font of social virtue. The family becomes a microcosm of what the larger society should be, a network of loving and peaceful relationships.

Popular culture has also perpetuated the folklore about larger moral communities, often times set in a past idyllic setting. The myth of the stable pre-industrial farm or small town community has persisted in popular culture, probably because it seems a nostalgic alternative to the impersonality and sterility of city and suburb. The community around *Little House* or *The Waltons* has its problems, but the solid virtue and the calm of most community members has nostalgic appeal. We still react warmly to Norman Rockwell paintings, Wilder's *Our Town,* and news stories about small town or country people. The "good old days" still occupies a place in our imagination as the setting for a moral community which we do not have now. Our ambivalence about "the machine in the garden" stems from this pastoral nostalgia.[7]

The importance of the dream

These two aspects of the dream are sometimes complementary,

sometimes conflicting sides to the Dream. In our folklore, materialism and moralism will often form the basis for dramatic conflict. The businessman, for example, can be envisioned as either heroic achiever and creator of material bounty or as villainous greedy exploiter who undermines the moral community. The conflict in the American cultural drama is over reconciling material and moral quests, or ensuring that the side of the Dream one thinks preferable will triumph. This conflict over what America is and can be, is traceable back in our politics at least to Hamilton and Jefferson. In both popular culture and politics, the Dream(s) have been represented by and articulated by heroes. If we take sides over the Dream, we respond to heroes and villains who dramatize the conflict.

Popular heroes enacting the cultural drama in past settings are then a major part of our mythic heritage. Some of our most important mythic heroes — real figures such as John D. Rockefeller or legendary ones such as Daddy Warbucks of *Little Orphan Annie* — symbolize our desires to see the Dream realized. Indeed, we change over time as to what dimension of the Dream we believe in. In some eras, we want heroes who achieve material or technical heights, and in others we desire heroes who seek moral values. Even though our socialization affects which aspect of the Dream we are drawn to, we are also affected by changing social and economic conditions. It was no accident that the businessman declined as a heroic type after the collapse of the business system in 1929, and became in, for example, 1930s movies either a villain or a fool.[8] Since then, achiever-heroes have tended to be technocrats who do something which draws upon the virtues associated with the myth — hard work, ingenuity, initiative — but which is directed to enterprises other than acquiring money.[9] Still, there are many popular manifestations of the traditional materialistic myth, and in the 1970s and 1980s with the advent of the "Me" Decade and the New Right, there was new salience accorded it.

Nevertheless, popular culture since the Depression has preferred heroes who were in the tradition of morality. Businessmen became the villain who, because of greed, undermined the realization of the moral community. For example, take one familiar genre — the private detective story. The private eye moves through the mean streets of the city as an unwitting agent or morality. Villains tend to be businessmen who are either gangsters or involved in some immoral scheme to make money. By foiling their evil plans, the private eye serves the values of the moral community.

The political importance of the dream

It is our argument that popular culture dramatizes cultural myths of importance to masses of Americans, and that we "segment" as a people by the popular dramas and heroes we prefer. We are heirs to a dual myth we have termed the American Dream, both aspects of which are treated in popular culture. The survival of the two sides of the Dream in the present points up the amazing continuity of popular folklore. It also suggests the political importance of folk myths that popular culture helps to keep alive. The political heroes of different eras represent one side of the myth of another. Now it is true that politicians will appeal to both material and moral myths, but they come to represent to many people the myth that they believe in and want to see realized through public policy.

The fact that we vacillate back and forth as to which aspect of the Dream we want emphasized politically can be illustrated by recent presidential contests and the changing images of Presidents. Now presidential candidates, like other politicians, cast themselves as heroes in the political-cultural drama, and thus as representative of one aspect of the Dream. Their rhetoric will tend to appeal to realization, and their past will often exemplify one aspect over the other. Let us refer to the presidential politics of the last several elections as examples of the political salience of the dual Dream.

Now presidential candidates attempt to self-cast themselves as advocates of both myths, but they most certainly emphasize one or the other, and win or lose elections on the basis of which aspect of the Dream is of most concern to voters at that time. Presidential contests are often characterized by a conflict that breaks down fairly clearly on lines of the two dimensions of the myth. In 1972, for example, Nixon ran clearly as an advocate of the materialistic myth, appealing to achievement, the work ethic, and free enterprise; McGovern ran as a moral reformer, emphasizing the moral evils of war, racism, and poverty. But the American people, apparently tired of the moralistic movements of the 1960s, chose Nixon, the paradigmatic example of material achievement and social power. But the failure of the moral reform spirit of the 1960s persisted, and the Watergate scandal raised again the question of the adequacy of the achievement ethic devoid of morality.

Indeed, the perception of institutional power bereft of democratic values was treated in 1970s popular culture. Movies of the period such as *Chinatown, The Conversation,* and, of course, *All the President's Men* depicted a world without heroes in which, like

Watergate, immoral elites exercised power for evil purposes. Other movies such as *The Godfather* and *Big Jake,* depicted powerful leaders who defended their material interests by immoral means. The many "disaster" movies of the period may also have indicated the sense that building material temples such as *The Towering Inferno* on immoral grounds leads to disaster.

It was in this political atmosphere that shows like *The Waltons* and *Little House* became popular, auguring a chance in mass opinion for the rise of a hero who revive the moral side of the Dream. Like John-Boy Walton or Pa Ingalls, he would appeal to conscience rather than pocketbook, and thus restore the moral force that many of us believe essential to the Dream. Such a figure has been referred to as a "Heidi redeemer," someone who leads people to the creation of a moral community through example and persuasion. In 1976, the political search was for a "good man," someone who would restore the "Old Values" that we believed to reside in rural and small town moral communities where religion, family, and democratic good feelings tempered the quest for power and money. Harry Truman was revived as a moral hero in popular culture. Gerald Ford tried to convince us that he was such a good family man of small town roots, but we slightly preferred Jimmy Carter, who as a "Heidi redeemer," told us he would never lie to us and would give us a government as good as our people. Throughout his presidency, Carter appealed to morality, asking us to curb our material desires, make sacrifices for the good of the whole community, and conserve fuel as "the moral equivalent of war."

But the limitations of the moral aspect of the Dream were revealed again in the recession and inflation of the late 1970s. Appeals to conscience fall flat when money is dear, and appeals to peace and love turn sour in the wake of aggressive and hostile acts such as the Iranian seizure of the American hostages and the Soviet invasion of Afghanistan. Carter attempted to revive the moral quest with his "crisis of confidence" speech, but it didn't work, and he was challenged first by Kennedy and then Reagan on the material question — physical security from attack and economic stability. People began to talk about the necessity of being "hardline," read the "success" books, and watched the rich and materialistic Ewings of *Dallas.* In that popular atmosphere, Reagan won easily in 1980, emphasizing the state of the economy and the need to return to economic fundamentals, appealing to material symbols such as "free enterprise" and lightening the tax burden.

It is true that Reagan, like all the other candidates of recent times, also had the other side of the Dream represented in his political coalition. The "Moral Majority" and other groups committed to some moral issue backed him, but one may argue that he won on the votes of those concerned about the economy. In any case, the candidate comes to "represent" a popular mood at a time which is also reflected in popular culture. If one sees one aspect of the Dream or the other become pre-eminent in popular culture, then one may well infer that some popular mood is changing which may have political ramifications in the future.

The dialectic of the dream

If it is the case that political and popular heroes represent different aspects of the Dream, then one wonders whether they can be truly satisfying to us in their quest, since they must de-emphasize or ignore the other important side of the myth. It may even be suggested that the duality of the Dream places us in cycles of political schizophrenia, in which heroes and the political mood that brings them to power prove by necessity failures, since they cannot satisfy the other part of the myth. The dramatic tension between the parts of the myth we see again and again in popular culture also may be central to American politics. This may be especially so when the gap between the aspiration of the Dream and the actuality seems great. If it is to be — as many who study the future think — that the next decades will be characterized by both economic troubles such as inflation, scarcities, *and* rapid changes in manners and morals, then it may well be that we may worry over both, and seek successive popular and political heroes who represent an aspect of the myth.

In that case, we should remind ourselves that heroes, political or popular, are objects with which we play because we derive something from them. Our anxieties about the economic or moral future will mean that we will play with heroes who dramatize what we want. Their quest will symbolize through play our quest for economic or moral well-being. And if they cannot represent the Dream in full, and must emphasize one part or the other, they leave by necessity unsatisfied desires nagging at us.

It is in this atmosphere of the eternal duality of the Dream that both popular culture and politics proceeds. Whatever pattern is ascendant at the moment, the presence of the other reminds us of the promise of its fulfillment. In times of scarcity, the popular depiction of opulence on television shows reminds us that mass prosperity is a promise of the Dream. In times of moral regression, the depiction of moral courage reminds us of the promise of a moral community. Such reminders in popular play keep alive that dimension of the Dream, and render it capable of being mobilized into politics by a new political hero. In such a way, then, popular culture becomes a vehicle of our political folklore by treating the old themes of material and moral quests in new ways.

The relationship between the two parts of the Dream are therefore *dialectical.* By seeking one, we are haunted by the neglect of the other. Soap operas eternally show us how those who seek money, pleasure, and glory are haunted by the absence of morality, true love, and the simple life, and vice versa. To use religious language, if it is true that when we pursue one we are troubled by the other, then we are in the realm of "sin." We suffer like the soap opera hero, because by choosing one we have ignored the other. Rich Americans feel good because they have achieved wealth through "individual effort," but bad because they no longer feel part of an egalitarian community. Businessmen who go through "mid-life crisis," give up the "rat race," and adopt a new "lifestyle" may be playing with choices about the Dream.

The dialectic of the Dream seems then to dominate different political eras. And again, popular culture may give us clues as to the mood of the period. Material-oriented political periods are "softline" and moral-oriented periods are "hardline." President Kennedy's "Camelot" was hardline, seeking moral reform and a tough stance against communism, vowing that we would "pay any price, bear any burden" in the fight. The subsequent events of the 1960s and early 1970s involved an intense conflict between "hardline" and "softline" conceptions of what should be done both domestically and in foreign policy.[10]

But the 1970s became a softline era, and it was evident in popular culture. People watched *M*A*S*H* rather than war movies, drank Perrier water and white wine rather than martinis, and read *Doonesbury.* The popular folklore of the period was dominantly softline, with the moral orientation toward self and good relations. But the popular culture, and the politics, of the 1980s may turn out to be hardline, with pragmatic, "conservative," and more mundane concerns. The dialectic shifts so that hardline interests are dominant for awhile, but the presence of softline moral concerns eventually returns.

Conclusion

The past participates in the political present, then, by the inheritance and use of a mythic legacy. The popular folklore and heroism we played with in the past persists in new forms, enacting the dialectical cultural drama of material and moral quests. The dual American Dream has both popular and political salience, and appears likely to continue into the future. Americans will continue to enact material and moral dramas, to vacillate between hardline and softline eras, and to feel guilty about the failure to realize the Dream. Since popular culture is a major forum in which such cultural mythology is enacted, it serves as a major reminder (and indicator of cultural and political change) of our legacy. We may expect that, like the past, both our popular culture and our politics will continue to belie our frustrations with the dual Dream.[11]

Notes

[1]George Herbert Mead, *The Philosophy of the Present* (Open Court, 1959).

[2]See, variously, Patrick Gerster and Nicholas Cords, *Myth in American History* (Glencoe Press, 1977); Robert Jewett and John Shelton Lawrence, *The American Monomyth* (Doubleday Anchor, 1977); Frank McConnell, *Storytelling and Mythmaking* (Oxford UP, 1979); Dan Nimmo and James Combs, *Subliminal Politics: Myths and Mythmakers in America* (Prentice-Hall Spectrum, 1980).

[3]Richard Dorson, *American Folklore* (University of Chicago, 1959); Jan Brunvand, *Folklore: A Study and Research Guide* (St. Martin's Press, 1976); Alan Dundes, *The Study of Folklore* (Prentice-Hall, 1965); Marshall McLuhan, *The Mechanical Bride: Folklore of Industrial Man* (Vanguard Press, 1951); R. Bauman, "Differential Identity and the Social Base of Folklore," *Journal of American Folklore,* Vol. 84 (1971), pp. 31-41; T.W. Adorno, "The Stars Down to Earth: The Los Angeles *Times* Astrology Column," *Jahrbuch fuer Amerikastudien,* Vol. II (1957), pp. 19-88.

[4]Joseph Campbell, *The Hero with a Thousand Faces* (World Publishing, 1970); Dixon Wecter, *The Hero in America* (Ann Arbor Paperback, 1963); Lord Raglan, *The Hero: A Study in Tradition, Myth, and Drama* (Vintage Books, 1956); Orrin Klapp, *Heroes, Villains, and Fools* (Prentice-Hall, 1962); Dorothy Norman, *The Hero: Myth/Image/Symbol* (World Publishing, 1969); Harold Schechter, *The New Gods* (Bowling Green University Popular Press, 1980); James Combs, "Television Aesthetics and the Depiction of Heroism: The Case of the Television Historical Biography," *Journal of Popular Film and Television,* Vol. VIII, no. 2 (1980), pp. 9-18.

[5]This conception is tracable to Alexis De Tocqueville's classic Democracy in America (1835-1840). The theme runs through much contemporary interpretation of America: Walter R. Fisher, "Reaffirmation and Subversion of the American Dream," *Quarterly Journal of Speech,* Vol. 59, no. 2 (1973), pp. 160-167; Seymour Martin Lipset, "A Changing American Character?", Chapter 3 in *The First New Nation* (Norton, 1979), pp. 101-139; the problem is implicit in such works as Louis Hartz, *The Liberal Tradition in America* (Harcourt, Brace, & World, 1955); David Riesman, *The Lonely Crowd* (Yale U.P., 1961). See also Irvin G. Wyllie, *The Self-Made Man in America: The Myth of Rags to Riches* (Rutgers U.P., 1954); James J. Clark and Robert H. Woodward (eds.), *Success in America* (Wadsworth, 1966); Herbert J. Gans, *More Equality* (Vintage Books, 1974); Richard Weiss, *The American Myth of Success* (Basic Books, 1969).

[6]See the changes gleaned by Kim Ezra Shienbaum, "Popular Culture and Political Consciousness: Ideologies of Self-Help, Old and New," *Journal of Popular Culture,* Vol. 14 (Summer 1980), pp. 10-19; and Madonna Marsden, "The American Myth of Success: Visions and Revisions," in Jack Nachbar (ed.) *The Popular Culture Reader* (Bowling Green University Popular Press, 1978).

[7]See Leo Marx, *The Machine in the Garden: Technology and the Pastoral Ideal in America* (Oxford U.P., 1964).

[8]Leo Lowenthal, "Biographies in Popular Magazines," in Bernard Berelson and Morris Janowitz (eds.), *Reader in the Public Opinion and Communication* (The Free Press, 1953), pp. 289-298.

[9]One of the key popular figures in this change was Lindbergh. See John W. Ward, "The Meaning of Lindbergh's Flight," *American Quarterly,* Vol. 10 (1958), pp. 3-16.

[10]Peter W. Kaplan, "The End of the Soft Line," *Esquire* (April 1980), pp. 41-47.

[11]The student interested in studying the popular culture of the American past will be pleased to know that quite a literature exists among historians, folklorists, and pop culturists. We can mention only a portion of it here. A reader of general interest is Norman F. Cantor and Michael S. Werthman (eds.), *The History of Popular Culture* (Macmillan, 1968), 2 vols. Some interesting studies of American popular culture in the past include Russell Nye, *The Unembarrassed Muse* (Dial, 1970); Rhys Isaac, "Dramatizing the Ideology of Revolution: Popular Mobilization in Virginia, 1774 to 1776," *William & Mary Quarterly*, Vol. 33 (1976), pp. 357-385; T.H. Breen, "Horses and Gentlemen: The Cultural Significance of Gambling among the Gentry of Virginia," *William & Mary Quarterly*, Vol. 34 (1977), pp. 239-257; Andrew Saxton, "Blackface Minstrelsy and Jacksonian Democracy," *American Quarterly*, Vol. 27 (1975), pp. 3-28; Robert C. Toll, *Blacking Up — The Minstrel Show in 19th Century America* (Oxford U.P., 1974); Rhys Isaac, "Preachers and Patriots: Popular Culture and the Revolution in Virginia," in Alfred F. Young (ed.), *The American Revolution* (DeKalb, Ill., 1976); Sisley Barnes, "Medicine Shows Duped, Delighted," *Smithsonian* (January 1975), pp. 50-54; Irving Wallace, *The Fabulous Showman: The Life and Times of P.T. Barnum* (Knopf, 1959); Otto L. Bettmann, *The Good Old Days — They Were Terrible* (Random House, 1976); J.C Furnas, *The Americans: A Social History of the United States, 1587-1914* (Putnam's, 1969) and Great Times: *A Social History of the United States, 1914-1929* (Putnam's, 1975). A series of articles which deal with how to approach historical questions about popular culture is collected by Susan Tanke and William H. Cohn, "In Depth: History and Popular Culture," *Journal of Popular Culture*, Vol.XI (Summer 1977), pp. 139-280. The movies are one of the major popular forms which has been used to interpret the past. See such works as Larry May, *Screening Out the Past: The Birth of Mass Culture and the Motion Picture Industry* (Oxford U.P., 1981); John E. O'Connor and Morton A. Jackson (eds.), *American History/American Film* (Frederick Ungar, 1979); Andrew Bergman, *We're In the Money* (Harper Colophon, 1971); Robert Sklar, *Movie-Made America* (Vintage, 1975); David Manning White and Richard Averson, *The Celluloid Weapon* (Barnes and Noble, 1972); Lawrence Suid, *Guts and Glory: Great American War Movies* (Addison-Wesley, 1978); Michael T. Isenberg, "An Ambiguous Pacifism: A Retrospective on World War I Films, 1930-1938, *Journal of Popular Film and Television*, Vol. IV (1975), pp. 98-115; Ina Rae Hark, "The Visual Politics of *The Adventures of Robin Hood,"Journal of Popular Film and Television*, Vol. V (1976), pp. 3-18. The historical interpretation of other media include such studies as Peter Rollins, *"Victory at Sea:* Cold War Epic," *Journal of Popular Culture*, Vol. VI (1973), pp. 463-482; Richard Gid Powers, "J. Edgar Hoover and the Detective Hero," *Journal of Popular Culture*, Vol. IX (1975), pp. 257-278; Arthur Frank Wertheim, "Relieving Social Tensions: Radio Comedy and the Great Depression," *Journal of Popular Culture*, Vol. X (1976), pp. 501-519; J. Fred McDonald, "The Cold War and Entertainment in Fifties Television," *Journal of Popular Film and Television*, Vol. VII (1978), pp. 3-31; Richard A. Oehling, "Hollywood and the Image of the Oriental, 1910-1950," *Film and History*, Vol. VIII (1978), pp. 59-67; Daniel Mishkin, "Pogo: Walt Kelly's American Dream," *Journal of Popular Culture*, Vol. XII (1979), pp. 681-690; Susan Sontag, "Science Fiction Films: The Imagination of Disaster," in Alan Casty (ed.), *Mass Media and Mass Man* (Holt, Rinehart, and Winston, 1968), pp. 131-142; Jeff Peck, "The Heroic Soviet on the American Screen," *Film and History*, Vol. IX (1979), pp. 54-63; Gerald Herman, "For God and Country: Khartoum (1966) as History and 'Object Lesson' for Global Policemen," *Film and History*, Vol. IX (1979), pp. 1-15; Harold Schechter, "The Myth of the Eternal Child in Sixties America," in Jack Nachbar (ed.), *The Popular Culture Reader* (Bowling Green University Popular Press, 1978), pp. 64-78; Henry M. Littlefield, *"The Wizard of Oz:* Parable on Populism," *American Quarterly*, Vol. XVI (1964), pp. 47-58. See also such other works as Maurice Horn, *The World Encyclopedia of Comics* (Chelsea House, 1978); Bud Sagendorf, *Popeye: The First Fifty Years* (Workman Pubco, 1979); Reinhold Reitberger and Wolfgang Fuchs, *Comics: Anatomy of a Mass Medium* (Boston, 1972); David M. White and Robert H. Abel (eds.), *The Funnies: An American Idiom* (New York: 1963); Tony Goodstone, *The Pulps* (Chelsea House, 1970); J. Fred MacDonald, *Don't Touch That Dial: Radio Programming in American Life from 1920 to 1960* (Nelson-Hall, 1979); Eugene Rosow, *Born to Lose: The Gangster Film in America* (Oxford, 1978); Jack Shadoan, *Dreams and Dead Ends: The American Gangster/Crime Film* (MIT Press, 1979); Charles Champlin, *The Movies Grow Up, 1949-1980* (Swallow Press, 1981).

We have introduced in this chapter the concept of myth, which has elsewhere been defined as "a credible, dramatic, socially constructed representation of perceived realities that people accept as permanent, fixed knowledge of reality while forgetting (if they were ever aware of it) its tentative, imaginative, created, and perhaps fictional qualities," in Dan Nimmo and James

Combs, *Subliminal Politics* (Prentice-Hall, 1980, p. 16. We use it here in the same spirit, but emphasize its presence in popular culture. We play with myths no less than, say, primitive man, only that now popular culture becomes the medium that teaches us both old and new myths in changing form. The student interested in pursuing the idea of myth might look at some of the major statements and applications of mythic thought: P.B. Stillman, *Introduction to Myth* (Hayden, 1977); Ernst Cassirer, *The Philosophy of Symbolic Forms*, Vol. II, *Mythic Thought* (Yale U.P., 1966) and *The Myth of the State* (Doubleday, 1955); Kenneth Burke, *Attitudes Toward History* (Beacon, 1961); Mircea Eliade, *Myth and Reality* (Allen & Unwin, 1964); Sir James Fraser, *The Golden Bough* (Macmillan, 1934); Joseph Campbell, *The Masks of Gods* (Viking, 1959) and *Myths to Live By* (Bantam, 1973); Northrop Frye, *Anatomy of Criticism* (Princeton U.P., 1957); Alan M. Olson (ed.), *Myth, Symbol, and Reality* (Notre Dame, 1980); A.J.M. Sykes, "Myth in Communication," *Journal of Communication*, Vol. 20 (March 1970), pp. 17-31; Jacques Ellul, "Modern Myths," *Diogenes*, No. 23 (Fall 1958), pp. 23-40. For specific political applications, see Henry Tudor, *Political Myth* (Praeger, 1972); Bill Kinser and Neil Kleinman, *The Dream That Was No More A Dream: A Search for Aesthetic Reality in Germany, 1890-1945* (Harper & Row, 1969); W. Lance Bennett, "Myth, Ritual, and Political Control," *Journal of Communication*, Vol. 30 (1980), pp. 166-179; Murray Edelman, "Language, Myths and Rhetoric," *Society* (July 1975), pp. 14-21; Gregory Casey, "The Supreme Court and Myth," *Law and Society Review*, Vol. 8 (1974), pp. 385-419.

Chapter Three

PASTPOP:
The Western Myth and American Politics

In the last chapter, we pointed to two key American myths that form the dual quest called the American Dream. The conflicts over realization of the Dream is a cultural theme that we have inherited from both past popular culture and politics, and which seems sure to continue. The mythic quests we discussed have remained important partially because popular culture serves as a vehicle of folklore, keeping the myths and the heroism of their quest alive. Now popular culture has placed these quests in many past, present, and future settings.

In the past, one could see both my themes in a variety of historical settings — The Revolution, The Civil War, the Immigrant Slum. But we will contend here that there is one generalized setting — a mythic time and place — in which the heroic quests which define us as Americans is most deeply rooted in our collective consciousness. This is the winning of the West, the long and inclusive cultural drama of the march of people across the American continent. The Western drama is central to our mythic heritage, our self-image, and our political culture and actions. With that in mind, this chapter will attempt to outline something of the political legacy the Western myth brings to the present and future, and what this means for our politics.

The west as epic

The story of the West is deeply imbedded in our consciousness as a people, and has long been a subject for popular culture. Take, for example, the *Leatherstocking Tales,* the Ned Buntline dime novels, pulp magazines, Wild West shows, Frederick Remington paintings, endless movies, and even a Puccini opera, "The Girl of the Golden West!" Millions of people around the world have seen Western movies made in France, Italy, Japan, and Romania, and generations of Germans, including Adolph Hitler, have read about the West through the novels of Karl May.

The great and longstanding appeal of the West stems from its *epic* nature. The winning of the West is our primal adventure, an epic quest in scope, a drama of mythical heroes, villains, and fools in a conflict set in a mythic time and place. The West is thus a powerful story with metaphorical uses for subsequent generations. We cannot only marvel at the exploits of those gigantic figures who walked the earth in that time; we can learn from them. These legendary figures from the West, and the folklore that surrounds them, constitute a cultural myth that may well be the American contribution to the world's mythology, ranking alongside the stories of Ulysses, Aeneas, Roland, King Arthur, Siegfried, and Robin Hood.

Our topic here is the political significance of the epic tale. A myth of such power and ubiquity survives not by accident, but because it relates important cultural themes, and indeed becomes a vehicle for the depiction of tensions that trouble later generations. Any current social problem can be given a "displaced" setting in the West where it can then be more safely treated for the entertainment and instruction of audiences. But the point is that the West is a mythic reference point, a standard by which we judge the conduct of people and society in the present. The tradition of the West affects our politics by its "presence" as a referent.

The West, then, is an epic "picture" in our heads. As Americans, we cannot escape its effects, either positively or negatively. We all recognize it when we see it — in Marlboro ads, Western dress, country and Western music, Western fiction, endless television shows, and playing cowboys and Indians as children. And most of all from the movies — that little stagecoach winding its way through Monument Valley in *Stagecoach,* the drovers in *Red River* finding the railroad tracks in Kansas, Gary Cooper alone in the street to face the outlaws in *High Noon,* John Wayne standing in the empty doorway at the end of *The Searchers*. Its power over us, as either a positive or negative symbol, is still great.

A moment's reflection on the dramatic logic of the Western myth should tell us why. The West in American history has always been a "country of the mind," a concept as much as a place. Its psychological core is optomism, the human capacity to believe that there is adventure and a "fresh start" somewhere else, in our case to the West. The West quickly became a symbol of what we have called the American Dream. The dramatic possibilities were soon celebrated in story and song: man vs. nature, civilization carved out of a savage wilderness, the discovery of natural virtue and freedom in nature, the rise of elemental heroism in the "taming" of a wild environment. It was a democratic drama of ordinary people who did extraordinary things in the creation of America. The dramatic possibilities were soon recognized by our emerging popular culture, and a myth-hungry people began to consume narratives of Indian hostage-taking, tall tales about frontier characters such as Davy Crockett and Mike Fink, and later the vast outpouring of popular materials which gave shape to the Western myth. It is astonishing how much self-promotion as instant legends was done by those actually involved in the West, such as Wild Bill Hickock.

The Western myth is one in which we can all participate and feel good about. Both the materialistic myth and the moralistic myth can be celebrated, and indeed even reconciled at times. The American Revolution is another mythic time, but is an elite drama that is too remote and venerated to be easily reduced to popular dramas. The Civil War is too divisive, involving the issue of race which still afflicts us. Many of our wars have not been good fare, since they were disillusioning. World War II, the war we feel the best about, has even been used as the setting for anti-war stories. The Western myth, on the other hand, is so democratic and flexible as to attract every possible kind of story, and no group is excluded — men and women, lawyers and doctors, soldier and Indian, black and Mexican, businessman and laborer — all can be cast as hero, villain, or fool in the drama, and each generation or group can play with the Western for its own purposes. In short, the Western myth made us all part of the epic of America.[1]

The political significance of the western myth

If the Western story is central to our mythic legacy, then it follows that it may well have deep, if subtle, political significance. As mythic reference point, the Western story gives us a folktale which includes a dramatic fantasy about how the real world ought to turn out. If the Western is a "deep" picture in our heads, then the myth of the epic past can be compared to the present and the future. Furthermore, the creators of popular culture can manipulate the myth to speak to problems which beset us in the present, as if placing those problems (racism, for example) in our mythic time allows us to see how Americans then would solve what we in the present apparently cannot. The Western is a durable myth precisely for that reason.

This "comparison" of the myth of the West with current reality may occur in popular images of politics. If we play with both popular culture and politics as worlds remote from our immediate experience, we may think that the latter world can or should "live up to" the standards of the former. The implicit question applied to politics is, why don't things work out the way they do in the movies? Why doesn't the cavalry come in time? Why can't heroes bring about denouements as in the Western?

Let us offer an example. After the seizure of the hostages in Iran in 1979, there was much rage and hand-wringing about what to do. Apparently many Americans wanted some sort of heroic action — a showdown, perhaps — which brought about the safe release of those held, or even just plain old violent retribution. Shortly after the takeover of the embassy, a conference on terrorism was held. One of the participants said prophetically that we want "cinemaphotogenic solutions."

> ... We want 'cinemaphotogenic solutions! ... We want solutions in the way John Wayne and Errol Flynn produced them. The cavalry rides in ... People like this because it is like the movies. If that is inapplicable, we have a sense of national frustration because we can't play Wild West there. Teheran is a big city, close to the U.S.S.R. We can't just jump in and say, 'We'll show those bastards whose mythology should prevail.'[2]

Now recall that these remarks were made *before* the attempted commando raid on Teheran in 1980. We can only speculate how much the pressures of a public desire for a definitive and heroic end to the crisis affected the Carter Administration's decision to try the raid, but the "logic" of the political action does seem to conform to the logic of the Western folktale. Subsequently, of course, we elected President a candidate who had long talked of heroic intervention in foreign crises and was closely associated in the public mind with the West and the Western perspective. This seemed to dramatize once again the salience of the myth.

However, the Western myth is a complex one, and its potential effects on American politics goes far beyond heroic intervention. Let us point to some aspects of the myth that are important for American politics through their persistence in the American imagination. In turn, we will discuss the West as pastoral dream, as righteous empire, as heroic morality play, as a symbol of the "American spirit," a symbol of freedom, and a symbol of community. We will also point to how these mythemes are relevant to politics and public policy.

The west as pastoral dream

The West survives as an image in the American mind of a *pastoral ideal,* a spectacular and raw landscape which held adventure, riches, and even salvation. It was the last natural setting — a "virgin land" — in which a heroic drama of conquest could be enacted. The power of that drama has occupied the American imagination ever since. The virtually unspoiled and often spectacular landscape gave birth to an American version of romanticism, in both the idealization of Nature and the kind of "ideal self" that one could realize in it. American myths about the "New Land" and the "New Man" sprang from the Edenic quality of the landscape, and the dream of an American Adam who would be spawned in it. The religious metaphor was not lost on Americans; at whatever point the expanding country stood, from the Puritan "City on a Hill" to the "Golden Country" that was California, there was the image of an Arcadia to the West. Either as Garden of the World, an agrarian Utopia, or as the freeroaming untamed Desert, the West became the symbol of the pastoral dream to be realized. There was always beauty, prosperity, a fresh start, in the West.

This idea was to have many complex political and social effects, but here let us point to two: the myth of *unlimited prosperity,* and the myth of *environment.* The West often came to be in the popular mind a symbol of prosperity, a land of milk and honey whose bounty was inexhaustible. The generations to come would prosper in the wake of the creation of the Midwestern Garden of the World, Texas beef and then oil, Western gold and silver, Northwestern timber, and so on. The myth was to have great effect on government policy and political rhetoric. The poetic idea of the West inspired the Homestead Act, the building of the railroads linking the continent, and indeed many of the ideas of the populist and progressive movements. Since the promise of the West offered the eternal growth of prosperity stemming from the Garden, popular logic dictated the creation of dramas which depicted and celebrated the myth. Beginning with the fantastic tales of early explorers, through the popular books set in the West such as *The Virginian,* up to movies such as *Shane* or *Jeremiah Johnson,* the Arcadian myth has persisted in popular culture.

But the drama meant that the land was to be exploited, and the prosperity created. The sodbusters had to clear the land, the miners mine, the lumbermen cut. But very soon the natural abundance ran out. The "Dust Bowl" of the 1930s, the recurrent depression in farm prices, the depletion of soil, forests, species, and oil kept disconfirming the myth. Continued prosperity meant continued exploitation, with, for example, the spread of suburbs and retirement communities and the use of new natural resources such as oil shale. But this engendered a political reaction that was to be manifest in various environmental movements — the movement early in this century to create national parks, environmental groups such as the Sierra Club, the fight to "save" Alaska, and so on. And popular culture reflected the environmental concern. Joni Mitchell sang that "they paved Paradise and put up a parking lot" and John Denver sang of "sunshine on my shoulder." Oil companies and strip miners became the villains of television shows, and even *Dallas* had a family battle over Ewing Oil's attempt to "develop" a wilderness area.

This conflict over the West reflects the two aspects of the American Dream we discussed in the last chapter. The exploitation myth is one that promises material prosperity. The environmental myth is one that offers peace and moral community. By preserving Nature, one saved our heritage as a people in the wilderness and allowed us to stay close to nature. Nostalgic shows like *Little House on the Prairie* were always set in a bucolic unspoiled environment. Popular "back to nature" movements recurred in American society, in which the celebration of the natural was prevalent. In the 1970s, the spread of "natural" foods, water, and childbirth, at least in advertising, gave us renewed awareness of the myth. "Marlboro country" was still the imaginative place of peace and beauty, and many were drawn, from hippies to retirees, to attempt to live in such communities again.

The West remains the center of the clash in America over material prosperity and thus exploitation of the environment versus moral community through the preservation of nature. Many celebrity environmentalists, such as Denver and Robert Redford, live in Western states. Yet opposition to environmentalism is centered in Western states, which disliked President Carter's environmental policy involving water development and Alaska and voted solidly for Reagan. In any case, both visions are legitimate parts of the American Dream, and underscores the West as the continuing symbol of the realization of one aspect of the dream or the other.[3]

The West as righteous empire

The West persists as a symbol of *righteous empire,* our destiny as a people to expand and dominate territories and people because of our superior values, both materialistic and moralistic. People do not like to think of themselves as crass imperialists, so there is a tendency, in political rhetoric and popular culture, to transform conquest into a heroic and noble adventure. The popular poetry of Rudyard Kipling did this for the British, and various popular media did this for us. The Western drama was the most important of these, since it dramatized the very imperial conquest under way. Indians, Mexicans, and outlaws became villains, and settlers and lawmen became the heroes. The drama was violent, but the violence was sanctioned by the larger social purpose of creating a new country which it was our "manifest destiny" to realize. This conception, then, gave the winning of the West a transcendant purpose, and justified it as something majestic.

The Western myth of righteous empire still gives us a sense of mission which did not end with the closing of the frontier. For a myth persists because it dramatizes in an idealized past something of use to successive presents. Righteous empire persists because it gives mythic support to American foreign ventures and our role as a dominant power in the world during what some thought would be "The American Century." Thus, our various overseas ventures are not expansive interventions, but rather missionary help for good people to defend themselves against evil. The myth helps to make such adventures from Cuba to Vietnam justified conquests, in which innocent power and honorable violence could be exercised with "cool zeal" for good defensive purposes against bad aggressive ones. Thus, our imperial ventures are not for material gain, like other empires, but rather for a moral purpose, to bring that aspect of the American Dream to the Filipinos or Vietnamese.

The redemptive theme in the Western is perfect for certain political purposes. The classic Western story provides a mythic background for the translation of our wars, for instance, into "noble causes" in which God is on our side and our enemies are evil. It was no idle plot twist during World War II for Nazi and Japanese spies to show up in B-Westerns and be bested by Gene Autry and Roy Rogers. And it was fitting that the actor who came to be the symbol of the Western hero, John Wayne, should star in the only pro-Vietnam War movie, *The Green Berets*. Indeed, the President who conducted the Vietnam intervention, Lyndon Johnson, was a Texas rancher who was fond of using frontier imagery to justify the war. It is true that not all Americans shared the enthusiasm for such imperial ventures, and after wars, popular Westerns appear which reflect disillusionment with righteous empire. For example, in the classic formula the cavalry is the symbol of empire which protects and advances American civilization, and is chivalric and responsible. But during the disillusionment over Vietnam, Westerns appeared with anti-imperial themes. In *Soldier Blue,* the cavalry is a savage band that massacres and rapes; in *Little Big Man,* Custer is a pompous egoist who uses the Indian wars for his political ambitions. In such times, this use of the Western signals that the mythic supports for righteous empire have eroded.[4]

The Western as symbol of the American spirit

The classic Western is a morality play in which a new human spirit is manifest in the pastoral setting of the conquest of empire. The American Dream is to be seen at work there in the creation of a democratic man and woman with simple but powerful virtues, who bring about the creation of a new and superior civilization. The Westerner comes to be something of a role model, an example for us to emulate in the present. The Western drama provides a story of prowess, fearlessness, bold striving against natural and human challenges and dangers, self-reliance and fresh starts, creativity and adventure. Popular culture celebrates the sturdy democratic virtue of the pioneers, their commitment to simple but time-tested values, and their plebian common sense. In later times, the memory of the Western adventure was forever renewed by Western movies, books, and dress.

The survival of the myth of the Western spirit in popular culture is paralleled by political rhetoric. Politicians like to use the imagery of renewal, and the frontier metaphor is perfect. That most urbane and Eastern of Presidents, John F. Kennedy, styled his program "The New Frontier." His successor, Lyndon Johnson, used the metaphor in his famous "Perdenales River" speech, in which he evoked the spirit of his frontier forebears in Texas as inspiration for his "Great Society." As a rhetorical device, the Western spirit can be used to contrast the present negatively with that past. In 1968, Richard Nixon asked in his television campaign ads, "Did we come all this way, across the oceans, across the prairies, across the mountains, for this?" The implication that the heroic struggle of the pioneers had been betrayed suggests that we had better return to that reservoir of the American spirit for sustenance.

It is still common, then, for us to appeal to the Western spirit. The astronauts came to be seen as carrying on the spirit of adventure we associate with the West, and the moon landing was celebrated as an old American story. But perhaps the most astounding recent example of such an appeal was utilized in a newspaper ad the Central Intelligence Agency took out in 1979, appealing for applications from "special men and women who still have a spirit of adventure." They asked for "bright, self-reliant, self-motivated" people, which is almost a portrait of the frontier spirit.

The appeal to the Western spirit is often used for two political purposes: as a symbol of freedom, and as a symbol of community. The freedom that the spacious and rich West offered included mobility and opportunity. The West as a "land of opportunity" evokes the materialistic myth of individual achievement in a competitive environment. The rancher, the sodbuster, the gambler even could find riches in the raw West. But the West is also a symbol of mobility, of our freedom to "move on," to roam, to seek adventure. Popular culture treats this nowadays with tales of truckers, a surviving vestige of the romantic roaming cowboy. The political consequence of the freedom motif is evident in two controversial areas of public policy: gun laws and energy conservation. For many Americans, gun ownership is a symbol of freedom, the freedom to defend oneself in the tradition of the West through individual violence. Many people seem to still believe in the Western-inspired "six-gun mystique," by which private violence metes out simple, direct justice in "vigilante" tradition. Even though we do not live on the frontier, now, and our murder rates with handguns are astronomical, the Western myth helps to prevent gun controls.

Too, there seems to be a relationship between the automobile and the Western myth of freedom to roam. Americans value their mobility, and the automobile became the ultimate vehicle of individual freedom to roam the country. But such an impulse deeply affects governmental attempts to conserve energy. It was the conservative Western states that most disliked the 55-mile-an-hour speed limit, and the Republican platform of 1980 made reference to the automobile as a "symbol of freedom." Like the Westerner, the car gives us choices on the "open road." Thus, it becomes difficult for politicians to tell us that we should not drive as much at our pleasure; it is like telling the cowboy he can't "drift" because we're short of hay!

The West is also a symbol of community which collectively realized the moral promise of the American spirit. The spirit was one of mutual help for one's neighbors, a sense of belonging, and a commitment to moral standards and manners defined and obeyed by everyone. This aspect of the myth imagines a world of gentleness, religiousness, and neighborliness which we no longer have. People trusted each other, and didn't lock their doors; problems were solved by everybody pulling together. Popular culture since has celebrated the simple pieties of such communities, as in the familiar roles in the Western of the schoolmarm, the preacher, and storekeeper. But it should also be remembered that in the Western story community was achieved by the violent purgation of evil.

That evil had to be purged to keep the community "pure" is a mytheme that has political consequences. The Western story survives in the belief that bad people of some sort — alien intruders — prevent the realization of community. So some groups — Indians, blacks, foreigners, communists — become the threat to the moral community. That such a threatening group cannot be "integrated" into nor does not accept community values is upsetting. Like the hero-deliverer of the Western myth, political heroes can promise to protect and purge the community from those that threaten it. The "logic" of the story lingers in our politics: just as there has to be a Lone Ranger, that the cavalry comes in time, so too there has to be some Bad Guys. The American spirit can only be saved by defeating them, since they threaten the "perfection" of the community. Such a popular story line, if believed to apply to politics, may contribute to political persecution and violence.[5]

Recent complications in the myth

The Western myth has been in recent years attacked and ridiculed. That audiences of college students laugh and snicker at classic Westerns is an indication of the decline of the power of the story. We have seen the decline of the pastoral dream with the destruction of the environment and the demise of rural culture. The trauma of Vietnam and the rise of new centers of political and economic power in the World has shaken the myth of righteous empire. And politicians and pundits never cease telling us about the "crisis of the American spirit," and indeed there have been recent doubts about "frontiers" and the consequences of handguns, overconsumption of gasoline, and social prejudice toward those different.

This change in American public opinion was expressed in new Western tales which reflected a new consciousness. Western movies and books became more violent, cynical, and nihilistic. Western movie heroes such as Clint Eastwood and Charles Bronson often did not redeem any community, and distinguishing the heroes from the villains became difficult. There was often no moral community to save, and material prosperity was not a promise but a curse. Violence became an end in itself, without any point save individual power over others. A depiction of such an immoral and frightening world has sent the creators of Westerns to seek new stories, what we may call the Protector motif and Professional motif.

In the new Western, the *Protector* centers around an individual "strong man" who heads some sort of empire he himself has built. He is good because he is powerful, and protects his charges against external threats. The Protector runs a cattle empire or ranch like a benevolent despotism, protecting those who are loyal and defending the empire by violent power. But the empire (such as the late Wayne movies, *Chisum* and *Big Jake*) is not righteous, and the moral of the story is that we have to put ourselves under the protection of a strong Godfather in order to survive.[6]

The *Professional* defends no empire and furthers no moral. Rather he is simply skilled at what he does, and is interested in conquest, money, and even destruction. He is either an individual (Eastwood's "man with no name") who survives by skill, or is part of a team (Butch Cassidy and the Sundance Kid, the James gang) which is skillful but holds loyalties only to the professional group, be they outlaws or lawmen, committed to some enterprise. Like corporation executives or astronauts, the Western Pro team is a master of technique. The Western in this format celebrates technical heroism without a moral.[7]

The political corollary to these changes is not hard to draw. If we find the world out there threatening, as the new Westerns suggest, then we may be drawn to a Protector, a strong leader who guarantees us safety and peace in exchange for obedience. The Protector presides over a Hobbesian world as a political authority based on pure power. On the other hand, the Professional motif suggests that we can withdraw from the world into the comradeship and expertise of a group of pros who succeed by their wits. But such teams of Pros, such as the "Plumbers" of the Nixon Administration, may be irresponsible and amoral, with contempt for values and those they rule. The political consequences of such leadership is not hard to calculate.

The fate of the myth and American politics

Confusion and role-reversal in our most powerful folk myth does augur changes in social and political attitudes. But such a powerful myth does not die easily, and indeed it will be an indicator as to the course of American life and politics over the next decades as to what themes emerge in the Western. For at this writing it is not clear whether the Western has reached its end, has been perverted, or is on the verge of revival. We might speculate a bit on these alternatives.

When John Wayne died in 1979, many speculated that his death symbolized the end of the Western myth, since he was the embodiment of what they wished the heroic time of our past to have been. Since he had depicted so well the heroism of the myth and seemed likely not to be replaced, it was thought that his death augured the demise of the myth itself. Indeed, in his last film, *The Shootist,* his death at the end in a turn-of-the-century Western town suggests that the myth has run its course and now will be replaced by civilization.[8]

Others have argued that the Western myth survives, but in perverted form. Apart from the movies we mentioned above, one might point to the enormously popular television series, *Dallas,* as an example of this argument. *Dallas,* of course, is set in the modern Sunbelt, with the melodrama centered around the rich and powerful Ewing family, who pursue money, fame, sex, and power shamelessly. The Ewings seem to represent something of the contradictions we now feel as a people: they give us a link with the Western past, and live out at least the materialistic pole of the American Dream. But if they as Westerners are the end product of the myth, then the American Dream has indeed gone sour. J.R. Ewing is not John Wayne. Wayne at least represented a right-wing and hawkish political position in defense of America. J.R. represents political nihilism, the pursuit of power for its own sake.[9]

But maybe it is merely the case that the Western myth has become pathetic. The phenomenon of the "urban cowboy," cowboy dress among urban dwellers, the popularity of country-and-Western music among suburbanites, the popular celebration of trucker culture, all point to the pathetic survival of the myth in urban settings. Those people who work in plants and offices who don Western clothes, dance in urban country-and-Western bistros, and ride mechanical bucking broncos seem a parody on the heroism of the myth. Yet in their own way, perhaps they yearn for the adventure and heroism the myth promised, and feel lost that their own lives lack such meaning. Such boredom suggests that they would like to see the myth revived, politically or otherwise.[10]

But it may be the case that we are on the verge of an attempt to revive the myth. The Western myth has a powerful hold on the American popular mind, and will not die easily. For the myth is closely linked to our desire as a people to feel good about ourselves and our country. The various political, economic, and social shocks we have felt in the last decades have increased public alienation and disillusionment, but maybe not our desire to believe in the restoration of something we feel we have lost, and even a happy ending to the American story.

Certainly the election of Ronald Reagan in 1980 is closely linked both to that deep desire for patriotic reaffirmation and belief in the Western myth. Reagan played Western heroes in many movies, such as *Cattle Queen of Montana,* and hosted *Death Valley Days* on television. He wore Western dress, loved to horseback ride, and associated himself with the Western myth. His favorite television show was *Little House on the Prairie.* His most solid base of political support was in California and the West. He often couched his conservative and hawkish stands in Western imagery. Thus, the perceived decline in American domestic values and "respect" overseas in the 1970s gave new salience to both Reagan and the Western myth which he seemed to embody.[11] Perhaps this was best expressed in some remarks he made in an interview shortly after the election:

> In recalling the America of his youth, the President talks with conviction and nostalgia. 'Everybody says we've run out of time,' Reagan says. 'But I remember back when I was a boy and you'd go to the movies and they were silent and they had subtitles on the screen. But you'd go there and, of course, Westerns were the big fare, and there was a line that was the cliche in every one.
>
> 'Always there'd be a scene with the outlaws and then one fellow, while they were planning their crime, would suggest robbing the mail train. And invariably the cliche was when the outlaw leader would turn to him and say, "Don't be stupid." '
>
> 'He'd say, "Look, the bank is all right, the stagecoach, but you don't monkey around with Uncle Sam." And everybody in the theater would cheer and break into applause no matter how many times they'd heard it. And that was the way we felt about our national government. How long has it been since anyone felt that way about our national government? But it was that, by golly, you don't futz around with Uncle Sam.'[12]

Reagan, the embodiment of the Western popular hero, appealed directly to the myth, and won in the wake of the popular feeling that America was being pushed around. In times of crisis, perhaps it is the case that people return to a deeply held cultural myth for reassurance. The empire strikes back at its enemies or critics by reference to the root metaphor that justified its ascendancy. Reagan's confident assurances that both the moral and materialistic myths will be revived fell on receptive ears among a mass public desperate and confused. The Western hero always had in him elements that were both nostalgic and hopeful, and its revival in the 1980s was no accident in either popular culture or politics.

The search

The persistence of the Western myth is not only related to political crises but also to the larger question of the cultural search for an American identity. If America was to be the embodiment of the pastoral dream, the realization of a righteous empire, and to bring a unique democratic spirit into the world, then the Western myth survives because it still reminds us of that promise, and thus the necessity of searching for that happy ending. The Western, after all, is a symbolic drama of reconciliation, and reminds us of the possibility of resolving the quest for material and moral resolutions. We still want the play-world of the myth to "work out" in reality.

It is said that the young filmmakers who emerged in the 1970s were all admirers of a classic 1956 John Ford Western called *The Searchers*. The plot involved an obsessed man (John Wayne) searching for his niece kidnapped by Indians after they murdered their family. But as the story progresses, and she has passed puberty, it becomes clear that Wayne doesn't want to rescue her, rather he wants to kill her. When he finds her, she doesn't even want to be rescued. But in the end, she is rescued rather than killed by Wayne, and returned to a white family. The plot is simple enough, but it appears to have attracted these young directors since it spoke, as popular culture often does, to the anxieties of time present. The story of *The Searchers* appealed to them, and us, because we are aware of searching for something dear that we fear we have lost. In the movies that these directors made — *Star Wars, The Deer Hunter, Taxi Driver, Hardcore,* and others — the basic theme remains: an attempt to regain something near and dear to us that is lost.[13] We are all much aware of the tremors of change which break up families and communities, of kids running away from home. Parents are afraid that their young will reject them, and that when they search for them when they flee from them and what they value, they will not want to return. Politically, we are afraid our search has been a failure, and want to recover what was lost in the last several decades. We thought we "lost" China and "lost" Iran as if they were our children. Like the Indians who infest the Garden, we are afraid of non-European peoples who pose a political and even sexual threat to us and those we love. We fear that the Garden will not be realized, that the righteous empire has become mere empire, that the American spirit is dispirited. Somewhere along the way, we have become confused over the goal of the search, and less confident that the search is noble. Politicians sense it: remember George McGovern's call to "Come Home, America," Jimmy Carter's "crisis of confidence" search, and Reagan's promise to "make America great again"? The story of *The Searchers* rings true for us now because our cultural and political search for the reconciliation that the Western myth promises is still unfulfilled.[14]

Notes

[1]The literature on the Western myth is vast. See, variously, Henry Nash Smith, *Virgin Land* (Vintage Books, 1950); Richard Slotkin, *Regeneration through Violence: The Mythology of the American Frontier, 1600-1860* (Wesleyan U.P., 1973); Richard Etulian and Rodman W. Paul, compilers, *The Frontier and the American West* (AHM Pubco, 1977); David Noble, *The Eternal Adam and the New World Garden* (George Graziller, 1968); Frank Bergon and Zeese Papanikolos, *Looking Far West: The Search for the American West in History, Myth, and Literature* (Mentor, 1978). More general but related interpretations of American mythology include Ernest L. Tuveson, *Redeemer Nation: The Idea of America's Millenial Role* (U. of Chicago P., 1968); R.W.B. Lewis, *The American Adam* (U. of Chicago, P., 1955); Robert Jewett, *The Captain America Complex* (Westminster, 1973); Robert Jewett and John S. Lawrence, *The American Monomyth* (Doubleday Anchor, 1977); Leo Marx, *The Machine in the Garden* (Oxford U.P., 1964).

[2]Frederick J. Hacker, quoted in "Terrorism: Mindless Violence or New International Politics," Chicago *Tribune*, November 29, 1979, sec. 2, p. 3.

[3]Marx, *op. cit.*, explores the tension between technology and pastoralism; see also the section "The Dream of the Garden," in Bergon and Papanikolos, *op. cit.*; Frederick I. Carpenter, " 'The American Myth': Paradise [To Be] Regained," Proceedings of the Modern Language Association, LXXIV (December 1959), 599-606; see also Peter J. Schmitt, *Back to Nature: The Arcadian Myth in Urban America* (Oxford U.P., 1969).

[4]See Frederick Merk, *Manifest Destiny and Mission in American History* (Knopf, 1969); Albert K. Weinberg, *Manifest Destiny: A Study of Nationalist Expansionism in American History* (Quadrangle, 1963); and the study of one of the major movie treatments of righteous empire, Robert Sklar, "Empire to the West: Red River" (1948), in John B. O'Connor and Martin A. Jackson (eds.), *American History/American Film* (Frederick Ungar, 1979), pp. 167-182.

[5]The "dark side" of the Western myth has been dealt with various authors, such as Slotkin and Jewett, as well as Jenni Calder, *There must be a Lone Ranger* (McGraw-Hill, 1974), and Richard Merelman, "Power and Community in Television," *Journal of Popular Culture*, Vol. 2 (1968), pp. 63-80. The Indian was the chief victim of the myth. See Leslie Fiedler, *The Return of the Vanishing American* (Stern and Day, 1968).

[6]See John G. Cawelti, "Reflections on the New Western Films" in Jack Nachbar, Ed., Focus on the Western (Prentice-Hall, 1974), pp. 114-117.

[7]Will Wright, Sixguns and Society (University of California P., 1975).

[8]James Combs, "The Higher Meaning of John Wayne: Searching for the Searcher," *The Cresset*, Vol. XLII (February 1980), pp. 13-14.

[9]James Combs, "Play, Soap Operas and the *Dallas* Phenomenon: The Sociological Significance of J.R. Ewing," *The Cresset*, Vol. XLIV (January 1981), pp. 16-18.

[10]Aaron Latham "The Ballad of the Urban Cowboy: America's Search for True Grit," *Esquire*, September 12, 1978, pp. 21-30.

[11]James Combs, "Ronald Reagan and the Collapse of the Categories: Show Business and Politics in America," *The Cresset*, Vol. XLIV (February 1981), pp. 29-31.

[12]Ronald Reagan, quoted in the Chicago *Tribune*, February 8, 1981, sec. 2, p. 1.

[13]Stuart Byron, " 'The Searchers': Cult Movie of the New Hollywood," *New York*, March 5, 1979, pp. 45-48.

[14]Further reading on the West will take the interested student into a vast and fascinating

literature. Along with the literature we have already mentioned, you might look at the bibliographic essay by Richard Etulian, "The Western," in M. Thomas Inge (ed.), *Handbook of American Popular Culture* (Greenwood Press, 1980), pp. 355-376. Some debunking accounts of the "real West" include Dorothy M. Johnson, *Western Badmen* (Ballantine, 1970) and Eugene Cunningham, *Triggernometry* (New York, 1934). The myth of the Western hero is treated by Kent L. Steckmesser, *The Western Hero in History and Legend* (University of Oklahoma P., 1965). See also the following: William Goetzman, "Mountain Man as Jacksonian Man," in Lawrence Levine and Robert Middlekauff (eds.), *The National Temper* (Harcourt Brace Jovanovich, 1977), pp. 132-144; H.L. Carter and M.C. Spender, "Stereotypes of the Mountain Man," *Western Historical Quarterly*, Vol. 6 (January 1975), pp. 17-32; Phillip D. Jordan, "The Pistol-Packin' Cowboy: From Bullet to Burial," *Red River Valley History Review*, Vol. 2 (1975), pp. 64-91; J.O. Robertson, "Horatio Alger, Andrew Carnegie, Abraham Lincoln and the Cowboy," *Midwest Quarterly*, Vol. 20 (Spring 1979), pp. 241-257; W.M. Clements, "Savage, Pastoral, Civilized: An Ecology of American Frontier Heroes," *Journal of Popular Culture*, Vol. 8 (Fall 1974), pp. 254-266; Kenneth Munden, "A Contribution to the Psychological Understanding of the Cowboy and His Myth," *American Image*, Vol. 15, no. 2, pp. 2-16; P.A. Hutton, "From Little Big Horn to Little Big Man: The Changing Image of a Western Hero in Popular Culture," *Western Historical Quarterly*, Vol. 7 (January 1976), pp. 19-45. Many of the myths about the West are in Patrick Gerster and Nicholas Cords, *Myth in American History* (Glencoe Press, 1977); see, too, C.L. Sonnichsen, "The West that Wasn't," *American West*, Vol. 14 (November 1977), pp. 8-15, and B.A. Rosenberg, "Custer and the Epic of Defeat," *Journal of American Folklore*, Vol. 88 (April 1975), pp. 165-177. In the literature on the Western in the movies and TV, see, along with the aforementioned Wright, *Sixguns and Society*, op. cit., John Cawelti, *The Six-gun Mystique* (Bowling Green U. Popular Press, 1970) and his *Adventure, Mystery and Romance* (U. of Chicago P., 1973); C. L. Sonnichsen, *From Hopalong to Hud* (Texas A & M Press, 1979); Ralph and Donna Brauer, *The Horse, the Gun, and the Piece of Property* (Bowling Green U. Popular Press, 1975); Philip French, *Westerns: Aspect of a Movie Genre* (Oxford U.P., 1977); Jim Kitses, *Horizons West* (Indiana U.P., 1969); John H. Lenihan, *Showdown: Confronting Modern America in the Western Film* (U. of Illinois P., 1978); F. E. Emery, "Psychological Effects of the Western Film: A Study of TV Viewing," *Human Relations*, Vol. XII (1959), pp. 195-232; Peter Homans, "Puritanism Revisited: Analysis of the Contemporary Screen-Image Western," in William Hammel (ed.), *The Popular Arts in America: A Reader* (Harcourt Brace Jovanovich, 1977), pp. 97-112; John Wiley Nelson, *Your God is Alive and Well and Appearing in Popular Culture* (Westminster, 1976), pp. 30-86; Ralph Brauer, "The Fractured Eye: Myth and History in the Westerns of John Ford and Sam Peckinpah," *Film and History*, Vol. VII (Dec. 1977), pp. 73-85. See the discussion of "dime novels" in Russel Nye, *The Unembarrassed Muse* (Dial Press, 1970), and the University Microfilms collection of dime novels. Two interesting books on stereotyping in Western movies are Gretchen M. Bataille and Charles L.P. Silet (eds.), *The Pretend Indians: Images of Native Americans in the Movies* (Iowa State U.P., 1980) and Arthur G. Pettit, *Images of the Mexican American in Fiction and Film* (Texas A & M P., 1981). The "search" now reaches into outer space: see William Blake Tyrell, "Star Trek as Myth and TV as Mythmaker," *Journal of Popular Culture*, Vol. 10 (1977), pp. 711-719. See also the forthcoming book on the captivity fantasy, John S. Lawrence and Bernard Timberg, *Visual News: Images of Captivity from the Woodcut to Network TV.*

Chapter Four
JOCKPOP: Popular Sports and Politics

In the last two chapters, we began to sketch some of the areas of popular play that help to shape how we think about politics. We pick up popular folklore about what our country is all about, what heroes are supposed to be like, what the American Dream is. We learn about the West by playing cowboys and Indians, reading comics, and so forth, and thus "know" what the Western myth means. And there are other areas of popular play, too, that affect our political ideas and images, not the least of which is sports.

Sports and learning

In the famous opening sequence of the movie *Patton,* General Patton (George C. Scott) delivered a speech to an audience of soldiers. He said in part:

> Men, all this stuff you've heard about America not wanting to fight, wanting to stay out of the war, is a lot of horsedung. Americans traditionally love to fight. All real Americans love the sting of battle. When you were kids you all admired the champion marble shooter, the fastest runner, the big league ballplayers, the toughest boxers. Americans play to win all the time. I wouldn't give a hoot in hell for a man who lost and laughed. That's why Americans have never lost, and will never lose a war, because the very thought of losing is hateful to Americans.[1]

Let us reflect a moment, as General Patton urges, on growing up. When we were kids, we all quickly learned the importance of sports. Playing was fun, and indeed gave us a chance to prove ourselves. We discovered that organized sports at school and the Little League gave us an opportunity to play. We discovered that some could play better than others, that winning was valued, that there was a huge adult interest in sports. We found that there was a big world of sports in which adult athletes played before gigantic audiences for large amounts of money and glory. We adopted heroes among athletes in high school, or more remotely in the pro leagues. We attempted to bat, or dribble, or pass like them, even to act like them. If we hung around locker rooms or played, we heard the slogans: "Quitters never win, and winners never quit." Some of us experienced the "thrill of victory and the agony of defeat." We heard the speeches at sports banquets. We won letters, were cheerleaders and pompom girls, went to the school games. We talked about sports, followed college and pro sports, maybe even dreamed dreams of athletic glory.

And what effect did it all have on us? Specifically here, what impact does the play-world of sports have on politics? Like the other areas of the American play-world, popular sports is not "just a game." Rather, we learn much about the world from sports. Whether consciously or not, the "lessons of sports" help to orient us to the world. It is not an idle metaphor when we speak of the "game of life." For games, and what we are told about games, gives us much learning about life, and even politics. Sports is a form of play which we early on learn is important, come to value, and link to "real life."

Sports and drama

The root of this may well be in the fact that sports are dramatic. Games are an organized play-area, in which dramatic struggle (*agon*) occurs. The game becomes a public arena for the enactment of the more interesting aspects of human life — competition, teamwork, risk-taking, aggression and defense, winning and losing. Because sports dramatize in microcosm both eternal human truths and specific cultural truths, we are drawn in the same way we are drawn to drama. The drama "represents" life, lets us look at a heightened reality which dramatizes in the story what we want to know about life. Popular drama like soap operas dramatizes exemplary situations with which we can identify. Similarly, sports interest us because they possess such dramatic qualities. We learn from the "story" of a game because we can relate it to our lives.

Sports and cultural myths

Sport is an integral part of our American mythic legacy. In our popular folklore, alongside Daniel Boone, Paul Bunyan, and Wyatt Earp stands Jim Thorpe, Babe Ruth, and Jack Dempsey. The most popular sports — baseball, football, basketball, boxing — have their own mythic heritage, a history of heroics and legends that are part of the cultural legacy to which we are all heir. Each sport, in its own way, tells us something about an aspect of American mythology, and thus by inference about politics. This can range from the most subtle interpretation of what a sport "means" to the most obvious use of sports for political purposes, but in any case, the linkage is there.

Sports help orient us to social values. The rhetoric of the sports banquet speaker typically extols the "values" that we learn from sports. But the values that are part of a cultural mythology are not simple. They are often complex, conflicting, and difficult to live up to. Did we learn from high school sports the value of individual effort or teamwork, the superiority of power or skill, the importance of obeying the rules or the necessity of bending them to advantage, sportsmanship, or nasty aggressiveness? Like other play-arenas of popular culture, the cultural message of sports is often ambiguous and variously interpreted. But we certainly can see the extent to which that sports are linked to the two major dimensions of the American dream, the materialistic myth and the moralistic myth.

Sports and the materialistic myth

If material prosperity is part of the promise of American culture, then surely sports is one of the major play expressions of this. The emphasis on winning, on individual or team achievement, is part of our success ethic. When we see slogans in the locker room such as "When the going gets tough, the tough get going," we are in touch with the cultural value of achievement and reward through effort. Even though we all start out as "equals" on the football squad, excellence and effort are rewarded, and the best wind up becoming the stars. We learn that life is competition, and that achievement and hustle are good. We learn that luck is part of the equation, but that winners usually come out on top through hard work. Sports then provides our culture with a dramatic example of how the real world is supposed to work.

Popular sports continually provides us examples of social mobility, of how poor individuals with talent and ambition can rise in the world. Everybody is equal to compete on the playing field, and the success of someone from the slums dramatizes to us that the American Dream still does work. As an example, think a bit on the history of our first national folk sports drama, professional baseball. Baseball is a distinctly American game, which began to flourish in the cities of the Industrial Revolution of the late nineteenth century. It was popular among working-class men, many of whom were immigrants who came to American in search of the Dream. Baseball offered them not only recreation from their hard labors, but also gave them dramatic example of what they hoped to achieve themselves. It was no accident that the first baseball heroes in Boston, Cincinnati, Chicago, and so on were Irish and Germans like so many of the new immigrants — Bresnahan, Delahanty, Wagner, Ewing. By their success on the playing field, and the large salaries they began to command, they symbolized what everyone hoped to be the fruition of the material dream. In succeeding generations, other urban ethnic groups that had migrated to such cities found the same message in sports heroes drawn from their group. Poles and Italians could admire Kurowski and Musial and Lazzeri and DiMaggio. Blacks and Latins could find hope in Mays and Aaron and Aparicio and Carew.

But if baseball communicated to us something of economic individualism, football has given us a somewhat more up-to-date message. The structure of football is more "corporate," and thus may appeal because we live in a highly bureaucratized, technological, corporate society. Football then tells us that material acquisition through aggressive play is good, but unlike baseball, football emphasizes teamwork. The team is divided into highly specialized skills, all coordinated by a rationalized system. Success is then a product of group effort. The "material" acquired — yardage and points — involve individual heroics, to be sure, but the individual acts only as part of a disciplined unit. Football then tells us something about the corporate world: one acquires material rewards only as part of a team, which is the most rational approach to business activity in a complex economic world of competition. Football also suggests something of the price one must pay for corporate materialism. For critics argue that football involves a kind of corporate fascism — as with, say, the Dallas Cowboys — in which the individual is subordinated to group discipline and authority because the group can only succeed by the suppression of individualism. Other modern institutions, such as the military and universities, have also taken on some of these qualities.

What does basketball tell us? It is a game that involves close teamwork, but also much more improvisation than football. In inner slums, black children play schoolyard basketball with great intensity; it is one of the few tickets out of the ghetto. Thus, it is part of the dream of individual achievement. Basketball also involves the idea that a team can achieve a collective dream. For any small high school or college can, in theory, overcome the odds and become a champion. After all, small schools such as Indiana State and DePaul have become NCAA champions. In any case, basketball combines elements of individualism and corporatism.

If it is true that there are subtle cultural myths implicit in these widespread American sports, then it may be that there are many latent political messages that people may draw from them. It is no accident that such sports folk dramas occur in a country that values the materialistic myth, and thus one should expect that they will reflect it. Nor should it surprise us to pick up the sports page and read about the importance of money in sports.[2]

Sports and the moralistic myth

The sports folk drama also communicates to us things about the moralistic myth. We should not be surprised that many conflicts involving moral questions should be dramatized in sports. For the American moral code includes values such as fair play, equality, sportsmanship, and the like, all of which are reflected in and learned from sports. Thus, the locker room slogans and sports banquet rhetoric may include talk about character, honor, winning and losing with grace, and how we are all equal on the playing field.

With these moral values implicit in sports, it should be expected that sports would involve tensions over violations over the code. If, for example, a football coach brutalizes his players, teaches them to cheat on the rules, slugs photographers, insults the press, equates football with war, suggests that black players are dumb, and so forth, then one can expect that people will be upset. (One does not "build character" among players that way!) Similarly, if society has racial or sexual tensions, then sports is clearly going to become one of the battlegrounds in which the tensions are dramatized. It is appropriate that the post-World War II civil rights movement began in baseball when the Dodgers fielded Jackie Robinson in 1947. Despite resistance from players and fans, the moralistic myth of equality was invoked: like any American, Robinson had the right to compete fairly in the game of baseball or life.

Similarly, in recent years American society has experienced tensions over the changing role of women. Sports has reflected something of the role structure of a male-dominated society. High school sports, for instance, used to emphasize male sports; the girls played volleyball, or more importantly, provided support for male sports as cheerleaders and pompom girls. One's femininity was thought to be threatened by being a jock. Indeed, many girls felt more comfortable playing the more "sexual" role of cheerleader or pompom girl. Critics have argued that one of the first lessons for girls was to be passive and support the men. But in recent years women have become more active in demanding equality in sports. Since women now want to compete in social activities, sports has become a natural place for them to want to prove themselves. Even though many men still resent it, the presence of women in sports has grown dramatically, reflecting the extent to which women have sought equality (and achievement, too, of course) in the drama of sports and life.[3]

Sports and politics

The dramatization of the American Dream in sports suggests that sports has important meanings for us. It is likely that we "read into" sports a variety of messages, including political ones. So we should expect that sports would have political meanings and realize that these meanings have not been lost on politicians and observers of politics. Sometimes the sports-politics connection is obvious, sometimes subtle, but it is nevertheless there. For if sports is a key part of our cultural mythology, and is a play-setting for the dramatization of American myths, then its relevance for the world of politics and government exists. Therefore, we can explore some of the political meanings and uses of sports: sports as a setting for political *ritual;* as a metaphor for political *rhetoric;* as a dramatic microcosm of political *conflicts;* and as a political *resource.* We will consider these in turn.

Sports as a setting for political ritual

Remember that we have stressed the ways that popular culture is a political teacher. We learn things about ourselves as political beings from the social messages that a popular play-form communicates. An important part of our political socialization was through patriotic ritual at school — saluting the flag, saying the Pledge of Allegiance, school spirit assemblies. But this is not the only setting for such symbolic dramas. We all remember the patriotic rituals attached to sporting events — the national anthem, raising the flag, color guards, and so forth. We would feel uneasy if a high school or college football game did not include such patriotic rituals.

These generalized rituals are more or less universal. Indeed, we commonly expect sporting events to be clothed in not only political symbolism, but also religious symbolism as well. We all recall the invocations given before games, the players all praying in the huddle, and singing "God Bless America." Patriotic and religious symbols are, of course, closely linked in sports ritual. The presence of such ritual underscores that the event is not merely a game, but a play-event conducted with proper deference by participants and audience to transcendant values. The appeal is very largely to the moral community, as when the invocation prays that the players conduct the game with respect to moral values. Thus, the folk drama of sports comes to be imbued with patriotic rituals which remind us not only in what country the game is being played, but that the game occurs in the context of national values.

Now when a political crisis ensues, such patriotic ritual takes on a more intensely felt meaning. During the Iranian crisis, it was common for football game rituals to recognize the hostages through moments of silence immediately before the national anthem was played, a dramatic reminder with political significance. Immediately after the release of the hostages, the 1981 Super Bowl became a festive setting for the ritual recognition of that celebrated event — everyone there wore yellow ribbons, and even the Superdome had a massive yellow ribbon on the outside.

But when the country is divided over some political issue, political rituals at sports events can become controversial and excessive. During the height of the Vietnam War, there was a clear increase in the number of college football halftime shows that involved patriotic themes and pageantry. Indeed, in 1970 ABC refused to televise a halftime show planned by the University of Buffalo band which dramatized antiwar, antiracist, and antipollution themes through music and skits on the grounds that it would be a "political demonstration." But later that season ABC did televise a halftime show at the Army-Navy game which honored Green Berets who had just conducted an unsuccessful raid on a prisoner of war camp in North Vietnam, including statements by military officers critical of antiwar activity at home. So it depends upon whose moralistic myth is to be ritualized! Such incidents do remind us that sports involve the affirmation of cultural myths, since sports "participate" in the social order. Thus, "negative" rituals which celebrate a counter-myth conflict with the traditional patriotic function that sporting rituals have served.

In the past, political rituals which celebrated the symbols of government seemed especially appropriate for sporting events, since major sports seemed to embody so nicely aspects of the American Dream. If myths of the State come to be disbelieved or doubted, then such rituals may ring hollow for many people. One may wonder what sorts of feelings playing the national anthem before a game conjurs up in our breasts. But whether we still believe or not, the fact remains that sports is a major stage for the dramatization of political symbols.[4]

Sports as a metaphor for political rhetoric

Politicians like to draw upon familiar symbols to illustrate some political point, and sports offer familiar and widely-used metaphors. The language of the locker room permeates politics. Sports is a major repository of American mythology, so politicians can utilize the analogy safely assuming wide familiarity with the "lessons" of sports. Since politics has many game-like aspects, reference to the dynamics of sporting games as similar to "the game of politics" is natural. Both coaches and political figures seem to believe in the necessity of inspiration, which is the most common political use of sports analogies, allegories, parables, and so on.

The "values" of sports can also be for a variety of political uses. In particular, sports can illustrate the "truth" of either moralistic or materialistic myths. The American sports creed includes many tenets, most of which can be used to support or illustrate different political messages. Even though there is wide popular consensus that sports makes us "better citizens," what that means is subject to interpretation. For instance, Americans repeatedly agree on the positive lessons of sports: e.g., sports are worthwhile because they teach us "self-discipline"; sports are good because they promote "fair play"; and sports are positive because they teach "respect for authority and good citizenship."[5] However, such virtues can be variously interpreted.

Let us illustrate this by reference to two often competing aspects of the sports creed: sportsmanship and winning. The ideal of sportsmanship has persisted in political rhetoric as a norm by which the game is supposed to be played, i.e., that one plays fair, enjoys the contest, and accepts victory with magnanimity and defeat with grace. Being a "good sport" was a trait admirable in all areas of life. The "truth" of sports was not whether one won or lost, but how you played the game. A "sportsman" was a gentleman committed to excellence, but within ethical bounds and without cheap tactics. Such an image smacks of the "Ivy League" pop books of an earlier age about sports heroes such as Frank Merriwell.

This venerable notion has been applied to democratic politics again and again. In a classic book about democracy, we learn that sportsmanship, on the field or in politics, consists of such attitudes as tolerating and honoring the opposition; being a gracious winner and loser; and playing "the game of politics" within the bounds of rules and fair play.[6]

This motif is complicated by a conflicting norm: winning. Winning isn't everything, goes Lombardi's Law, it's the only thing. Nice guys, Durocher's Dictum has it, finish last. The winning motif is related to the idea of sports as war, in which winning takes precedence over gentlemanly traits, and indeed where sportsmanship is a hindrance to victory. The implicit locker room message is often that since winning is paramount, any means, including bending or breaking the rules, unfair play, and intimidation, are justified. At the extreme, this can justify the virtue of sheer winning in politics. Indeed, the Nixon Administration's fondness for sports metaphors was thought to have contributed to the "Watergate mentality," i.e., that the political world is a game of winners and losers locked in relentless strife, and since the "other side" are rogues and will do anything to win, we are justified in being just as nasty as them in order to win. The famous "Plumbers" office in the basement of the Nixon White House, consisting of those assigned to conduct break-ins, dirty tricks, and the like, had a sign that paraphrased Lombardi: "Winning in politics isn't everything, it's the only thing."

The sportsmanship theme is explicitly stated in political rhetoric, but the winning theme, by emphasis, implicitly suggests to us the necessity of aggressiveness, cunning, and even violence. In areas such as business and politics, the sports metaphor reflects the tension we feel about these two values.[7] In business, for example, we believe that pursuit of material goals all should be bound by the competitive rules of capitalism and moral rules derived from, say, religion; but we also recognize and even admire the business sharpie who makes lots of money by circumventing the rules, participating in underhanded and even illegal deals, and perhaps even using intimidation and violence. Our fascination with the superrich, instant millionaires, and gangsters stems in part from the popular belief that one cannot make it without being a scoundrel. Similarly, it has been widely believed since Machiavelli that one cannot acquire and use power unless you are not bound by moral rules. Since politics, like sports, is a mean and competitive world, the winners have to be equal to the task. Getting the "material" of power and prestige in politics requires violating morality. Like the Godfather, you have to make people offers they can't refuse.

In American culture, our attitudes toward the conflicting values have roots in the world-view termed social Darwinism. As a metaphor drawn from the theory of evolution, the social Darwinists argued that business and politics were hard struggles in which the fittest survived and dominated. For this viewpoint, sports offers evidence that life is like that, and thus politics is by necessity that way. Therefore, we want people in charge who use power less bound by moral restraints. But if we take the more "civilized" view of the sportsmanship motif, business and politics, like sports, should be tamed and made fair. For the political rhetorician, sports offers analogies of both motifs, although the "winning" ethic is usually not blatantly said. In any case, it is an indication of a tension in our attitude toward American politics as to which sports metaphor we think most applicable to politics.

Sports as a dramatic microcosm of political conflicts

The old saw has it that sports reflect society. If sports is a mirror of our conflicts, certainly when our divisions are politicized, sports become a dramatic microcosm of political conflicts. If groups experience material or moral lapses, they may be dramatized on the playing field. We have already mentioned how the post-World War II civil rights revolution was reflected in sports. Many other domestic conflicts work their way into sports. For example, it is nowadays popularly thought that America is a society of litigants, eternally suing each other. Certainly this is reflected in sports, which involves a great deal of litigation over the status of players, franchises, fans, the media, and so on. If Americans think that as a people we spend a great deal of time in court, they certainly are reinforced in that view by reading the sports page.

Perhaps the most spectacular way in which sports come to be infested with politics involves international political conflicts. It is no secret that international sports — the Olympics, international track and field meets, even professional sports — often become embroiled in political controversies between nations.

The quadrennial Olympic games are the most important dramatic forum with political overtones. Nations are interested in "proving" the superiority of their political values by success at the Olympic games. The Nazis tried to prove the superiority of the "Ayran race" at the 1936 Olympics, but the dramatic scenario backfired somewhat by the success of American black runners.[8] Communist countries such as the Soviet Union and East Germany invest great resources into Olympic success, since this dramatizes the alleged superiority of "socialist man." Terrorists are attracted to such games to dramatize their cause, as was the case with the Palestinian group that kidnapped the Israeli athletes at the Munich Olympics of 1972.[9]

But the most memorable recent incident involving the United States occurred at the 1980 Winter Olympics. In late 1979, in an already volatile Middle East following the Iranian Revolution and the hostage crisis, the Soviet Union invaded Afghanistan. This was the culmination of a complex series of political events that signified the crisis of "detente" between the United States and the Soviet Union, and brought the world into one of those periods of international tension. Further, it was an election year in the United States, which made the role of American public opinion all the more crucial in the crisis. It became politically important for President Carter to respond to these developments, given the chauvinistic and retributive mood of the country. So he dispatched the fleet, agitated for Persian Gulf resistance to Soviet expansion, and cut off the shipment of some trade materials to the Russians.

But he did something else too: he called for a boycott of the 1980 Summer Olympic games in Moscow. He sent boxer Muhammad Ali to Africa to enlist support for the boycott. He advocated and arranged "alternative" games to be held somewhere other than Russia. He pressured NBC to not televise the Soviet Olympics, and stopped American companies from Olympic-related shipments to the Soviets. He sought the support of the athletes themselves, and of the international sports community. The political purpose, of course, was to symbolically (and in some measure, tangibly) "punish" the Soviets for the Afghanistan intervention.

In the midst of the new tension, a dramatic sports event occurred which demonstrated how play can have political significance. At the Winter Olympics in Lake Placid, New York, the American hockey team unexpectedly upset the Soviets, 4-3. This triumph, and then later when the Americans won the gold medal by defeating the Finns, brought an outpouring of rejoicing and national pride. This outburst, which included many people who knew absolutely nothing about hockey, was clearly related to the new international tensions with the Soviets. The defeat of the Soviet hockey team was not "just a game." Boycotting the Olympic games for political reasons dramatized the importance accorded international sporting matches. Inviting the triumphant U.S. Winter Olympic team to the White House, including the cowboy-hatted hockey team, became the focus for national congratulations, and gave a dramatic role to a President up for re-election.

An international sporting event conducted in the midst of a political crisis, then, can take on an intensely patriotic flavor, and if victorious, people can feel as if through play they have "won" some sort of political victory. It focuses political emotion onto the play drama of the game, and thus gives us deep patriotic pride. Politicians and the news media recognized the political significance of the event, and gave it great play. The triumph gave occasion to a political ritual at the White House, associating the event formally with patriotic symbols and offering ritual thanks to the athletes. The drama did nothing to undo Soviet political intentions, but it did help people to deal with their anxieties about international tensions and their own country's worth. The Olympic triumph signaled a new patriotic fervor in the United States, and helped to revive the moralistic myth about our "mission" in the world and national superiority. The hockey match and the national outburst it caused was a dramatic microcosm of a political crisis.

Sports as a political resource

Since sports are valued popular play-activities, it is common for politicians to use sports and sports figures for a wide variety of political purposes. Like religion and show business, sports offer the politician association with something non-political that large numbers of people are attracted to. Not only do politicians use the rhetoric of sports for political purposes, they also express their interest in sports to dramatize their commonality. Candidates campaigning for office attend sporting events, mention the local team, and seek the endorsement of famous athletes. Endorsement-seeking illustrates how politics seeks out popular culture. The endorsement of a famous athlete somehow gives the aspiring politician a kind of popular status and humanity he might not enjoy otherwise. The athlete is an embodiment of both material and moral success on the playing-field, and the politician seems to think that with the association some of the heroic magic might rub off. And this is nothing new: both Al Smith and Herbert Hoover sought the endorsement of Babe Ruth in 1928! But it doesn't always work. Gerald Ford had an endless list of athletes who endorsed him in 1976, but he lost the election anyway. Ford and other politicians have been accused of being "jocksniffers," zealously exploiting their relationship to athletes and athletics, but the transfer of magic is not guaranteed.

President Carter did not appear to be a jocksniffer, but he was aware of the political uses of participation in sports. He cultivated his Southern regional tie, including hunting, fishing, and wading in hipboots for bait. He reigned over slow-pitch softball games between the White House staff and the press. He became the First Jogger, and was photographed jogging in long distance races with troops in Korea. President Reagan liked to ride, and professed himself a sports fan. (Many older Americans associated him with sports through his depiction of "The Gipper," since he played Notre Dame's famous George Gipp in *Knute Rockne of Notre Dame* as well as baseball pitcher Grover Cleveland Alexander in *The Winning Team*.) It is always difficult to tell the extent to which sports participation by politicians stems from their desire to stay healthy and enjoy strenuous activity, or from their awareness that such activities are popular, and by participating they communicate to the public their common human interest. In any case, most recent Presidents have cultivated some form of popular leisure activity — golf, touch football, sailing, etc. However, if some of the recent revelations about President John Kennedy's "favorite leisure activity" are true, then it must be said that although golf and jogging have their virtues as sports, so does his, although the former type is most politically acceptable and performable in public.

Since sports figures do become popular embodiments of heroic success, the celebrity status they enjoy can become a resource for successful political recruitment. Having played college football or even some professional sport seems to have helped a wide variety of political figures, ranging from Ford to Supreme Court Justice Byron "Whizzer" White (a former All-American) and former baseball pitcher and House member Wilmer "Vinegar Bend" Mizell. Former NBA star Bill Bradley became Senator from New Jersey at least partially on his sports celebrity. Congressman Jack Kemp of New York ran for Congress in the city he was an NFL quarterback, stressed how quarterbacking gave him leadership qualities, and used the rhetoric of football for political purposes.[10] It may be the case in the future that more politicians will be drawn from the ranks of well-known sports figures.

Conclusion

We have not exhausted the complex relationships between popular sports and political culture, but the above should give the reader the idea of some of the major linkages. As long as Americans are sports-crazy, we should expect that sports will have political relevance, and that "the game of politics" will be conducted in a culture that includes sports as a value. In that case, the play of sports and the political play will continue to affect each other.[11]

Notes

[1]General George S. Patton, quoted in Lawrence Suid, *Guts and Glory: Great American War Movies* (Addison-Wesley, 1978), p. 62.

[2]For the social importance of baseball, see David Voight, *America Through Baseball* (Nelson-Hall, 1976); Douglass Wallop, *Baseball: An Informal History* (Bantam, 1970); in more general terms, Michael Novak's romantic and indulgent *The Joy of Sports* (Basic Books, 1976); Wiley Lee Umphlett, *The Sporting Myth and the American Experience: Studies in Contemporary Fiction* (Bucknell University P., 1975); Leverett T. Smith, *The American Dream and the National Game* (Bowling Green University P., 1975); John Richard Betts, *America's Sports Heritage, 1850-1950* (Addison-Wesley, 1974); for football, see David Riesman and Reuel Denny, "Football in America: A Study in Cultural Diffusion, *American Quarterly,* Vol. 3 (1951), pp. 309-310; for a comparison of football and baseball, see Murray Ross, "Football Red and Baseball Green"; Jacque Barzun, *God's Country and Mine* (Knopf, 1956), pp. 159-165, for a comparison of cricket and baseball; Peter Grella, "Baseball and the American Dream," *Massachusetts Review,* Vol. 16 (Summer 1975), pp. 550-567.

[3]See Richard Lipsky, *How We Play the Game* (Beacon, 1980); Harry Edwards, *Sociology of Sport* (Dorsey Press, 1973); R.K. Haerle, "Athletes as Moral Leader: Heroes, Success Themes, and Basic Cultural Values in Selected Baseball Autobiographies, 1900-1970," *Journal of Popular Culture,* Vol. 8 (Fall 1974), pp. 392-401; C. Messenger, "Tom Buchanan and the Demise of the Ivy League Athletic Hero," *Journal of Popular Culture,* Vol. 8 (Fall 1974), pp. 402-410; Ronald Cummings, "Playing for 'God's Squad': The All American Dream Team," *Indiana Social Science Quarterly,* Vol. 26 (Winter 1973-1974), pp. 65-73; Jack Scott, *The Athletic Revolution* (Free Press, 1971); classic linkages between democratic values and sports include John R. Tunis, *Democracy and Sport* (Barnes, 1941) and T.V. Smith and Edward C. Lindeman, *The Democratic Way of Life* (Mentor, 1963). An interesting view of women in sports is in Joanna Bunker Rohrbaugh, "Femininity on the Line," *Psychology Today* (August 1979), pp. 30-42.

[4]The ritual origins and aspects of sports are treated in works such as Thorstein Veblen, *The Theory of the Leisure Class* (Random House, 1899); Allen Guttman, *From Ritual to Record* (Columbia University P., 1978); Edwin Cady, *The Big Game: College Sports and American Life* (University of Tennessee P., 1978); Gregory F. Stone, "American Sports: Play and Dis-play," *Chicago Review,* Vol. 9 (Fall 1955), pp. 83-100; John Lahr, "The Theatre of Sports," *Evergreen Review* (November 1969), pp. 39-76; Novak, *Joy of Sports, op. cit.;* the classic Lewis Spence, *Myth and Ritual in Dance, Game, and Rhyme* (Watts & Co., 1947); the presence of magic in sports is treated in William A. Gamson and N.A. Scotch, "Scapegoating in Baseball," *American Journal of Sociology,* Vol. 70 (1964), pp. 69-72; George Gmelch, "Baseball Magic," *Transaction,* Vol. 8, no. 8 (June 1971), pp. 348-353.

[5]See the discussions in Edwards, *op. cit.,* pp. 63-83; Eldon Snyder and Elmer Spreitzer, *Social Aspects of Sport* (Prentice-Hall, 1978), pp. 23-38; D. Stanley Eitzen and George H. Sage, *Sociology of American Sport* (Wm. C. Brown, 1978), pp. 59-78.

[6]Smith and Lindeman, *op. cit.,* "Democracy as Sportsmanship," Chapter 5, pp. 65-88.

[7]See Ike Balbus, "Politics as Sports: The Political Ascendancy of the Sports Metaphor in America," *Monthly Review,* Vol. 26 (March 1975), pp. 26-39.

[8]Richard Mandell, *The Nazi Olympics* (Macmillan, 1971).

[9]See Richard Espy, *The Politics of the Olympic Games* (University of California P., 1979); Richard E. Lapchick, *The Politics of Race and International Sport* (Greenwood Press, 1975).

[10]Martin Tocchin, "Jack Kemp's Bootleg Run to the Right," *Esquire,* October 24, 1978, pp. 59-69.

[11]Along with the works already cited, the reader seeking further enlightenment on the cultural significance of sport might consult some of the following. Other general treatments of value include: Gregory Stone (ed.), *Games, Sport, & Power* (Transaction Books, 1972); Eldon E. Snyder (ed.), *Sports: A Social Scoreboard* (Bowling Green University Popular Press, 1975); Donald Ball and John Loy (eds.), *Sport and Social Order* (Addison-Wesley, 1975); Marie M. Hart (ed.), *Sport in the Socio-cultural Process* (W.C. Brown, 1972); Eric Dunnig (ed.), *Sport: Readings from a Sociological Perspective* (University of Toronto P., 1972); Howard L. Nixon, *Sport and Social Organization* (Bobbs-Merrill, 1976); John W. Loy, et. al., *Sport and Social Systems*

(Addison-Wesley, 1978); John W. Loy and G.S. Kenyon, *Sport, Culture, and Society* (Macmillan, 1969); Hilmi Ibrahim, *Sport and Society* (Hwong Pub. Co., 1976); Jay J. Coakley, *Sport in Society: Issues and Controversies* (C.V. Mosby, 1978); Donna Miller, *Sport: A Contemporary View* (Lea and Febinger, 1971); John T. Talamini and Charles H. Page, *Sport and Society: An Anthology* (Little-Brown, 1973).

A wide-ranging essay on "Sports and Politics" is by Brian Petrie, in Ball and Loy, *op. cit.,* pp. 189-237. See, too, the chapter on sports by Christopher Lasch, *The Culture of Narcissism* (Norton, 1978), and H. Babbidge, "Athletics and the American Dream," in Jack Scott (ed.), *The Athletic Revolution, op. cit.,* pp. 23-34; also A. Lund, "Sports and Politics," in M.M. Hart, *Sport in the Socio-Cultural Process, op. cit.,;* A. Natan, "Sports and Politics," in Loy and Kenyon, *Sport, Culture, and Society, op. cit.,* pp. 203-210.

The literature cited in the first chapter on play certainly has applicability to cultural games, and perhaps the reader would like to look at serious work on the "higher meaning" of games. Game theory has been applied to both sports and politics, which might account for the rhetorical equation that is often made. In any case, one might start with Paul Weiss, *Sport: A Philosophical Inquiry* (Southern Illinois University P., 1969); Robert G. Osterhoudt, "What is a Game?", *Philosophy of Science,* Vol. 34 (June 1967), pp. 148-156; more formal is Henry Hamburger, *Games as Models in Poker, Business, & War* (Norton, 1950) and Michael Laver, *Playing Politics* (Penguin, 1979).

Although we are not directly concerned here with the role of the media in sports, the reader might like to look at the collection entitled "Sports: The Medium is the Stadium," *Journal of Communication,* Vol. 27, no. 3 (Summer 1977), pp. 127-174; and the latest attempt to link values and sports viewing, Robert H. Prisuta, "Televised Sports and Political Values," *Journal of Communication,* Vol. 29, no. 1 (Winter 1979), pp. 94-102.

Among the many journalistic accounts of sports, perhaps the best is James Michener, *Sports in America* (Random House, 1976), but much other useful material exists in such works as Robert Lipsyte, *Sportsworld: An American Dreamland* (Quadrangle, 1975); Neil D. Issacs, *Jock Culture, U.S.A.* (Norton, 1978); Glenn Dickey, *The Jock Empire* (Chilton, 1974). Among the many calls to reform that aspect of the American Dream that enjoins "competition," perhaps the best done is Terry Orlick, *Winning Through Cooperation* (Acropolis Books, 1978).

The literature — fictional, biographical, satirical, and so on — on sports is inexhaustible. The work I think best understands the mythical, gamelike, and even dreamlike aspects of sport is Robert Coover's novel, *The Universal Baseball Association, Inc., J. Henry Waugh, Prop.* (New American Library, 1968). A delightful satire on sports and politics is Howard Sensel's *Baseball and the Cold War* (Harcourt, Brace, Jovanovich, 1977).

More extensive bibliographic help is available in Robert J. Higg's article "Sports" in M. Thomas Inge (ed.), *Handbook of Popular Culture* (Greenwood Press, 1979), pp. 275-291.

Chapter Five
GODPOP: Popular Religion and Politics

Americans are the most actively religious people among the Western industrial countries. According to a 1979 national poll, 94% of Americans believe in some form of god, and more than 80% believe Jesus Christ to be divine. Seventy percent believe in Satan or evil as a force in the world, and nearly half of American adults hope to go to Heaven. About one-third of us claim to have had some sort of "life-changing" religious conversion, such as being "born again."[1] Such beliefs, combined with widespread church attendance, monetary and volunteer support, and religious proselytizing, makes the United States far more supportive of religion than, say, Britain or Germany, not to mention the Soviet Union.

Yet, is this not the same country of the "age of the secular city," the hedonistic Babylon of greed, lust, and rock 'n roll? Can a country that claims to embrace such exalted religious ideals also be the country that values and practices rampant capitalism, including the exploitation through advertising of every human need and desire? As Tocqueville long ago understood, Americans are a contradictory mix of the sacred and the secular, the noble and the base, the high-minded and low-aimed. We took to religion with the same gusto we took to business and politics, and indeed, as we shall see, these three characteristically American activities have been thoroughly intermingled.

America is the land, as nowhere else on earth, of popular religion. Religion is part of our great national heritage, both in terms of our "faithful fathers" and our tradition of religious toleration. Both of these legacies are in part mythical, but they contribute much to our self-image as a "nation under God." Religion has been caught up, just as the Western mythic drama and sports, in the "logic" of popular culture. This should not surprise us, since a

71

religion cannot escape being part of the secular culture in which it must operate, no matter how other-worldly it may be; so the many different religions that Americans have adhered to take on aspects of the popular culture that "surrounds" them.

Popular religion and politics

Americans have always made a linkage between religion and politics. It is central to our popular folklore to imagine the Puritans, the Founding Fathers, and such figures as Washington and Lincoln at prayer. The rhetoric of sermons and religious literature still abounds with the interweaving of God and Government. Observers of American politics have long noted that religious imagery — what is variously termed "civil religion," "religious nationalism" and "civic piety" — inform political rhetoric and policies. Despite our official "separation of church and state," American civil religion is the complex mythic basis for popular religion's involvement in politics and government.[2]

This relationship involved something more than constant public reassurance by political figures that they believe in God, they go to church, and that the State plays proper deference to God. Rather, it is the belief that America is a country singularly blessed by God and has been singled out for a Divine Mission. We turn wars into "crusades" and believe, as boxer Joe Louis said during World War II, that "God's on our side." The moralisms of Presidents such as Lincoln, Wilson, Carter, and Reagan abound in Biblical imagery applied to American mission. Reagan in 1980 conjured up the Puritan dream of a "City on a Hill," suggesting that America was part of a Divine Plan. Indeed, with the new political involvement of evangelical Christians, most presidential candidates so openly speak of their relationship to God, and how they are "born again," that it is difficult to find a presidential candidate who had been only born once!

American religiosity has meant that religious groups not only want public obeisance to religion by political figures. They also want sectarian ideas directly written into public policy. This involves not only such matters as the legal status of parochial schools, but also "moral" issues such as legal abortion. It is highly symbolic to such people that "creationism" be taught in public schools along with evolution, and indeed one of the most spectacular trials in American history, the Scopes trial in 1925, centered around a law in Tennessee that forbade the teaching of evolution at all.[3] Finally, the status of prayer in public schools, currently forbidden by the Supreme Court, is an example of a public issue which involves religious nationalism. For some supporters of prayer in public schools include the argument that America will magically prosper again, and children will respect traditional values, if we re-institute prayer in schools.

Popular religion and political learning

Even without official school prayer, we learn a great deal about government through religion. Many of us have gone to religious schools, and with the proliferation of the evangelical "Christian schools" of recent years, many more of us will. Thus, our participation in church activities — Sunday schools, catechisms, church camps, revivals, crusades, and so on — probably has an effect on how we feel about government. If we believe that "God blesses America," it is likely that we learned that in part through religion. If religious values are important to us, then they may well affect what we think the proper agenda of government should be. If our church or minister takes a stand on a public issue or candidate, we often take the same stand. If we watch the "electronic church" on television, we may get a view of government different than, say, that of CBS News or the local newspaper. If we take a religious rather than secular view of the world, then our perspective on politics is colored by that.

Popular religion and political drama

In particular, a religious perspective on politics makes it part of a larger sacred drama. If we share a popular image of America as having a quasi-religious "mission" in the world, this may well stem from a religious conception of the drama of history. By listening to evangelical preachers who preach that we are in "the last days," we may expect nuclear war to be imminent and act accordingly. By reading such pop religious books as Hal Lindsey's *The Late Great Planet Earth,* we may see world politics as part of the grand drama of the struggle between God and Satan, culminating, as one wag has it, at the Gunfight at the Armageddon Corral.[4] Politics is seen as part of the religious drama of history, which means we interpret what happens in politics in terms of that grand story. By naming the Soviet Union as "Anti-Christ," or Islamic oil sheiks as villains because they are "un-Christian," then such political casting stems from our ideas about religious dramaturgy. Catholic, "born-again," or whatever religious orientation by a political candidate may make him a hero, villain, or fool, depending upon your religious persuasion.

Popular religion and cultural mythology

The drama of religion also plays a role in the drama of American culture. By this we mean that American culture has utilized religion for a wide variety of cultural purposes — political, economic, social; you name it. American popular religion is the way it is not only because of tenets in sectarian doctrines, but also because it is a part of our culture. The Judaeo-Christian tradition has spread all over the world with its universal message, but each culture integrates it into their own way of thinking and doing. In America, religion has long been a form of cultural play with implications for our entire cultural mythology. By referring to religion as play we do not mean that it is frivolous. Rather, religion is a symbolic activity with which people play, not only for the sake of religious experience, but also relating religion to other areas of life. The "separation of church and state" does not forbid our linking the divine plans of God to our nation or indeed our own lives. Indeed, we interpret God's intentions as supportive of our differing interpretations of the American moralistic and materialistic myths.

God and the politics of the materialistic myth

From Puritan divines on, Americans have made a connection between God's blessing and the material bounty of America. But the bounty given by God is not free, goes the myth; we must work for it. Indeed, Christian virtue — piety, sobriety, perseverance, godliness — are keys to material success. If it is true that the "spirit of capitalism" evolved out of the puritan work ethic and lifestyle, then that spirit is emboldened by the myth. The myth justifies material acquisition as godly, as one's reward for being virtuous. One does not have to feel bad for achievement and reward, since they are part of God's economy. If American businessmen were troubled by greed and exploitation, those doubts could be allayed by "the gospel of success," wherein religious logic supports business logic by providing the "morality" of materialism.

American popular religion abounds with figures who preach the gospel of success, and by extension, the political ideology which support it. The idea that "God blesses business" has always found a ready audience in the American middle-class and especially among the captains of industry who sought ideological myths to reinforce their achievements. Those ministers of the gospel who provided the proper rhetoric of godly materialism could always find a ready audience among those with wealth and those who fantasize about becoming wealthy.

There have been many such figures in the American past, such as Reverend Russell H. Conwell and his famous "Acres of Diamonds" lecture. But more recent divines — Norman Vincent Peale, Reverend Ike, and Robert Schuller — have updated the doctrine. Peale's "power of positive thinking" updated the gospel of success for the corporate age, including psychological as well as material rewards that one could gain from climbing the corporate ladder. Schuller's "possibility thinking" is a descendant of Peale, and indeed Schuller's very method of success — merchandizing, advertising, promotional gimmicks, entertainment, hustle — symbolizes by church expansion an example of the business ethic in action.

The "religion business" itself has now reached astounding proportions. The "electronic church" takes in hundreds of millions of dollars annually. Billy Graham and other super-preachers appear before hundreds of thousands of people in stadiums. The marketing of religious materials, including bumper stickers, T-shirts, records, and books, has become big business. The popularization of religious symbols in popular culture reaches idolatrous and sacrilegious heights, as with Bobby Bare's lyrics about "Dropkick Me, Jesus, through the goalposts of life." Indeed, one of the classics in the religio-materialistic tradition was the 1920s book by Bruce Barton, *The Man Nobody Knows,* in which he portrays Jesus as a great businessman who sends traveling salesmen out in the world to sell his product. In a business culture, religious and capitalistic imagery converge.

The politics of the materialistic myth flow from this religious-business alliance. If God is a capitalist, it follows that He wants us to succeed through our achievements, which can only flourish in the absence of government "interference." Thus, the religio-materialistic myth enjoins "conservative" government which supports free enterprise and largely "leaves alone" business competition. Jesus Christ becomes a symbol of rugged individualism, achievement, and free enterprise. Christianity becomes an example of success, the ethic that guarantees worldly acquisition, and the theological justification for a conservative political ideology.[5]

God and the politics of the moralistic myth

Religion does not only participate in the economic structure of American culture. Religion is also a source of moral concern, and much of its activity as a cultural force is directed toward shaping the moral behavior of Americans. That this would involve them in political action is clear, although many clerics and churches have been reluctant to become heavily involved in politics. Religious groups of various stripes have defined a moral agenda which combines some version of American national mission with religious underpinnings. Thus, religious nationalism is expressed in a moralistic myth that foresees some sort of political reform.

Religions and religious leaders have become involved in moral reformist crusades with political overtones throughout our history. Some of these crusades have aimed at "liberal" reforms — abolitionism, prison reform, women's rights, civil rights, and so on. We associate such activities with the "social Gospel," which urged Christians to become involved in moral reform.[6] Such liberal activism includes much criticism of the materialistic myth, such as the responsibility of the rich toward the poor, and the right of the have-nots to share in the bounty of the haves. It was in this tradition that Reverend Martin Luther King, Jr., and the Southern Christian Leadership Conference pioneered the civil rights movement in the South.

Religion has also been involved in conservative or reactionary reform crusades, opposing alcohol, pornography, homosexuality, women's rights, abortion, and so forth. Drawn largely from evangelical churches, the political ideology of these groups is fairly uncritical of the materialistic myth and supportive of business. They believe that America requires "saving" and "revival" to restore a mythical past of "traditional" morality. The morality of capitalism is fine, but the morality of "liberal" secular behavior is not. Critics have charged that conservative religious moralists fail to see the connection between capitalist marketing and "immoral" consumption or activities. Advertising constantly enjoins us to consume by appeals to hedonistic pleasures such as sexual gratification. The consumer economy depends heavily on such enticing appeals.

In any case, religious people in America are much split over their interpretation of the moralistic myth. Both envision the creation of a moral community, but for the liberal activists, that community tolerates moral pluralism but is less tolerant of materialistic acquisition; for the conservative activists, the community tolerates materialistic acquisition but not moral pluralism. The competing moral agendas of these two religious camps makes them political adversaries that are likely to contend for political power in the years to come.

The electronic church and contemporary politics

It was not so long ago that the large number of people in the United States loosely classifiable as religious "fundamentalists" were largely politically submerged, unorganized, and quiescent. With the revival of religion in the 1970s, religious conservatives became politically active, opposing the passage of the Equal Rights Amendment, homosexual rights, and other moral questions. Further, they ventured into more unknown territory, fighting to get television stations not to show programs such as *Dallas* and *Soap,* and defining as "immoral" such political stands as the Panama Canal treaty and the recognition of the People's Republic of China. Their "fundamentals" were not just moral, but also economic and political, fervently pro-free enterprise and patriotic. They were a new grouping of popular religion that had become by 1980 politically important, when they claimed to have played a crucial role in the election.

The fundamentalist movement is held together not only by common values, but by their access to each other through various mass media, most notably the "electronic church." They form a "moral community" of sorts by their vicarious media experience which brings together many millions of people. The estimates are staggering: electronic evangelism generates a cash flow of more than a half-billion dollars a year; religious broadcasters spend over $500 million a year for air time; there are now over 1,400 radio stations and 30 television stations with a religious format; Jerry Falwell's "Old Time Gospel Hour" alone has 25 million viewers each Sunday; and some estimate that as much as 47% of Americans are "members" of some electronic church. Now there is even a Christian Broadcasting Network with a national news division, which will eventually use satellite to provide broadcast programs.[7]

The political clout that such organizations and their celebrity preachers might have stems from their ability to influence such massive audiences. Their appeal seems in part to stem from their adroit use of the media. On television, for example, the format of the most successful of the electronic churches obeys the canons of the medium. Some programs are directly modeled on the talk show format. Roberts, Schuller, and the others pay great attention to production values, a low-key intimate style, and making it a "good show." Electronic churches such as Falwell's offer people a symbolic reality, a pseudo-church in which they can vicariously participate. The shared illusion of the technological community is that one is part of something that is moral in a world that is immoral.[8] The drama that someone such as Falwell offers is a drama of authority, community, and hope. The church is authoritatively run, and the sermons center on moral absolutes and the need to restore the authority of church, family, and state; the broadcast communicates to the viewer the image of a traditional moral community extant; and the message is one of hope not only for eternal life but also national restoration. People can play with the program vicariously and satisfyingly at home, without the burdens of having to belong to a real church in their home town.[9]

Those electronic preachers who have chosen to politicize their message offer their viewers another symbolic drama, a drama of national revitalization. In many ways, the fundamentalist revival is a revolt against change and what the fundamentalists believe is decay and decline in American morals, material, and power, all of which are linked in their minds. Revitalization movements occur in the wake of great change in which people are confused about their identity and the drift of events toward what they envision as a dread outcome, both spiritually and nationally. The Ghost Dance movement among the plains Indians of the late nineteenth century stemmed from a religious fantasy about the return of the buffalo and the disappearance of the white man; the Islamic revival in Iran tried to reverse the influence of Western secularism and modernization. Contemporary American fundamentalism is a similar revitalization movement, fantasizing about the restoration of a mythical past of moral and material prosperity and identifying the devils of modernity that "liberalism" and "secular humanism" have created to undermine American moral and material strength. The symbolic drama of the electronic church then dramatizes itself as a moral community with which the individual can "belong," and also as the force which will exorcise the devils from America and revitalize the moral and material strength that we enjoyed in a mythical past.[10]

To this end, it is interesting how much Falwell and the other politically-conscious evangelical preachers identify popular culture itself as one of the enemies. They condemn not only popular depictions of religion (such as *Jesus Christ, Superstar*), but also popular activities such as rock 'n roll, disco, pop magazines such as *Playboy* and *Penthouse,* long hair on men and revealing dresses on women, television programming that deals with "explicit" themes, and so on. Popular fads and habits are as much a threat, it seems, as "socialism" and "humanism." In the drama of moral revival, popular culture, even though a product of capitalism, is one of the enemies, but may be one of the most difficult aspects of modernity to eradicate. People may heed the electronic church as to the hiring and firing of Presidents, but they may be more reluctant to give up the daily play of soap operas and rock music.

The political drama of the evangelical media-churches, then, is manichean, a drama of religious and national good versus irreligious and unpatriotic evil. This makes for a simple conflict of good and evil, in which the forces of God, wrapped in a mantle of electronic righteousness, not to mention three-piece suits and blow-dried hair, contest against the "enemies" who are either conscious or unwitting allies of Satan. Like Satan's hordes, the enemies are identifiable and palpable: television network programmers, Hugh Hefner, women's libbers, liberal politicians, and so on. In the face of inchoate change, such figures become convenient scapegoats, dramatic villains on whom the righteous can visit their moral wrath. Like the "communists" or other witches of the past, such figures are by definition guilty. And like such figures in the past, they are in places of power, affecting both public policy and popular culture. Falwell said in January 1980, that "255,000 secular humanists have taken 214 million of us out to left field." If the drama is a "holy war" against those evil people who have led the nation astray, then it includes not only identifying the guilty, but also persecution, punishment, and victimage.[11]

In any case, the politically aroused evangelical groups, led by celebrity preachers, have become a new and uncertain force in American politics. They formed lobbying organizations designed to support not only conservative but specifically "born again" candidates who agreed with their agenda in detail. Christian Voice organized as a pressure group on behalf of "Christian morality" in government. The "Moral Majority," led by Falwell, campaigned with the warning that "Our grand old flag is going down the drain" because of "immorality" — abortions, smut peddlers, homosexual rights, the absence of "voluntary prayer" in school, the SALT treaty. In April 1980, 200,000 of their numbers gathered for a "Washington for Jesus" rally at the nation's capitol. "In a time of crisis in our land, to come and say, 'God of our fathers, you will save us' — that is why we are here," said Pat Robertson, president of the Christian Broadcasting Network.[12]

Such activities and the new political agenda of the evangelicals caused concern in various quarters, including religious ones. The National Council of Churches, a mainstream and ecumenical body of thirty-two church bodies, criticized the right-wing Christian organizations for seeking "to 'Christianize' the government," and thought it "arrogant" for them "to assert that one's position on a political issue is Christian and that all others are un-Christian, secular, humanist, immoral, or sinful. There is no 'Christian' vote or legislation."[13] Others have even seen in the evangelical political movement the seeds of a kind of Christian fascism intolerant of religious or political diversity, and point out that such groups are heavily supported by some of the most reactionary big businesses in the country.

The charge of fascistic overtones was given credence by the uncompromising — some would say fanatical — commitment of the evangelical Right to "pure" versions of the American materialistic and moralistic myth. Such a monistic stance led some of their numbers to regard as "un-Christian" politicians who were avowedly and publically Christian, such as John Anderson, Senator Mark Hatfield, and President Carter. Critics charged that the religious conservatives were also astonishingly uncritical of their candidate in 1980, Ronald Reagan. Reagan, after all, is the first divorced President. He spoke to the Moral Majority about morality in government the same day he lunched with the executive board of the Teamsters union, including four convicted felons! His convention acceptance speech touched on themes dear to the religious Right, while his wife sat next to Elizabeth Taylor (not exactly Mother Elizabeth Seton) and his guest of honor was Frank Sinatra (not exactly St. Francis). His income tax return for 1979 revealed that he had donated less than one percent of his income to charitable and religious causes, not exactly the 10% tithe favored by evangelicals. But for the moment Reagan became the political hero of the movement because he preached the political gospel they wanted to hear.

There was likely something else in the attraction to Reagan. As a popular religious and political movement, the religious Right has developed and utilized the methods of show business. The electronic church uses entertainment appeals, including the appearance of "acceptable" celebrities who were born again. Electronic church audiences apparently are as attracted to and awed by celebrities as the rest of us. Singer Anita Bryant, Pat and Debbie Boone, Roy Rogers and Dale Evans, famous converts such as Eldrige Cleaver, Susan Atkins, and Charles Colson, right-wing activists such as Phyllis Schafley, and politicians such as Representative Phillip Crane and Senator Jesse Helms frequently appear on such televised shows. Thus, this show biz connection made the attraction to

Reagan all the more solid. For he had "made it" in much the same way Robertson and Falwell had, through the adroit use of television.

The electronic church is a genuine popular movement made possible by the mass media. Through the electronic dramas it performs, it mobilizes the religious play of millions of people into a symbolic drama with both religious and political consequences. It is an authentic American popular drama with roots deep in our culture. It taps a deep desire in many of us for national revitalization, and appeals to moral and material myths rooted in the popular mind. It is the old-time religion tailored for a mass-mediated culture, and its roots in and use of American popular culture makes it one of the remarkable American popular dramas of our time.

Civil religion and the American political order

The ardent political agitation for change by this new popular movement brings into question again the relationship between church and state in a secular country. It is time, said Pat Robertson, "to put God back in government." "We want," said Jerry Falwell, "to bring America back ... to the way we were." The difficulty is that putting God back in government involves Constitutional and political questions, not to mention whose God is to be "put back" into government. The moralistic myth includes, for instance, the popular — and mistaken — notion that the Founding Fathers were "godly men," and that our troubles stem from our current lack of such godly politicians. Similarly, the more general dream of bringing America back "to the way we were" belies a popular nostalgia for a Walton-like past of moral rectitude that certainly never existed.

The political aggressiveness of the evangelical movement augurs a new test for the American tradition of "civil religion." The tradition persists around an unwritten "contract" between church and state about the nature of the separation and respective jurisdictions of God and Caesar. The balance is delicate and permeable, but certainly it included an "agreement" that government is secular, and could not be "Christianized" by some sectarian definition. The contract has always been tentative, dependent upon popular support and elite consensus.[14] As history careens us toward the evident and upsetting changes in world and domestic politics, and in such areas of life as popular culture, it may be that the appeal of something more elemental and certain which symbolically unites God and Government in a holy alliance will overwhelm tradition. If that is the case, it may well stem from the popular religions movement, discussed here, armed with Holy Book and television technology, which would lead us back into their image of the Promised Land. The serious popular play of a revitalized religious fundamentalism given political power augurs attempts to impose a new contract. Such a drama would bring great changes in both our politics and our popular culture. The political activism of the fundamentalists (or any other group armed with a religious doctrine they want translated into public policy) raises again the question of what God "wants" us to do "as a nation," and whether or not we are again playing with God's mysterious "intentions." The contemporary religious activists, playing with popular media technique and political ambitions, might well ponder Luther's ringing injunction to "let God be God!"[15]

Notes

[1]Jack Houston, "Americans 'Most Religious' People: Poll," Chicago *Tribune*, December 19, 1979, section 4, p. 24.

[2]See William G. McLoughlin and Robert N. Bellah (eds.), *Religion in America* (Boston: Beacon Press, 1968); Russell E. Richey and Ronald G. Jones (eds), *American Civil Religion* (New York: Harper & Row, 1974); Charles Glock and Robert N. Bellah, (eds.), *The New Religious Consciousness* (Berkeley: University of California, 1976); Sidney E. Mead, *The Nation with the Soul of a Church* (New York: Harper & Row, 1975); Michael Novak, *Choosing Our King* (New York: Macmillan, 1974); Cushing Strout, *The New Heavens and New Earth* (New York: Harper & Row, 1974); and Robert N. Bellah, "Religion and Legitimation in the American Republic," *Society*, Vol. 15 (May 1978), pp. 16-23.

[3]Ray Ginger, *Six Days or Forever?* (Oxford University P., 1974).

[4]John Wiley Nelson, "Hal Lindsey and the Late Great Planet Earth: UnCivil Civil Religion," paper delivered at the 1980 Popular Culture Association meeting, unpublished.

[5]See Moses Rischlin (ed.), *The American Gospel of Success* (Quadrangle, 1965); Madonna Marsden, "The American Myth of Success: Visions and Revisions," in Jack Nachbar, ed., *The Popular Culture Reader* (Bowling Green University Popular Press, 1978), pp. 37-50; Robert Friedman, "Inspiration, Inc.," *Esquire* (September 1979), pp. 24-33; the classic criticism of philistinism is Sinclair Lewis, *Babbitt* (New American Library, 1961).

[6]For a study of religious involvement in the Prohibition movement, see Joseph R. Gusfield, *Symbolic Crusade: Status Politics and the American Temperance Movement* (University of Illinois P., 1966).

[7]Bruce Bursman, "A New Crusade," Chicago *Tribune*, August 31, 1980, sec. 2, pp. 1-2.

[8]This notion about television was first explored by Donald Horton and R. Richard Wohl, "Mass Communication and Para-Social Interaction: Observations on Intimacy at a Distance," *Psychiatry*, Vol. 19 (1956), pp. 215-229.

[9]Charles E. Swann, "The Electronic Church," *Presbyterian Survey* (October A.D. 1979), pp. 17-20.

[10]See Anthony F.C. Wallace, "Revitalization Movements," *American Anthropologist*, Vol. 58 (April 1956), pp. 264-281.

[11]The quote and the "holy war" idea are from Martin E. Marty, "Fundamentalism Reborn: Faith and Fanaticism," *Saturday Review* (May 1980), pp. 37-42; see also the article on Falwell by Mary Murphy, "The Next Billy Graham," *Esquire* (October 10, 1978), pp. 25-32; for an incisive treatment of the roots and drama of fanaticisms, see Eric Hoffer, *The True Believer* (Perennial Library, 1966).

[12]Associated Press, "200,000 Christians Pray for U.S. during Daylong Rally in Capital," Chicago *Tribune*, April 30, 1980, sec. 1, p. 2.

[13]*Ibid.*

[14]Roderick Hart, *The Political Pulpit* (Purdue University P., 1977).

[15]The literature on popular religion should include such classical works as Max Weber's writings on religion, primarily his famous *Protestant Ethic and the Spirit of Capitalism* (many editions) and the essays on religion in H.H. Gerth and C. Wright Mills (ed.), *From Max Weber: Essays in Sociology* (Oxford University P., 1958). See also such important works as Karl Mannheim, *Ideology and Utopia* (Harcourt, Brace & World, n.d.); Micea Eliade, *The Sacred and the Profane* (Harcourt, Brace & World, 1959); Peter L. Berger, *The Sacred Canopy* (Doubleday Anchor, 1969); related is the insightful study of group faith, Leon Festinger, et. al., *When Prophecy Fails* (Harper Torchbooks, 1964).

The cultural and political role of religion has received much attention. Perhaps the most provocative religious interpretation of American politics is Robert Jewett's *The Captain America Complex: The Dilemmas of Zealous Nationalism* (Westminster Press, 1973). The status of "civil religion" has received much attention: besides the works cited above in footnote 2, see Sidney E. Mead, *The Old Religion in the Brave New World* (University of California P., 1977); Lloyd Warner, *The Living and the Dead* (Yale University P., 1959); Robert Alley, *So Help Me God: Religion and the Presidency* (John Knox P., 1972); Robert N. Bellah, *The Broken Covenant: American Civil Religion in a Time of Trial* (Seabury Press, 1975); Conrad Cherry, *God's New Israel: Religious Interpretations of American Destiny* (Prentice-Hall, 1971); Sherwood Eddy, *The Kingdom of God and the American Dream* (Harper & Row, 1941); Alan Heimert, *Religion and the American Mind* (Harvard University P., 1966); Martin Marty, *Righteous Empire* (Dial Press, 1970); Richard E. Morgan, *The Politics of Religious Conflict* (Pegasus, 1968); Roy I. Nichols, *The Religion of American Democracy* (Louisiana State University P., 1959); Elwyn A. Smith (ed.), *The Religion of the Republic* (Fortress Press, 1971); Charles H. Lippy, "The President as Priest: Civil Religion and the Folklore of the American Presidency," *Journal of Religious Studies* (October 1980); M. Darroll Bryant, "America as God's Kingdom," in *Religion and Political Society*, J. Moltmann, et. al. (eds.) (Harper & Row, 1974); Conrad Cherry, "Two American Sacred Ceremonies: Their Implications for the Study of Religion in America," *American Quarterly*, Vol. 21 (Winter 1969), pp. 739-754; William A. Cole and Phillip E. Hammond, "Religious Pluralism, Legal Development, and Societal Complexity: Rudimentary Forms of Civil Religion," *Journal for the Scientific Study of Religion*, Vol. 13 (June 1974), pp. 177-189; Roderick P. Hart, "The Rhetoric of the True Believer," *Speech Monographs*, Vol. 38 (November 1971), pp. 249-261; Robert E. Stauffer, "Civil Religion, Technocracy, and the Private Sphere: Further Comments on Cultural Integration in Advanced Societies," *Journal for the Scientific Study of Religion*, Vol. 12 (December 1972), pp. 218-225.

The religious component of politics and government has been explored in other cultures. See for instance, Edward Shils and Michael Young, "The Meaning of the Coronation," *Sociological Review*, Vol. 1 (December 1953), pp. 66-70, reprinted in J. Combs and M. Mansfield (eds.), *Drama in Life* (Hastings House, 1976), pp. 302-314; and Ernest B. Koenker, *Secular Salvations* (Fortress Press, 1965).

Much excellent work is subsumed under the Chicago History of American Religion Series, Martin E. Marty, editor, at the University of Chicago Press. Other presses — Westminster, Fortress, and others specialize in religious studies. There is now a literature appearing on the "religious vote," such as Albert J. Menendez, *Religion at the Polls* (Westminster, 1978). But there needs to be more attention paid to religion as pop culture. A good place to start is John Wiley Nelson's *Your God is Alive and Well and Appearing in Popular Culture* (Westminster, 1976). Studies of the "electronic church" include work on the forerunners of media religion, such as Billy Graham and Bishop Fulton J. Sheen. On Graham, see Marshall Frady, *Billy Graham: A Parable of American Righteousness* (Little, Brown, 1979); Frady, "The Use and Abuse of Billy Graham," *Esquire*, April 10, 1979, pp. 25-44; Michael R. Real, "Billy Graham: Mass Medium," in his *Mass-Mediated Culture* (Prentice-Hall, 1977), pp. 152-196. A critical examination of the electronic church is Virginia Stem Owens, *The Total Image: or Selling Jesus in the Modern Age* (William B. Eerdmans, 1980) while a defense is Ben Armstrong, *The Electric Church* (Thomas Nelson, 1979). See also Jerry Sholes, *Give Me That Prime-Time Religion* (Hawthorn Books, 1979); Malcolm Muggeridge, *Christ and the Media* (William B. Eerdmans, 1977), and Donald Meyer, *The Positive Thinkers: Religion as Pop Psychology from Mary Baker Eddy to Oral Roberts* (Pantheon Books). See the discussion of Fulton J. Sheen in J. Fred McDonald, "The Cold War as Entertainment in Fifties Television," *Journal of Popular Film and Television*, Vol. 7 (1978), pp. 22-24. On cults see Christopher Evans, *Cults of Unreason* (Delta, 1980). An interesting piece on a theological theme latent in a television show is James E. Ford, "*Battlestar Galactica* and Mormon Theology," *Journal of Popular Culture* (forthcoming, 1981). A famous interpretation of the religiosity that re-emerged in the 1970s is Tom Wolfe, "The 'Me' Decade and the Third Great Awakening," (New York, August 23, 1976), pp. 26-40.

Part II

Popular Media and the Drama of American Politics

The first part of the book dealt with American popular dramas that have implications for politics. What we learn through popular culture about the American past, especially the Western myth, affects our image of ourselves as a people and thus what we expect out of politics. Similarly, what we learn through participation in popular sports and popular religion has impact upon our political values and actions. Such popular activities form part of our cultural mythic legacy which helps to shape our orientation toward politics.

Now let us turn to the drama of American politics as it is presented in the popular media. The mass media both shape and reflect American popular culture, creating and exploiting themes and moods in the popular consciousness and presenting them in popular form for the consumption of mass audiences. In a wide variety of media, mass communication organizations create symbolic dramas for people to play with. These mediated dramas — television programs, rock music, ads, night club comedy, science fiction, or whatever — include cultural messages which are a source of political learning. For we learn a great deal, as yet uncalculated precisely, about politics through the mass media, in either direct or indirect ways. This makes sense because of the awesome amount of time and attention we give to popular culture in our lives. Our playing with popular dramas communicated to us through the media suggests that either consciously or unconsciously it helps to shape our image of the political world.

In this part of the book, then, we will focus on some of these play-dramas of mediated popular culture which have political consequences for mass audiences. First, we will examine some

86

characteristics of the depiction and reporting of politics through the mass media. Then we will look at political propaganda as popular art. Next, it seems worthwhile to trace something of the connection between show business and politics. And, given the proliferation of American popular culture overseas, we should point to some of the political aspects of this. Finally, we will look at the vision of the political future in science fiction.

Chapter Six:
POP MEDIA: The Depiction and Reporting of Politics in the Mass Media

It is now a cliche to say we live in a "media society." Most of us are familiar with the mass media, take them for granted, use them in our daily lives. Consider for a moment the extent to which most Americans expose themselves to mass media today. We wake up in the morning to a wake-up radio, watch snatches of a television morning show as we dress, read a newspaper as we eat breakfast, listen to a disc jockey on the car radio as we drive to work, maybe catch a soap opera at lunch, the evening news at night, and then watch prime-time television, go to a movie, or listen to pop records. During the course of the day, we see thousands of ads, watch several hours of television, have the radio on for long periods, read a variety of popular newspapers and magazines, in short use multiple media in the interludes of our day. As the day progresses, we keep up with the news, hear several news broadcasts, a newspaper, and news programs and newsbriefs at night. We live in the constant, taken-for-granted "presence" of the mass media.

Mediated messages are central to the "play" of our day. We "keep up" with the news, our favorite disc jockey, soap operas, situation comedies, and magazines. And, as this book has stressed, we learn from this daily fare. Some of the things we learn from the mass media we are aware of, other things we are not. We call the former overt learning, the latter covert learning. But in both cases, what we learn by playing with the mass media affects how we imagine the world. In both direct and indirect ways, the images shaped by the media affects our attitude toward politics. This chapter will explore this. We will first examine popular depictions in the mass media which have political consequences. Then we will look at popular news reporting for the same reason. We cannot be exhaustive, so we will stick to some examples which will illustrate how the process works.

Media logic and play

American mass media are business organizations that market

and sell products to consumers. They are selling entertainment in the form of dramatic stories. The movies, radio, television, the news media, even pop music are storytellers. They are marketing stories for mass audiences, and thus seek common denominators which they think will appeal to mass audiences. The medium utilized defines in some measure the kind of story that is told: a pop record has to be a short tale of romance, a television show includes visual images, a newspaper can include a wide variety of stories, and so on. But certainly the audience is not simply a passive consumer of popular culture creations.

What we are talking about is *media logic*.[1] People are attracted to the products of the mass media industry because the stories told are entertaining. The logic of the creators of popular culture and the logic of the medium itself are supplemented by the logic of the consumers. The creators of mass media stories are interested in how to use a medium to tell stories that will sell. The consumers of this medium are interested in selecting which tales they want to be entertained by. If they find each other, the logics of both have converged: the play-object and the play-consumer engage in popular play. Audiences converge on mass media stories, but their collective logic is not the same. For the mass play of popular culture involves a variety of psycho-logics, different "reasons" why people select and play with a pop creation. The mass media create symbolic realities and appeal to the collective imagination of people, but the play-fantasies of those people may vary. Consequently, what people "get out" of a news program or movie may vary considerably.

Nevertheless, the logic of the creators of mass media stories impels them to appeal to collective fantasies by creating a play-world with which a mass audience can relate. To that end, they attempt to create dramatic *formulas* which "work" with mass audiences. Media formulas involve stereotyped stories and roles which entertain a mass audience. The logic of a media formula is that it includes identifiable cultural myths or personal desires. The play-world created is a formulaic fantasy with which people play and learn.[2]

The consumers of the mass media, then, are active learners. We may seek and select those media stories which reinforce what we already believe, or find new learning, but in either case the media teach us. They give us messages about what the world is like, what values are important, and what the political world is like. We learn about politics by playing with the mass media. It is clear that the media may present a distorted image of politics, but that may be what we want! If mass media organizations are selling entertainment, they may overdramatize or oversimplify political reality.[3] Their media logic is not truth or verisimilitude, but success with a mass audience. Therefore, they may well stereotype politics and politicians for their purposes — and ours — thus giving us a political play-world but not in some way a "real world." So what we learn from media shows, including news shows, may be only an ambiguous, or even deliberately distorted, image of a more various and complex political world.

The mass media and cultural mythology

The dramatic formulas of the mass media revolve around the two broad dimensions of the American Dream we have identified, the materialistic myth and the moralistic myth. The endless variations of the American Dream are the stuff of television shows, news, records, pop books, movies, and so on. Popular stories treat the conflicts, efforts, and sometimes resolutions of the myth. Media formulas are cultural stories, teaching us a good bit about what it means to be an American. These cultural tales include both direct and indirect messages about politics and government with which we can conjur. By linking politics to both positive and negative treatments of our mythology, we then learn something about the role of things political in our culture.[4]

The mass media industry is part of American culture, and are sensitive to the necessity of interweaving identifiable cultural themes into dramatic stories. But the industry is also sensitive to the times in which we live, and thus "responds" to mass trends and moods. Thus, their presentations "play" with both the old and new, with both the cultural myths to which we are heir and the time which gives them new definition. Popular culture responds to and helps to shape people's play-responses to our life at the moment. This includes how we think about and act toward politics.

Let us take the soap opera as an example again. The soap formula, first on radio and now on television, has evolved over the years, retaining some of its features and values but also adapting to changing social conditions in order to "keep up" with its wide audience. Much of the success of the soap opera stems from its eternal "play" with the American moralistic and materialistic myths. Both old and new moralities work and don't work; success and affluence are both good and bad. We are depicted as needing moral roots but wanting moral freedom; of both enjoying wealth and sophistication, but also being corrupted by it. If the soaps are a source of learning for us, we may pick out a wide variety of messages. There certainly may be indirect learning that has political consequences. The constant depiction of moral lapses — abortion, extramarital sex, drugs and alcohol abuse, child abuse — may convince us that "traditional" morality has broken down and that "new" morality leads to license, and direct us toward politicians who urge the restoration of the old morality.

The soaps may also directly depict politics. Many shows have characters — usually males — who run for office (D.A., state senator, etc.). Such episodes often involve the candidate's chances for election entangled in personal love affairs, such as his wife's mental health, the exposure of a love affair, and so on. For the soaps, the central issue in a campaign appears to be personal morality. If people learn from that, then they may "transfer" that from the play-world of the soaps to the real-world of politics, and evaluate political candidates not so much by their political stances as by their personal rectitude.[5]

Although popular culture has at times directly depicted American politics, on the whole indirect popular depictions probably have a great deal more "suggestive" influence. The soaps, like other movies and television shows, pop music, and so forth, are not primarily "about" politics. Yet, their attitude toward American morality and materialism has political consequences. Let us point so some typical media depictions which may contribute to popular political learning.

TV formulas and role stereotyping

Television shows use formulas which appeal to segments of their mass audience. These formulas evolve over the years, but include *role stereotyping,* wherein certain social types or jobs are depicted as typical. Television roles thus may confirm or disconfirm stereotypes held by mass audiences. If women are depicted as dopey and impulsive (as *I Love Lucy*), as competent but still dependent on males (*Mary Tyler Moore Show*), or as sex objects (*Charlie's Angels*), this may reinforce male stereotypes about what women in general are like. The use of female stereotypes in television shows gives shape to people's cognition of "what women are like," and thus indirectly helps form their attitudes toward "women's issues" in politics.[6]

Television formulas and stereotypes, then, are not harmless. Indeed, much attention has been directed toward such shows to determine what in fact is learned from them. The formula that has been studied the most is the "law and order" show — cops and robbers, police vs. criminals, private eyes, and so on. Television never tires of variations of this theme, and we never tire of watching them. Such shows have adventure, mystery, romance. They appeal to the Western moral of the individual hero who defeats evil, but now they are set in an urban setting. They have action, violence, and chases. They often take us to exotic places. And they appeal to our abiding interest in evil, criminals, and "The Mob."

A steady diet of such shows for the habitual viewer does seem to have its toll. Careful studies of the people who are "heavy" users of television indicate that their image of the world differs from "light" users. Heavy users think the world more dangerous and threatening than light users. They don't trust their fellow citizens as much, think that cities are bad places, that violence is endemic and needs violence to suppress it, that they themselves are in danger. Frequent viewers are angrier, more paranoid, and indeed even more prone to violence than those who watch little television. Heavy viewers agree more with the view that "the lot of the average man is getting worse," and that "politicians aren't really interested in most people's problems." They are more prone to buy guns for protection; they are more afraid of walking alone at night; they are likelier to expect that the United States will fight another war in the near future. And they overestimate the percentage of private detectives in the population, the amount of crime, the number of criminals. Such learning may well mean that the fears generated for such people will make them more prone to support "law-and-order" politicians and perceive as a major political issue the "crime wave."[7]

As with the soap, there are even more subtle twists to the law-and-order formula and role stereotypes that may have political consequences. It used to be that the policeman or private detective was a model of moral rectitude, but that is not always the case now. The variation appears to be linked to our changing attitude toward authority. The heroes of such shows must appeal to the "play" people want at the time. Thus, more recent variations include heroes who are less clearly "authoritative" — rebels (*Baretta*), cynics (*Kojak*), slobs (*Columbo*), nice guys (*Barney Miller*), and so forth. There is also the tradition of vigilantism, in which a private eye (*Mike Hammer*), renegade cop (*Dirty Harry*), or private citizen (Charles Bronson in *Death Wish*), takes the law into his own hands. Indeed, the television crime formula, with its accent on violence, the authority of crimestoppers is such that they are allowed considerable latitude in what they do, much more so than in real life. A study of fifteen prime-time police programs during one week found no less than forty-three separate scenes in which the police violated the rights of a suspect, including 21 clear constitutional violations, seven omissions of constitutional rights, and fifteen instances of police brutality and harassment![8] The traditional moralistic myth of the Western "lawman" apparently permits the authority figure to stop crime any way he or she can.

The criminal in such shows is obviously a violator of morality, but variations in his or her depiction may affect our social perceptions. The criminal is often a perverted seeker of the materialistic myth, and his root motive is almost always greed. Often the criminal is already wealthy, enjoying the creature comforts of penthouses, limousines, and plush offices. People may well conclude from such depictions that wealth is evil, the wealthy got that way by crime, and thus that the materialistic myth has clearly bad features. If such a message is representative of reality, one has to violate common morality to achieve material prosperity, and only the moral authority of the crimestopper brings justice to such criminals.

It is obvious that such stereotyped depictions distort reality. The evidence that people get many of their ideas about the world from such shows has led to widespread monitoring of such shows by interest groups. Everybody appears to object to some depiction — unions to the depiction of workers, Italian-Americans to Mafioso, the PTA to violence, and so forth. Based on their definition of the moralistic myth, the "Moral Majority" and such groups want a great variety of shows off the air. But the depictions many such groups would prefer to see would likely be as stereotyped and distorted as the current fare, and simply perpetuate other myths.[9] Whomever's myths get aired, they are likely to have subtle but nevertheless real effects on our attitudes toward the social and political world.

Two examples

Let us discuss two shows which have been much studied as examples of formulaic stereotyping and potential political effect. First, there is the celebrated case of the Archie Bunker role on Norman Lear's highly successful television series, *All in the Family*. Lear's intention was didactic: to make fun of lower-middle-class white bigotry and narrow-mindedness, and thus teach people that bigotry was bad by making fun of a character — Archie — who was a bigot. The show was inspired by similar shows in England and Germany. Like Archie, these characters were ignorant and bigoted working-class males. (The German character, "Alfred Tetzlaff," bears a resemblance to Adolf Hitler!) Lear's intention, then, was "liberal": to satirize conservation, or at least mindless, patriotism, racial prejudice, and intolerance, and thereby make an implicit political point. (Lear is a well-known liberal political activist.) Archie's "reactionary" version of the Dream is negatively juxtaposed by Mike's and Gloria's "liberal" version, thus teaching us that the latter is good.

A study of the viewers of *All in the Family* found, however, that a lot of viewers did not share the stereotype of Archie that Lear was trying to communicate. Only ten percent of a sample of American adolescents thought Archie was the character most often made fun of. Many viewers identified with Archie, saw Archie as the "winner" in their debates, and saw nothing at all wrong with Archie's bigotry and intolerance. Those who were highly prejudiced themselves were the ones most likely to identify with Archie. Indeed, those people most likely to watch the show were already highly prejudiced to start with, and were drawn to the show because they liked Archie! The researchers concluded that, contrary to Lear's intentions, the show did more to *reinforce* bigotry among the mass television audience than to satirize it successfully.[10] In the realm of media depictions, intent does not guarantee effect. Stereotypes and formulas may have an implicit political consequence not desired by the creators of media depictions.

Another popular depiction with political significance was the television mini-series *Roots*. At one point, *Roots* was watched by around 130,000,000 Americans, and became one of the media phenomena of our time. It gave many people, both black and white, a look at the historical spectacle of the black experience in America for the first time. It followed the formulaic canons of the "mini-series," with stereotyped social types. It may give blacks a mythic Eden with which to play — an idyllic Africa from which Kunta Kinte is cruelly taken. However, the formula may have had an effect on mass consciousness about the bitter experience of black people in America by identifying with the victims. In other words, for many people it was the first time they saw the history of America from the point of view of the slaves. (It is interesting to note that the only show to approach *Roots* in mass television audience is the movie *Gone With the Wind*, which depicts the relationship between slave and master very differently.) The successive generations of the "Kinte family" struggle against the institutional power of the system, and one is compelled to identify with their plight and see a glimpse of the evils of slavery and segregation.[11]

A national survey of viewers of *Roots* found that they both reacted to and learned from the show. The study found that among both blacks and whites, the mass audience responded with sadness (92%) and anger (71%), and many admitted to crying over such memorable scenes as the passage of Kunta Kinte to America on the slave ship, the sale of Kizzy away from her family, and the final triumph of Chicken George. Black families treated the series as a major social event, encouraging their children to watch it, and discussing it with them afterwards. Blacks were most likely to become emotionally involved with the show, but did not increase their anger toward whites. Whites reacted with increased sympathy toward blacks, but thought the show was too "one-sided," portraying whites as too evil. In any case, it appears that the show excited many people, they wanted to talk about it, and even learned something from it. Blacks explicitly wanted their children to learn from it, but many whites seemed to have learned from it, too. Such a popular show, then, by the success of a stereotypical historical tale, may have had the effect of making "real" for many Americans an episode in our history often submerged, and perhaps even increasing racial tolerance. The historical accuracy of *Roots* may be questioned, but the power and effects of its stereotyped dramatization is quite real. For many, it showed that blacks are a part of the American experience, and want to share as much as others in the Dream. It showed the "roots" of racial bigotry and exploitation, dramatizing the moral and material deprivation of one race by another, thus denying hope for the Dream. But it also showed that the Dream lives in the survival power and grit of the family, and eventually in the end is somewhat realized by freedom and property. By personifying good and evil, *Roots* offered us a depiction of black people's distance from the Dream in moral terms identifiable by a mass audience. Whether it and other shows like it, with positive depictions of blacks and other minorities, will have long-term effects on racial prejudice remains to be seen.[12]

Popular reporting and politics

News is part of the play of our lives. We learn much of what we know about the world outside our immediate experience from the stories told to us by news media—newspapers, radio and television news, newsmagazines. The news business gives us their depictions of the social and political world for the same reason that non-news media do — to make money. News is thus entertainment — stories about "what's happening now" — which will hold the attention of an audience and thereby their advertising accounts. News is marketed to the extent that research is done on what kind of news mass audiences want to see reported. That such news is selected, geared toward popular common denominators, the sensation-alistic, biased, and misleading is obvious. The press receives the same criticisms that groups express about popular media depictions of the world. The news media are charged with distortion, persecution, superficiality, rumormongering, and just plain sloppy reporting. Politicians constantly berate and intimidate the media, and even attempt to suppress news stories. Yet they also try to use and manipulate the media for their own political purposes.[13]

The principle of media logic applies as much to the news business as other kinds of mass media. The process of newsmaking involves a variety of business, journalistic, political, and interest group pressures. News is "selected" with those pressures in mind. The news media are storytellers drawn to dramatic formulas and stereotyped roles.[14] They are also part of American culture, and thus tend to hold attitudes toward and depict in various ways aspects of the American Dream.[15] Their popular audiences can "play" with both positive and negative treatments of the materialistic myth and moralistic myth and relate this "news" to their images and actions concerning politics. To a large degree our reactions to popular news depends upon how they treat the meaning and interplay of our myths.

Our belief in and interest in the American Dream becomes the basis for typical news stories, either in the realization of material or moral worth or in their absence. Think of the "stuff" of news stories on, for example, the television network news. In one way or the other, television news stories are typically a tale of someone trying to realize the American Dream, for good or ill. A story about the poor struggling to survive in the wake of budget cuts may suggest to some of us that not all share in the material Dream, and for others that the poor are immoral and could get out of their fix if they had initiative. A "liberal" may play with the story as to how society is immoral if it doesn't help the poor, a "conservative" that society is immoral if it does. The news story may be played by the reporter and program one way or the other, but that does not guarantee that the mass audience is going to get the implied message; we read into it what we want. In any case, we learn from it something that affects our attitude toward the Dream.

Popular reporting, then, is a process by which the mass media create stories about how current events affect the American Dream. A story may tell of a small town (a "moral community") disrupted by big business moving in (the "material community"). Is it a threat or a promise? Is capitalism responsible or not? What values realize the American Dream? The extent to which such stories have mass impact, and become part of our political learning, probably has bearing on the course of American politics. Most of us probably select and play with those news media which tell stories that dramatize what we already believe. But we cannot avoid coming into contact with news stories about the conflicts and failures of the Dream, and that disturbs us. If we think that some aspect of the Dream is being unrealized, we may seek politicians who promise us that they will fulfill it.

A non-political story may also have political implications because popular news audiences give it political play. If a story dramatizes something about the status of the American Dream, then many of us are quite capable of seeing the political implications. Take for example the coverage of the nuclear power plant accident at Three Mile Island in 1979. Different media covered the story different ways, and indeed in terms of this event's relationship to American mythology, it could be dramatized in different ways. For some reporters, the "story" was the immorality of the material community: big business had built a Frankenstein monster for profit in the middle of a peaceful garden, the monster got loose, and the innocent peasants had to flee. Or the story might focus on the concern for safety on the part of the business, reflecting the responsibility of material elites. Stories could represent either the compatibility or incompatibility of the nuclear plant and the surrounding community, reflecting an old theme in the American Dream, the relationship between the Machine and the Garden. In any case, dramatizing the relationship of the accident to the Dream does have political fallout, depending on how we "read" the story.[16]

The direct coverage of politics usually includes definitions of what is valuable in the American Dream. The "moral of the political story" dramatizes how some political event, at home or abroad, affects our national fate, both morally and materially. The Mideast oil crises, for example, include sober speculation in the news about how this affects the American material community, and indeed the moral community. Why can't the material community provide us with gasoline? Are Americans immoral for consuming so much energy? Does the American Dream include our right to squander gas as we see fit (in, for instance, big gas-guzzlers)? What does energy shortages tell us about the future of the American Dream? If one candidate tells us that with the proper incentives free enterprise will discover enough oil for our lifestyle, does our reading of news stories about this affect our choice of candidates?

How a particular political story is dramatized has a great deal to do with our reaction to it, both emotionally and eventually politically. The coverage of the Iranian hostage crisis evoked this reaction. Much of the coverage was "sensational" in the sense that the visual coverage depicted Iranian hatred and defiance of the United States. The scenes of Iranian crowds shouting anti-American slogans in front of the embassy, coupled with news reporter speculation about the threat to the hostages' lives, evoked intense reactions among much of the American audience. Such dramatic treatment of the story made for exciting news copy, but it also had political consequences. People "played" with what ought to be done, militarily or politically, to resolve the crisis. The more emotional the response, the more likely the television viewer wanted direct retribution ("Nuke the Ayatollah"). Thus, the coverage first contributed to Carter's rise in the polls and success in 1980 presidential primaries (a "rally-round-the-flag" effect), and then to frustration over his inability to resolve the crisis as the mass audience wanted it to be. In the long run, the coverage also revived popular political thinking about the morality of American imperial involvements abroad, and what sort of political moral should apply — the morality of saving the lives of the hostages, or the morality of national honor? Not only did the hostage crisis affect the 1980 election, the release of the hostages on election day brought brief popular outbursts of patriotic celebration over the "re-integration" of the American moral community.

The Iranian crisis was a spectacular, disturbing story given much play by the news media. ABC-TV, for instance, began to run a nightly late-hour program entitled "America Held Hostage." The story was "personalized" as a conflict between evil and violent fanatics holding innocent American victims. It revived one of the most enduring fantasies in American culture, the captivity story. The hostage story was especially disturbing, since it challenged our sense of national righteousness, that the American Dream of moral superiority and material wealth should be honored and copied abroad by our friends. Revolutionary Iran, however, offered us a dramatic story of a former "friend" who rejected American benevolence. Their televised hatred and defiance toward us helped to revive intense patriotic fervor in the United States, as if we desperately needed to reassert the American Dream in the face of an alien challenge. We may speculate that if the media had not "played" the story the way they did, it might not have had the mass political effect it did. By treating it as a personal drama rather than, say, a small incident in a larger world of Persian Gulf policy considerations, they sensationalized the story. By doing so, the media gave impetus to the mass feelings about the story, and wittingly or not affected public opinion about Iran and the general political mood of the time.

The media logic of popular news reporting thus includes treating stories in light of their relevance to the American Dream. News organizations, in the business of selling news, treat stories in various ways, realizing there may be mass responses, including political ones, to how a story is reported. News play with stories then not only shapes our ideas about the American Dream, but also what current events tell us about the politics of the Dream.

The confluence of popular news and politics

The confluence that results from the necessities of the news business and the necessities of politics is to be expected in a media society. Like symbiotic relationships in nature, the two enterprises need each other. Politicians must understand and use the media to be successful, and the media reporters must do the same with politicians. The result is cooperation in which both parties use each other. In campaigns, for example, the politician running for, say, President provides schedules, colorful "media events," news releases timed for the newspersons deadline, interviews, and so forth. The news organizations provide media forums for the candidate to reach popular audiences. Both the news organizations and the candidate's media advisers understand the media logic of campaigns. They realize that, for instance, television news had formulas for news programs, and both sides have a stake in the story being dramatic for a popular audience.[17]

This is not to say, of course, that there is not conflict between news and politicians. Take the case of campaigns again. The confluence is clear enough, but there is also considerable tension between the campaign organization and the press corps. The press wants to be "critical" and "objective," but the campaign organization dislikes criticism. More importantly, the campaign "flacks" want to influence how the press reports their candidate. If the press casts him as heroic, everything is fine; but if they stereotype him as villain ("wanting war") or fool (making dumb statements), then the tension rises.

There are other ways in which the press and politics have merged. Since the expansion of mass play with news, news reporters have become celebrities, being paid enormous salaries like athletes, becoming the subject of gossip columns, and intervening in political affairs. The role of television "media stars" in the peace negotiations between Egypt and Israel was remarkable. Figures like Walter Cronkite, Barbara Walters, and John Chancellor actually facilitated the negotiations between Begin of Israel and Sadat of Egypt, with Cronkite even acting as a go-between. As media stars, they were an integral part of the play, not only sustaining audience interest in what was a media drama but playing a part in that drama. Some critics thought this made the negotiations into a media event, undercutting the diplomatic authorities in the United States, and raising false hopes among their popular audience that media intervention could resolve the age-old conflict.

Somewhat the reverse of the political involvement of media stars is the transformation of political stars into media stars. NBC hired ex-President Gerald Ford and ex-Secretary of State Henry Kissinger to multi-million dollar contracts as "news commentator" and "special consultants for world affairs," wherein they were supposed to bring their political expertise to news programs. Even Watergate criminals signed lucrative contracts to give interviews, make speeches, and write books. But the media logic of it seems irresistible; if media stars can involve themselves in politics, why can't politicians involve themselves in the media?

But the overall importance of the confluence of media and politics in America may well be that politicians accept the "values" of the media. Their attempts at election, their daily schedule in office, their decisions, even their careers out of office all are affected by the demands of the popular news business. They come to feel they are media figures who must live up to the logic of the media. Presidential power now must include the depiction of the First Family in gossip magazines, news stories about their private lives, and the like. Apparently presidential families understand the media's and their mass audience's interest in playing with their private lives. Presidents and their families are, after all, political embodiments of the moral myth and the material myth, and the media's glimpses into how they live either confirms or denies that they are living up to that trust.

Newspeople and popular learning

The people in the news industry are as much products of popular culture as the rest of us. We may speculate that their self-image as journalists and their image of politics may be much affected by popular culture. In other words, reporters learn things about the news industry and the political world from popular sources. Think, for instance, how the movies and television depict reporters. From old movies like *The Front Page* down to the television series *Lou Grant,* it seems that three recurrent depictions may be observed. First, there is the traditional view of the reporter as an urbane, cynical, and worldly-wise *tough guy* who observes the corrupt world of politics with a jaundiced eye. Popular culture has also seen the reporter as a *crusader,* righting some social wrong by writing editorials and stories about moral corruption. Finally, there is the image of the reporter as *detective,* as someone whose hard digging for the facts uncovers an important story. These qualities, of course, may be combined in one fictional figure. Lou Grant, for instance, is a tough guy but also something of a crusader (the shows often involve some general social problem) and detective (there is often a mystery). These images may affect the self-image of reporters, and affect their attitude toward themselves, journalism, and politics.

Consider, for example, the degree to which the film *All The President's Men* helped to revive the romance of investigative journalism. Woodward and Bernstein were depicted as relentless detectives moving through a Washington of adventure, mystery, and romance. Both crusaders and detectives at the Washington *Post* then uncover the Watergate scandal and bring down a President. It was said that Watergate helped to boost enrollment in journalism schools, and this movie probably helped. For here the reporter is the moral hero, the agent who saves the moral community by uncovering political immorality. The *Post* reporters and editors become redeemer figures whose commitment to truth "though the heavens fall" brings down the President but preserves constitutional government and the freedom of the press. Such a romantic myth would indeed make journalism seem like an appealing career. It may also help reinforce the self-image journalists would like to hold about themselves.

Positive popular images of the journalist, then, is a potential source of learning for those in or considering journalism as a career. It makes them part of a moral community that dramatically fights social evils. However, popular culture includes many negative images of journalists, too. The savage movie satire of network news,

Network, depicted journalists as ambitious, greedy, and cynical. Other films, such as *The China Syndrome,* showed television newspeople covering "fluff" stories and yielding to intimidation by powerful organizations. Negative images may discourage those who had thought journalism was romantic and heroic. And it may also plant doubts in those journalists who think likewise. In any case, popular cultural treatments of the news world gives us images of it which may color our attitude toward the news. For example, popular depictions from which we learn may affect the extent to which we trust newspeople and the news. If we trust, or do not trust, the news, is it because of the impressions made on us by popular culture?

Television as ritual

Television news, as well as other forms of programming, is ritual play. We learn from it, but the learning is ritualized learning. We watch it habitually, and we expect the play of the show to have certain features. In particular, we expect the news to include certain cultural messages, most notably its depictions, both positively and negatively, of the American Dream. Television news follows a formulaic logic, presenting current stories with a mythological meaning. We attend to news shows, one may argue, because it ritually reassures us of our values. For some, watching the news may be a ritual of reaffirmation of the American Dream; for others, it may be a ritual of denial, in which the Dream is unrealized. In either case, the news teaches us about the current status of the Dream. We use television news to gratify our beliefs about ourselves and the world. We want that gratification to occur in a familiar pattern, in the ritualized structure of the news show. The ritual drama of the news show depicts for us a condensed world of political talks with the Soviets, the rise and fall of the Dow, the effects of politics and economics on ordinary people.

People play with the news, then, to ritualize their responses to the world "out there" beyond their immediate daily lives. The ritualized structure of the news show helps us to focus our distress about the change, the presence of enemies, and the confusing debate over what should be done in politics. The world may be threatening, but at least it is made predictable by its incorporation in the familiar formula of television news. The television news ritual dramatizes the life of American mythology, but also the ways the Dream is unheeded or unrealized. It communicates to us both our cultural values and the troubles those values are having in the present. It is a ritual both of reassurance and subversion.[18]

For some, the ritualization of news gives comfort — the world is troubled, but the values endure. For others, the evening litany of troubles is discomforting — things are getting worse, the people in charge can't cope, the Dream is becoming a nightmare. This dependence on the news ritual by both "optimists" and "pessimists" has inspired much speculation and study by students of the media. Some people may depend on the ritual of television news because it is less distressing than other forms of media news. Others may see in it the most frightful reminder of the terrible state of things. In either case, it may be that such dependence increases political malaise. In other words, people who participate heavily in the play-ritual of television news may be either satisfied or dissatisfied with the state of the American Dream, and thus conclude that things are either so good or so bad that no action is necessary or possible. People may "learn helplessness" through the news ritual. The news ritual teaches us that our participation in the life beyond our immediate experience is only possible as a passive observer. For this reason, the news ritualization of politics may contribute to popular political malaise.[19] It is not difficult to calculate what the political consequences of such a popular phenomenon might be.[20]

Notes

[1]David L. Althiede and Robert P. Snow, *Media Logic* (Sage, 1979).

[2]William Stephenson, *The Play Theory of Mass Communication* (University of Chicago P., 1967).

[3]See the thoughtful exploration of entertainment by Harold Mendelsohn, *Mass Entertainment* (College and University Press, 1966).

[4]Peter H. Wood, "Television as Dream," Horace Newcomb (ed.), *Television: The Critical View* (Oxford University P., 1979), pp. 517-535.

[5]On soap operas, see W. Lloyd Warner and William E. Henry, "The Radio Day Time Serial: A Symbolic Analysis," *Genetic Psychology Monographs,* Vol. 37 (1948), pp. 3-71; the articles in the section entitled "Daytime Serial Drama," *Journal of Communication,* Vol. 29 (Autumn 1979), pp. 66-88; the articles in Newcomb, *op. cit.,* Renata Adler, "Afternoon Television: Unhappiness Enough, and Time," pp. 74-86; and Dennis Porter, "Soap Time: Thoughts on a Commodity Art Form," pp. 87-96; Francine Hardaway, "The Language of Popular Culture: Daytime Television as a Transmitter of Value," *College English,* Vol. 40 (January 1979), pp. 517-521; Horace Newcomb, *TV: The Most Popular Art* (Doubleday Anchor, 1974), pp. 161-182; "Sex and Suffering in the Afternoon," *Time* cover story, January 12, 1976, reprinted in William Hammel (ed.), *The Popular Arts in America,* 2nd ed., (Harcourt Brace Jovanovich, 1977), pp. 287-297; see also Robert LaGuardia, *The Wonderful World of TV Soap Operas* (Ballantine Books, 1974) and Manuela Soares, *The Soap Opera Book* (Harmony Books, 1978). Too, consider the following quote from R.P. Cuzzort and E.W. King, *Humanity and Modern Social Thought,* 2nd ed. (Dryden Press, 1976), in discussing social theorist Hugh Dalziel Duncan's ideas about art, culture, and social action:

"A soap opera, for example, is not something which works just to amuse the frustrated housewife. The housewife may actually rely on the soap opera to gauge the nature of her own social existence. She may view the soap opera as a presentation of someone else's domestic problems, but she may also incorporate its value priorities into her own domestic problems. The soap opera and the "realities" of life are thus conjoined. It is not a mechanical connection. To the extent that the housewife acts out the concerns of the soap opera, art and life have come together. The woman's day-to-day existence is as much a reflection of art as art is a reflection of her life." (Pp. 298-299.)

[6]For studies of women in the media, see Gaye Tuchman, et. al., *Hearth and Home: Images of Women in the Mass Media* (Oxford University P., 1978); Kathryn Weibel, *Mirror Mirror* (Doubleday Anchor, 1977); Maurine Beasley and Sheila Silver, *Women in Media* (Women's Institute for Freedom of the Press, 1977); Judith S. Gelfman, *Women in Television News* (Columbia University P., 1980); Susan Franzblau, et. al., "Sex on TV: A Content Analysis," *Journal of Communication,* Vol. 27 (Spring 1977), pp. 164-170; symposium, "What Does 'She' Mean," Journal of Communication, Vol. 28 (Winter 1978), pp. 130-192.

[7]Since 1967, a team of researchers has monitored television violence at the University of Pennsylvania's Annenberg School of Communications. For a summary of the heavy user effect, see George Gerbner and Larry Gross, "The Scary World of TV's Heavy Viewer," *Psychology Today* (April 1976), pp. 42-45, 89.

[8]Stephen Arons and Ethan Katsh, "How TV Cops Flout the Law," *Saturday Review,* March 19, 1977, pp. 11-18.

[9]See the studies and propaganda generated by such interest groups as the International Association of Machinists, concerned with the image of labor on TV; the Congressional Black Caucus, which objected to a CBS program about a black Congressman, "Mr. Dugan"; the National Association of Arab Americans, which monitors anti-Arab depictions; the National Federation of Decency, which objects to sex and violence; the Parent-Teachers Association, which monitors and protests TV violence; and on, endlessly.

[10]See Neil Vidmar and Milton Rokeach, "Archie Bunker's Bigotry: A Study in Selective Perception and Exposure," *Journal of Communication,* Vol. 24 (Winter 1974), pp. 36-47; see also three studies of the Archie controversy in the *Journal of Communication,* Vol. 26 (Autumn 1976), pp. 61-68, 69-74, and 75-85.

[11]Phillip Wander, "On the Meaning of *Roots,*" *Journal of Communication,* Vol. 27 (Autumn 1977), pp. 64-69.

[12]National survey, Center for Policy Research, New York, reported in Kathy La Tour, " 'Roots' Postlude: Survey Charts Viewer Response," *The National Observer,* June 20, 1977, p. 2.

[13]The literature on the news process alone is vast. See Edward Jay Epstein, *News From Nowhere* (Vintage Books, 1974); David Altheide, *Creating Reality: How TV News Distorts Events* (Sage, 1976); and Gaye Tuchman, *Making News: A Study in the Construction of Reality* (The Free Press, 1978); Edith Efron, *The News Twisters* (Nash Publishing, 1971); C. Richard Hofstetter, *Bias in the News* (Ohio State University P., 1976); Robert Cirino, *Don't Blame the People* (Diversity Press, 1971); Edwin Diamond, *The Tin Kazoo* (MIT Press, 1975).

[14]David L. Eason, "Telling Stories and Making Sense," *Journal of American Culture* (1981, forthcoming); Gaye Tuchman, "What Is News? Telling Stories," *Journal of Communication* (Autumn 1976), pp. 94-97; James E. Combs, "Mass Communication and Political Drama," in *Dimensions of Political Drama* (Goodyear Pubco, 1980), pp. 106-137; Robert Brustein, "News Theater," *New York Times Magazine,* June 16, 1974; Paul H. Weaver, "Captives of Melodrama," *New York Times Magazine,* August 29, 1976; David L. Swanson, "And That's the Way It Was? Television Covers the 1976 Presidential Campaign" *Quarterly Journal of Speech,* Vol. 63 (October 1977), pp. 239-248.

[15]The "enduring values" that the news depict has been explored by Herbert J. Gans, "The Messages Behind the News," *Columbia Journalism Review* (January/February 1979), pp. 40-45; see also his book, *Deciding What's News* (Pantheon, 1979).

[16]James Combs and Dan Nimmo, "The Return of Frankenstein: The Aesthetic of Three Mile Island Coverage by ABC Evening News," *Studies in Popular Culture,* Vol. IV (Spring 1981), pp. 38-48.

[17]See Timothy Crouse's delightful account of the 1972 campaign, *The Boys on the Bus* (Ballantine Books, 1974).

[18]Gregor Goethals, *The TV Ritual* (Beacon, 1981); James Combs, "The Family Altar Under the Antenna: Television as Ritual," *The Cresset,* Vol. XLIV (April 1981), pp. 22-24.

[19]Grace Ferrari Levine, "Learned Helplessness and the Evening News," *Journal of Communication,* Vol. 27 (Autumn 1977), pp. 100-105; Lee B. Becker and Jeffrey W. Fruit, "The Growth of TV Dependence: Tracing the Origins of the Political Malaise," paper presented at the 30th conference of the International Communication Association, 1980.

[20]It is impossible here to detail the literature on the mass media and politics, but we can offer some suggested starting points. First, consult such media-oriented journals as the *Journal of Communication, Journal of Broadcasting, Quarterly Journal of Speech, Journalism Quarterly, Columbia Journalism Review, Communication Monographs, Communication Research, Human Communication Research, Public Opinion Quarterly, Central States Speech Journal, Southern Speech Communication Journal, Western Journal of Speech Communication, Political Communication Review,* and others. Extensive bibliographies on different subjects involving communication and the mass media are available from The Annenberg School of Communications, University of Southern California, University Park, Los Angeles, CA 90007.

Introductory books which relate aspects of mass media and popular culture are Francis and Ludmilla Voekler (eds.), *Mass Media: Forces in Our Society* (Harcourt Brace Jovanovich, 1978); Edward Jay Whetmore, *MediaAmerica* (Wadsworth, 1979); Fredric Rissover and David C. Birch, *Mass Media and the Popular Arts* (McGraw-Hill, 1977). A wide-ranging collection of material is in Ithiel de Sola Pool, et. al. (eds.), *Handbook of Communication* (Rand McNally, 1973). The most complete treatment of political communication is Dan Nimmo's *Political Communication and Public Opinion in America* (Goodyear, 1978), but see also the less formidable volume, Doris A. Graber, *Mass Media and American Politics* (Congressional Quarterly Press, 1980). A compendium of data on effects is Sidney Kraus and Dennis Davis, *The Effects of Mass Communication on Political Behavior* (Pennsylvania State University P., 1976). Another relevant collection is George Comstock, et. al., *Television and Human Behavior* (Columbia University P., 1978). Gaye Tuchman (ed.), *The TV Establishment* (Prentice-Hall, 1974) is a good place to start examining the media as institutions. The "great man" theory of media power is advanced by David Halberstam, *The Powers That Be* (Knopf, 1979). The latest treatment on presidential media is Michael B. Grossman and Martha J. Kumar, *Portraying the President* (Johns Hopkins University P., 1981). The work of media guru Marshall McKuhan, *Understanding Media* (Signet, 1964), and *The Gutenberg Galaxy* (Signet, 1969) is still provocative and controversial. Classics of interest here include Walter Lippmann, *Public Opinion* (Macmillan, 1922), Bernard Berelson and Morris Janowitz (eds.), *Reader in Public Opinion and Communication* (The Free Press, 1953), and Kurt and Gladys Engel Lang, *Politics and Television* (Quadrangle, 1968). The relationship between government and news organizations is explored in Leon V. Sigal, *Reporters and Officials* (D.C. Heath, 1973).

To gain a grounding in communication theory, the interested reader might consult David Berlo, *The Process of Communication* (Holt, Rinehart, and Winston, 1960); Melvin DeFleur, *Theories of Mass Communication* (David McKay, 1966); Ernest G. Bormann, *Communication Theory* (Holt, Rinehart, and Winston, 1980); but the most entertaining entry is Paul Watzlawick, *How Real is Real?* (Vintage 1976). George N. Gordon's *The Languages of Communication* (Hastings House, 1969) has much material relevant to the study of popular culture.

Much of popular culture studies involves study of the depictions in mass media, but unfortunately relatively few involve political interpretations. The aforementioned collection edited by Horace Newcomb, *Television: The Critical View, op. cit.,* is indispensable. Bradley S. Greenberg, *Life on Television: Content Analyses of U.S. TV Drama* (Ablex, 1980) is systematic and worthwhile, both for methodology and results. Almost every issue of the *Journal of Popular Culture* will include an interpretation of a media depiction, but the criteria for interpretation remains a murky and complicated issue. Nevertheless, a few examples may give the reader the idea and inspire him/her to try it. See J.D. Lechenby, "Attribution of Dogmatism to T.V. Characters," *Journalism Quarterly,* Vol. 54 (Spring 1977), pp. 14-19; B. Reeves and M.M. Miller, "Multidimensional Measure of Children's Identification with Television Characters," *Journal of Broadcasting,* Vol. 22 (Winter 1978), pp. 71-86, for attempts to systematize the relationship between depiction and audience. See also, C.N. Piltch, "Reassuring Role of TV's Continuing Characters," *USA Today,* Vol. 107 (March 1979), pp. 54-56; E.M. Becherman, "Superheroes, Antiheroes, and the Heroism Void in Children's TV," *Christian Century,* Vol. 96 (July 4, 1979), pp. 704-707. One of the most interesting episodes involved audience interpretation of the character of Archie Bunker of *All in the Family.* See Neil Vidmar and Milton Rokeach, "Archie Bunker's Bigotry: A Study in Selective Perception and Exposure," *Journal of Communication,* Vol. 24 (Winter 1974), pp. 36-47, and the three studies of the controversy in the *Journal of Communication,* Vol. 26 (Autumn 1976), pp. 61-68, 69-74, and 75-85. Another part of a *Journal of Communication* issue was devoted to *Roots:* see Phillip Wander, "On the Meaning of *Roots,*" Vol. 27 (Autumn 1977), pp. 64-69. With regard to what vicarious experience people obtain from media depictions, see John L. Caughey, "Artificial Social Relations in Modern America," *American Quarterly,* Vol. 30 (1978), pp. 70-89. The television "docudrama" has been explored: see James

Combs, "Television Aesthetics and the Depiction of Heroism: The Case of the TV Historical Biography," *Journal of Popular Film and Television,* Vol. 8 (1980), pp. 9-18; and Joseph P. McKerns, "Television Docudramas: The Image as History," *Journalism History,* Vol. 7 (Spring 1980), pp. 24-25, 40.

Analysis of depictions should be grounded in some of the conceptual approaches mentioned in the notes to Chapter One. See, for example, Milton C. Albrecht, "Does Literature Reflect Common Values?", *American Sociological Review,* XXI (1956), pp. 722-729; and the comparative study by Donald V. McGranahan and Ivor Wayne, "German and American Traits Reflected in Popular Drama," *Human Relations,* Vol. I (1948), pp. 429-455, as well as the works mentioned there.

There is much work on the culture of reporting and its relationship to politics, so again we want simply to mention works that will get the student started. A good place to start is W.A. Swanberg's biographies of press lords who transformed print into popular culture: *Citizen Hearst* (Bantam, 1971); *Pulitzer* (Scribner's, 1972), and *Luce and the American Century* (Bantam, 1974). Another absorbing tale is Robert Meta, *CBS: Reflections in a Bloodshot Eye* (Signet, 1975). More formal is Eric Barnouw's *History of Broadcasting in the United States,* 3 vols. (Oxford University P.); Edwin Emery, *The Press and America* (Prentice-Hall, 1972); John Tebbel, *The Media in America* (Mentor, 1974). A study of the press as institution is Charles S. Steinberg, *The Information Establishment* (Hastings House, 1979). Some good essays on cases of reportage are Edward Jay Epstein, *Between Fact and Fiction: The Problem of Journalism* (Vintage, 1975), and Ben H. Bagdikian, *The Effete Conspiracy* (Harper & Row, 1972). One of the most exhaustive case studies is Peter Braestrup, *Big Story: How the American Press and Television Reported and Interpreted the Crisis of Tet in 1968 in Vietnam and Washington* (Doubleday Anchor, 1978). Pieces discussing aspects of media as culture include, Harold L. Wilensky, "Mass Society and Mass Culture: Interdependence of Independence?", *American Sociological Review,* Vol. 29 (April 1964), pp. 173-196; George Gerbner and Nancy Signorielli, "The World of Television News," in *Television Network News,* ed. William Adams and Fay Schreibman (George Washington U., School of Public and International Affairs, 1978), pp. 189-196. An intriguing article on the question of objectivity is Gaye Tuchman, "Objectivity as a Strategic Ritual: An Examination of Newsmen's Notions of Objectivity," *American Journal of Sociology,* Vol. 77 (January 1972).

The reader will also benefit from more topical pieces that may whet the appetite for further empirical research by the interested student. See, for openers, Terri Schultz, "Bamboozle Me Not at Wounded Knee," (June 1973), pp. 46-56; Robert Brustein, "News Theater," New York *Times Magazine,* June 16, 1974, pp. 66-75; Tom Bethell, "The Myth of an Adversary Press," *Harper's,* January 1977, pp. 33-40; Michael Herr, *Dispatches* (Knopf, 1978), on Vietnam coverage; on war coverage in general, see Phillip Knightley, *The First Casualty* (Harcourt Brace Jovanovich, 1975); see the discussion of "The New Political Power of the Press," by Don Bonafede and Edwin Diamond, *Washington Journalism Review* (September 1980), pp. 25-37.

Chapter Seven

POLPROP: Political Propaganda as Popular Art

The popular media in America are part of the economy and culture of an advanced industrial society. A capitalist-consumer economy and democratic culture suggests that a great deal of effort is spent inducing people to do something they might not otherwise do — buy something, watch something, believe in something, vote for someone. This effort is termed *persuasion*.[1] In a wide variety of ways, media organizations use sophisticated techniques of *propaganda,* deliberate and usually dramatic communications to persuade popular audiences of something. We are constant targets of propaganda, being exposed to thousands of persuasive messages every day. The communication industry that produces the various kinds of propaganda — advertising, public relations, publicity — is vast and expensive. A consumer economy depends on us to consume more, different, and new products constantly — new cars, new clothes, new foods, new books. The "persuasion industry" whose job it is to ensure that we do consumer products means that our consumption habits are not left to chance. Indeed, popular culture producers themselves (movies, television, recordings, books, etc.) spend a great deal of money advertising their wares.

If we may speak of media logic, we may also speak of *propaganda logic*.[2] The logic of propaganda assumes that people do respond to persuasive messages, and that skill in presentation can make a difference in our consumptive habits, what we will believe, and toward what we are attracted. Thus, the propagandist's effort directs her to use the arts of persuasion to reach, and even create, audiences for her message. The logic is manipulative across mass audiences, appealing to common human desires and beliefs through the use of popular art forms. It is common to use dramatic formulas

and stereotypes in the presentation of propaganda messages. If we
do resist propaganda, it is not because they aren't trying: since the
message is persuasive, the most sophisticated means of persuasion
— depth psychology, cultural studies, public moods, exquisite
technology, even "subliminal" appeals — are used.[3]

The logic of propaganda also includes a propaganda *aesthetic*.[4]
The propagandist uses language and imagery to communicate with
popular audiences. As an art form, propaganda has developed its
own traditions, conventions, and aesthetic standards. The
"persuasion industry" values the artistry of great ads, public
relations episodes, and publicity campaigns. Advertising in
particular creates fantasy worlds which dramatize a product
through the use of art. Yet, the same aesthetic principle applies to
other forms of persuasion also. A publicity campaign that turns an
unknown actress into a "star" involves dramatizing her as having
sex appeal, acting ability, celebrity, and takes skilled
organizational coordination of popular communication. The star, as
much as the ad for denture cream or Twinkies, is an aesthetic object
created and communicated by propaganda artists.

Propaganda and learning

Propaganda is a source of popular learning.[5] We learn about our
culture, our time, the choices in our lives. Our constant exposure to
propaganda makes us used to it and responsive to it. We take it for
granted that we will learn from it. We play with it because it offers us
ideas and images about ourselves and the world. We can remember
ads, stars, and so forth because they captured our attention, taught
us something. The dramatic formula of the "spot ad" on television
amuses us, titillates us, impresses upon us that we can handle a
situation through the use of a certain product. We associate our own
lives with products, stars, and politicians which we are told possess
certain desirable qualities that we need. If we did not believe
propaganda, we might not consume or prefer the things we do. In
short, we have bought the logic of the propaganda by being
impressed with the aesthetic of its presentation.

Propaganda, then, is a source of popular learning because it is
play, offering us dramatic worlds to which we may vicariously
transport ourselves. It helps us deal with our identities and anxieties
by offering us dramatic "proof" of what we can be and do.
Propaganda is a world wherein many individual members of a mass
audience learn by playing with a created fantasy world which they
can then relate to their own lives. Why did we buy a particular brand

of designer jeans, or like a particular movie star, or vote for a particular candidate? For that matter, did we decide to go to a particular college because of the propaganda brochures they mailed to us?

Propaganda and cultural mythology

Propagandists use cultural mythology for their own persuasive purposes. Propaganda couches its appeals in terms of the moralistic or materialistic myth, and indeed suggests some of the conflicts in the Dream. Let us take the obvious example — the appeal to sex and marriage. All such propaganda revolves around the legitimacy of hedonistic materialism, and the morality of marriage and family. A perfume ad may suggest that wearing it leads to sexual success. An ad for a detergent may dramatize that a clean wash contributes to marital happiness. If we have anxieties and desires about either, this means that we share those feelings with most other people. It also means that propaganda offers us an ubiquitous source of dramatization of cultural myths with a persuasive purpose directed at us.

We play with cultural myths as presented in propaganda because the messages offer us hope of satisfaction. An ad typically presents a cultural problem about which we have deep fears and confusions — fear about social acceptance, financial success, our moral worth, the future of our country. The ad dramatizes our personal fear by offering a solution, or at least an outlet for our anxiety. This principle of propaganda logic is evident in both moralistic propaganda and materialistic propaganda. Think how much of "moral education" is propaganda — sermons, lectures at school, speeches by politicians, urging on us religious, educational, or political morality. More common on the ads we see every day is the promise of moral worth through consumption — from being accepted as an equal by our friends to being part of a moral community that eats only "natural" foods. If we are urged by the phone company to "reach out, reach out and touch someone," we are seeing use of the myth of a moral community of loving relations. If we are urged to drink a mass-produced wine because a "wine expert" advises us of its snob appeal, we are seeing use of the myth of material acquisition and deserved hedonism. Indeed, many propagandistic appeals will attempt to integrate both myths: a car ad may try to combine symbols of economy (our moral responsibility to conserve gas) with elegance (material luxuries such as velour seats).

Political propagandists use cultural mythology for their persuasive purposes. Since politicians are supposed to be "guardians" of American political myths, as they define them, they feel they have to use propaganda to "propagate" popular support for what they believe in. The logic of propaganda is an integral part of American politics. Politicians use propaganda to sell themselves — he is what he claims to be, she is a person of great ability, the President is the guardian of the American Dream. Bureaucracies use propaganda — the Pentagon is the guardian of American power, wealth, and moral purpose, NASA carries the American Dream of empire and adventure into space. Interest groups, parties, and other political organizations also use propaganda. Since they are all trying to "teach" people something about politics, political groups are drawn into the logic of propaganda, offering us dramatic evidence of how they are guarding the American Dream. The politician or political organization is thus linked to cultural mythology, appealing to our deepest and most widely held ideas and images about ourselves and our country.

Here we want to discuss briefly some political stages on which propaganda dramas are enacted. This will illustrate the political uses of popular propaganda: advertising in political campaigns, popular culture creations as political propaganda, and "semi-official" popular culture as political propaganda.

Political advertising in campaigns

We are all familiar with the flurry of political propaganda that emerges during campaigns for public office. In major campaigns, the advertising and other propaganda are quite sophisticated, utilizing the skills of propaganda experts, most of whom are drawn from advertising, public relations, and publicity. These "publicists" structure the campaign communications of the candidate, taping television ads and programs, staging campaign "pseudo-events," arranging itineraries, writing position papers, brochures, and speeches, doing polls, and so on. Altogether, the political persuasion industry has brought all the arts and logic of propaganda to contests for public office.[6]

Political advertising, especially on television, has become a major popular art form, deriving from the propaganda logic that publicists have brought to politics. The artistic skill that campaign ads contain are there to persuade us. The appeals typically relate the candidate and the current election to our political mythology. This is evident even in the simple campaign brochures that politicians commonly circulate. The candidate, it is claimed, is a man or woman who embodies those virtues of moral integrity and material achievement that made this country great.[7] In the 1980 presidential election, for example, campaign brochures emphasized these themes. John Connally's brochure said that he is "one who rose from a humble beginning as a barefoot farmboy to pinnacles of success ..." Many candidates emphasized their humble beginnings and nearness to the grassroots of America. The "man of the soil" myth is an old propaganda ploy in American politics, since it seems to be a political embodiment of the democratic myth of both moral worth in common people and their ability to achieve material success. John Anderson, for example, was proud to claim Illinois, the "Land of Lincoln" as his native state; his brochure claimed, "... and the parallels between Anderson and the first Republican President are not lost on some writers: tall, thin, brilliant lawyers and orators from humble beginnings in the Prairie State."

Similarly, campaign propaganda appeals to American mythology by pointing to the personal virtues and achievements of the candidate. In the 1980 brochures, for example, we learn that John Anderson was "A Man of Leadership, Experience, Principle, Character." George Bush is a man of "strength, candor, and effectiveness." Carter is your man "if you value the fundamental qualities of honesty, integrity, hard work, and fair play." Reagan is "open, forthright, and consistent." That such adherence to the moralistic myth is important was underscored by the failure of the candidacies of Senator Edward Kennedy and Governor Jerry Brown, who could not place themselves in the typical family portrait, since Kennedy and his wife were estranged and Brown was a bachelor who had a celebrated liason with singer Linda Ronstadt. But they could point, as all candidates did, to achievements, material accomplishments which help define their claim to leadership.

The brochures of 1980 also pointed to another key non-political achievement, one that is still apparently an important popular symbol: the war record. Anderson, we learn, served in the Army in World War II and was awarded four battle stars. Connally was "a decorated Navy hero of World War II." Bush was the "youngest Torpedo-Bomber pilot in the Navy" in World War II, and was "Shot down over [the] Bonin Islands" and received the Distinguished Flying Cross for heroism. The most blatant use of heroic service was claimed by Senator Bob Dole, with a brochure that pictures his hand crippled in combat, under the slogan: "You can sum up Republican presidential nominee Bob Dole with a four-letter word: GUTS. He proved it in Italy in 1945." The brochure then went on to tell the story of his war record, wounding, award of the Bronze Star, and rehabilitation. The claim in all cases appears to be that combat heroism is an achievement that tempers one for presidential heroism, and somehow proves one's patriotism and service. It is not absolutely essential, since the presidential winner that year had no war record, although he did star in some training films.[8]

Campaign propaganda deals with much more than the candidate's heroism. They offer visual and verbal images of the candidate in relationship to the American Dream. His version of the Dream is combined rhetorically with what he will do politically to realize it. In television ads, this may simply picture him talking to us about his commitment to the Dream. The sophisticated art of television advertising has taken presentation of this to new heights. The Nixon campaign of 1968 ran a television ad in 1968 that presented a series of still images while Nixon's voice was heard talking calmly. The ad first had a succession of negative images of riots, Vietnam, and urban and rural decay while Nixon talked of our plight ("Did we come all the way for this?"). Then the ad switched to a montage of "Creative and Contributing Faces" (as the script called them) who "give drive to the spirit of America . . . give lift to the American Dream . . . give steel to the backbone of America." After extolling the moral and material virtues of us (script: "Strength and Character of Americans — Busy factories, Farms, Crowds & Traffic, Etc."), the ad climaxed with a call to greatness (backed by a montage of "Scenic Values" — purple mountain majesties, amber waves of grain, etc.), concluding: "What America needs are leaders to match the greatness of her people." The ad thus associates the candidate with the Dream, but ambiguously enough that audiences which entertain different versions of the Dream can "read into" the ad whatever they want. The montage ad conjurs up a variety of popular images which touch deep chords in us, perhaps persuading us.[9] In any case, such a propaganda motif has been much copied. The 1976 Carter campaign used a similar ad, wherein Carter speaks of his "vision for America" while the camera fades to montage of landscape scenes, culminating in a shot of the heads of four Presidents carved on Mt. Rushmore, then fading back into a shot of Carter's head, subliminally suggesting that he might be the fifth head![10]

It is still disputed as to what extent campaign propaganda affects us. We all think we are resistant to advertising, but it may have effects we are not aware of. Our familiarity with propaganda in general makes us take it for granted, assuming that it doesn't affect us; but the influence on us may be real if subtle. Campaign propaganda, after all, does attempt to imaginatively associate the candidate with deeply held popular myths. To the extent that the propaganda is done well artistically, it does have a chance of succeeding. At least, candidates and their advisors, as well as the campaign industry, believe it does, and they spend much time and money on the assumption that popular propaganda can persuade us to think and do what they want. If we do believe in and want to see realized the American Dream, then propaganda logic dictates that such myths can be appealed to and direct political behavior, ultimately in the voting booth.

Popular culture creations as political propaganda

We are all familiar with the explicit propaganda of political campaigns. We are not as aware that implicit political messages may be implanted in popular culture creations — movies, television shows, songs, etc. Politicians and government agency heads have long understood the attraction people have for popular culture, and have used popular creations to propagate a political message. They often become aware that a particular popular culture magnate has a particular political viewpoint, and attempt to enlist him as a propagandist. Or someone may simply use a popular forum to propagate a political message, consciously or not.

In the last case, a creator of popular culture may have a covert political message and use his creation as a way to dramatize his viewpoint. For example, a popular story in parable or fantastic form may have wide appeal, yet still contain a propaganda message. Children still love Swift's *Gulliver's Travels* and Orwell's *Animal Farm,* unaware of the implicit political message contained therein. So it is with L. Frank Baum's *The Wizard of Oz.* Written in 1900, it immediately became a children's classic, but few realized that it included a latent political message. Baum was a Kansas populist who had witnessed the rise and fall of the Populist movement and the defeat of its champion, William Jennings Bryan, in the presidential election of 1896. Baum saw the moral community (midwestern and Southern farmers, urban labor, and even Indians) as exploited by the dominant material community of the East (bankers, industrialists, and their political allies). The Populists favored "bimetallism," using silver as well as gold as a monetary standard to make credit easier for farmers and wages higher for workers. The failure of the movement caused Baum to write a propagandistic parable about it. Dorothy symbolizes a kind of Kansas "Miss Everybody" who lives in bleak poverty with her virtuous but exploited aunt and uncle. The tornado force of events uproot her, and she finds herself in a strange land called Oz (the abbreviation for ounce, the standard measure for gold). She goes down the Yellow Brick Road (a la yellow bricks of gold), and meets the rusted Tin Man (symbolizing the urban worker, who showed he had no heart by voting for McKinley in 1896, and now cannot work), the scarecrow (the farmer, who showed he had no brains for the same reason, and now is pinned up in a cornfield and cannot farm), and the Cowardly Lion (Bryan). They go on to the Emerald City (green, the color of greenbacks) to meet the Wizard, who turns out to be a humbug who rules by deception (President McKinley). The slippers the witch gives Dorothy are silver, and by clicking them she can do magical things. The witches represent the economic forces of the four regions of the country, the bad witches from the East (the economic oppressors) and West (gold interests), and the good witches from the North and South (populist interests). Practically every figure or scene in the story appears to have some relevance to the political situation of the day. Thus, a delightful tale has an original, but now virtually forgotten, propaganda intent.[11]

In Baum's case, as with other political satirists, the political message is quite consciously created. In many other cases, however, the political content of a popular creation may be unconsciously included, an implicit message deriving from the social values held by the creator but without clear ulterior intent to persuade. This may be the case with groups such as television movie scriptwriters. A study of the attitudes of Hollywood writers found them to be politically "liberal" and that their values quite naturally found their way into scripts. For example, they tended to depict businessmen as bad guys, greedy, duplicitious, and violent. The poor and minorities tend to be depicted as victims who are rarely the perpetuator of crimes. Military officers are either pompous or vicious, and the military as an institution is rampantly committed to violence and suffering. They include openly sexual themes in much of their writing, and positively depict homosexuals, prostitutes, and extramarital lovers. It is unlikely that Hollywood script writers are part of some "value conspiracy," however. Like the rest of us, they write into story form what they believe. Nevertheless, in the long run a steady diet of such viewpoints broadcast on mass media might have a propaganda effect. People who watch the depiction of certain values, and the heroes and villains who embody them, may come to share them. No matter how unconscious or unintended propaganda may be, it still may in effect persuade us and thus have an indirect political consequence.[12]

A major example of a popular culture organization that carries a particular version of the American Dream, and its concomitant political viewpoint, is the Disney empire. Disney's version of the American Dream is traditional and nostalgic, celebrated in cartoons and feature-length movies. Traditional moral virtues, such as rugged individualism, patriotism, and thrift, are extolled in cartoon form. Disney thought himself to be an example of the Horatio Alger myth, and such cartoons as *The Tortoise and the Hare* suggest that victory in the social race goes to those who persist in their goal. During World War II, the government sought and Disney produced propaganda films which extolled the war effort. One of the most famous was his cartoon, *Der Fuhrer's Face,* a propaganda satire of Hitler and Fascism. He made a cartoon feature for Latin American consumption to shore up the United State's image there, especially in those countries flirting with Germany. Disney was courted by conservative politicians till his death, and Disney Studios continues to perpetuate a world-view supportive of the "conservative" version of the Dream. Disneyland and Disneyworld offer symbolic features that link us to the dreamed-of past (Frontierland), our political mythology (Mr. Lincoln), and the utopian future (Tomorrowland).

Disney and Disney Studios creations are therefore implicitly didactic. We learn about ourselves and the world through the characters (Mickey Mouse as American optimistic adventurer), songs (Whistle a Happy Tune), stories (Davy Crockett), environments (Liberty Square), and images of the future (Space Mountain). The Disney creations are implicit propaganda for an idealized universe of traditional morality, American benevolence, technological progress, and corporate responsibility. Disneyland and Disneyworld are almost shrine-like, symbolic universes of the American Dream to which people bring their children to learn through play and reassure themselves in the reality of the Dream.[13]

That the Disney symbolic worlds include implicit propaganda has not been lost on the creators of other "theme parks" — Great America, Six Flags, and so on. All seem to traffic in American mythology in the Disney vein. There are not theme parks that offer, say, different versions of the Dream, with exhibits and environments about poverty, racism, and war. Different popular ideologies can be represented in theme parks elsewhere. For example, the Soviet Union is building a communist version of Disneyland they call "Socialistland." Socialistland extols Soviet achievements and values, both the moral and material ideology of communism and Soviet society. Like American theme parks, Socialistland teaches patriotism by re-creating historical places and events. One can ride a miniature train which is a replica of the one that brought Lenin out of exile to the Finland Station in Petrograd. Visitors can cruise on a replica of the cruiser *Aurora* that fired the first shots of the Revolution, and twice daily can witness a battle between Red Army and Czarist White Army partisans, in which, of course, the Reds always win!

In other cases, the connection between popular culture and political propagandizing is much more overt. Perhaps the most famous example of cooperation between a government agency and the creators of popular culture for propaganda purposes was during the many years of J. Edgar Hoover's directorship of the Federal Bureau of Investigation. Hoover built the FBI into an American legend, and a large, heavily-funded federal agency, partly through the adroit use of popular culture. Hoover's public relations staff provided scripts, stories, dramatic devices such as the "Ten Most Wanted" list, examples of dramatic investigations and arrests, and so on. Comics, radio, movies, and then television dramatized the FBI agent as a federal version of the "action detective" symbolically fighting crime, subversion, and corruption. Hoover identified popular villains such as the Mafia, bank robbers, and the like as domestic adversaries, and foreign-controlled subversives, first the Nazis and then the Communists, as foreign adversaries. Thus, the stories the FBI provided depicted the agency as heroic, efficient, successful, the federal police defender of American myths. Hoover's political orientation meant that FBI approval on shows and scripts restricted them to certain themes, reliable cops-and-robbers-or-Reds tales. But there were few stories about civil rights violations, police brutality, or corporate crimes. Hoover assumed that the populace would rather see stories about people robbing banks than banks robbing people. Indeed, Hoover may have become a captive of the FBI myth himself. It is said that in the 1960s real FBI agents had to conform to the "Zimmy image" of actor Efram Zimbalist, Jr., who played Inspector Erskine on the television show *The F.B.I.!* Hoover's overt influence over how popular culture depicted the FBI did much for its reputation and popular and political support as the symbolic defender of the American Dream from those who would rob it of its morality and material wealth. In that sense, popular culture served the propagandistic purposes of a government agency.[14]

"Semi-official" popular culture as political propaganda

In a subtle sense, politicians use popular culture as political propaganda by associating themselves with popular figures and creations. By so doing, they give a "semi-official" sanction to popular culture which signals their approval or disapproval of social values and styles. The implicit political message is, by publicly demonstrating my affinity to a certain kind of popular culture, I am making a political statement. This may simply say "I approve of a certain style of life," since we associate certain forms of music, humor, dance, and other forms of entertainment with a certain segment of society. Or it may be that a politician will extol a particular creation as exemplary of some social or political virtue. Too, a politician may associate with popular figures and creations with the intent of demonstrating his or her approval of certain forms of popular culture to extend his political support.

The prime example of this use of popular culture involves who gets invited to and performs for Presidents on festive occasions. By a President watching and laughing at Bob Hope make jokes about antiwar demonstrators, hippies, and liberals, he is siding with those who dislike these moral lifestyles and criticism of American material power. By a President saying how much he likes the movie *Patton* (and then, as Nixon did, subsequently sending troops into Cambodia!), he is saying that American moral and material toughness is a virtue that should be part of foreign policy. By a President inviting and associating with stock car racers, square dancers, rodeo stars, country and Western singers, or whatever symbolizes his "like" for that form of popular culture and implicitly all those in the mass that do too. A politician who likes what we like must be a "regular guy" and thus wins our approval. Such popular associations do then have a propaganda intent. The President may actually loathe country and Western music but understand the propaganda logic of publicly demonstrating appreciation of it, and implicitly the moral and material values which surround it.

Conclusion

In these and many other ways, political propagandists use appeals to popular mythology in order to persuade. Popular communication in campaigns associates the candidate with popularly held values. Popular culture itself may contain overt or covert propaganda messages which celebrate aspects of the American Dream. By a politician adopting a type of popular culture as "semi-official," he or she communicates a propaganda message to the public. Through such play, we learn or re-learn about politics and politicians, and politicians teach us about what they claim to be and value. Propagandists try to use us through the play of propaganda, and we use propaganda to learn what to value and how to act. But it is the nature of propaganda to use rather than respect truth, so there is always the possibility that what we learn from propaganda is not true. And thus we may ask ourselves how much we know about the world, and politics in particular, by learning from propaganda, which is after all messages designed to persuade, and often to bamboozle, us.[15]

Notes

[1]George Gordon, *Persuasion: The Theory and Practice of Manipulative Communication* (Hastings House, 1971); Erwin P. Bettinghaus, *Persuasive Communication* (Holt, Rinehart, & Winston, 1973).

[2]This notion stems from sources such as Jacques Ellul, *Propaganda* (Vintage, 1973); Terence H. Qualter, *Propaganda and Psychological Warfare* (Random House, 1962); Jules Henry, "Advertising as a Philosophical System," in *Culture Against Man* (Random House, 1963), pp. 45-99, with his notion of "pecuniary truth," and Jeffery Schrank's idea of "pseudo-choice" in his *Snap, Crackle, and Popular Taste* (Delta, 1977).

[3]A controversial treatment of the power of subliminal ads is Wilson Bryan Key, *Subliminal Seduction* (New American Library, 1973).

[4]Some ideas about the aesthetics of advertising can be gained from Vance Packard, *The Hidden Persuaders* (Pocket Books, 1958); Michael J. Arlen, *Thirty Seconds* (Farrar, Straus & Giroux, 1979); Gary Yanker, *Prop Art* (Darien House, 1972); Erving Goffman, *Gender Advertisements* (Harper Colophon, 1976); Tony Schwartz, *The Responsive Chord* (Anchor Doubleday, 1974).

[5]Herbert E. Krugman, "The Impact of Television Advertising: Learning Without Involvement," *Public Opinion Quarterly*, Vol. 29 (Fall 1965), pp. 349-356.

[6]See Dan Nimmo, *The Political Persuaders* (Prentice-Hall, 1970); and Robert Agranoff (ed.), *The New Style in Election Campaigns* (Holbrook Press, 1976) for a glimpse of the campaign industry and technology.

[7]A historical treatment that finds recurrent mythic themes in the "official" campaign biography from Jackson to Kennedy is W.B. Brown, *The People's Choice: The Presidential Image in the Campaign Biography* (Louisiana State University P., 1960). The heroic cultural image he identifies can be seen in campaign bios, brochures, and films since.

[8]James Combs, "The Aesthetics of Political Fantasy: Themes in Popular Campaign Propaganda in the 1980 Presidential Race," paper delivered at the 10th annual Popular Culture Association meeting, 1980.

[9]James Combs, "Political Advertising as a Popular Mythmaking Form," *Journal of American Culture*, Vol. 2 (Summer 1979), pp. 331-340; the Nixon ad is described in Joe McGinniss, *The Selling of the President, 1968* (Pocket Books, 1970), pp. 91-95.

[10]Joseph Lelyveld, "Ford to Delay Ads on TV Until After First Debate," *New York Times*, September 14, 1976, p. 28.

[11]Henry M. Littlefield, "*The Wizard of Oz*: Parable on Populism," *American Quarterly*, Vol. 16 (1964); pp. 47-58.

[12]Ben Stein, *The View from Sunset Boulevard* (Basic Books, 1979); Michael J. Robinson, "Prime Time Chic: Between Newsbreaks and Commercials, the Values are L.A. Liberal," *Public Opinion*, Vol. 2 (May 1979), pp. 42-48.

[13]See Richard Schickel, *The Disney Version* (Avon, 1968); Robert Jewett and John Shelton Lawrence, "Disney's Land: Saints and Sanitary Animals," in *The American Monomyth* (Doubleday Anchor, 1977), pp. 125-141; Michael R. Real, "The Disney Universe: Morality Play," *Mass-Mediated Culture* (Prentice-Hall 1977), pp. 44-89.

[14]Richard Gid Powers, "J. Edgar Hoover and the Detective Hero," *Journal of Popular Culture,* Vol. IX (Fall 1975), pp. 257-278.

[15]The student interested in persuing topics in propaganda and political persuasion will find many topics and much data on persuasion, propaganda, advertising, publicity, public relations, and other aspects of the "consumer culture." Many journals, such as the *Journal of Advertising, Advertising Age, Journal of Marketing, Public Opinion Quarterly, Journal of Advertising Research,* and many others. A glance at advertising textbooks will give an idea of the technology, purposes, and ethics of the industry. An overview of literature can be found in Paul Kecskemeti, "Propaganda," in *Handbook of Communication,* I. DeSola Pool, et. al. (eds.) (Rand McNally, 1973). A classic textbook is Leonard Doob, *Public Opinion and Propaganda* (Archon, 1966). An interpretation that links the consumer culture with advertising is Stuart Ewen, *Captains of Consciousness* (McGraw-Hill, 1976). See the discussion of the "new men" in Andrew Hacker, "Liberal Democracy and Social Control," *American Political Science Review,* Vol. LI (December 1957). Related works include Herbert Schiller, *The Mind Managers* (Beacon, 1973); Stanley Kelley, Jr., *Professional Public Relations and Political Power* (Johns Hopkins, 1966); and Hans Magnus Enzensberger, *The Consciousness Industry* (Seabury Press, 1974). Relevant here too are Daniel Boorstin, *The Image* (Harper Colophon, 1964) and Aldous Huxley, *Brave New World Revisited* (Perennial, 1965). Critical analyses of the advertising culture include Samm Sinclair Baker, *Advertising: The Permissible Lie* (Beacon, 1970) and Arthur Herzog, *The B.S. Factor* (Penguin Books, 1973).

The pioneering work of Harold Lasswell is still useful. See his *Propaganda Techniques in the World War* (MIT Press, 1971) and "Propaganda and Mass Insecurity," *Psychiatry,* Vol. 13 (August 1950), pp. 284-285. Other classic works include Robert Merton, *Mass Persuasion* (Harper, 1946); Fred Bartlett, *Political Propaganda* (Cambridge University P., 1940); Leo Bogart, *Premises for Propaganda* (Free Press, 1976); Melvin DeFleur, *Theories of Mass Communication* (David McKay, 1970); Alexander George, *Propaganda Analysis* (Greenwood Press, 1959); J.A.C. Brown, *Techniques of Persuasion* (Penguin, 1963). Donald McQuade and Robert Atwan (eds.), *Popular Writing in America* (Oxford University P., 1977), had a section of prototypical ads and commentary on technique. An insightful "inside dope" look at the ad world is David Ogilvy, *Confessions of an Advertising Man* (Atheneum Publishers, 1963).

Some idea of the range, techniques, and ethos of advertising may be gained from the following works: Roger Barton, *Media in Advertising* (McGraw-Hill, 1964); Yale Brozen, *Advertising and Society* (University Press, 1974); Kenneth Longman, *Advertising* (Harcourt Brace Jovanovich, 1971); Maurice Mandell, *Advertising* (Prentice-Hall, 1980); C.H. Sandage and Vernor Fryburger, *Advertising Theory and Practice* (Richard D. Irwin, 1967). See too two works by Johnathon Price, *Television Advertising* (Penguin, 1978) and *Commercials: The Best Thing on TV* (Kingsport Press, 1978). See too Jib Fowles, *Mass Advertising as Social Forecast* (Greenwood Press, 1976), and Marjorie Burns, "The Advertiser's Bag of Tricks," in F. Rissover and D.C. Brich, *Mass Media and the Popular Arts* (McGraw-Hill, 1977), pp. 18-25. Two delightful studies of advertising are by Ron Rosenbaum, "Tales of the Heartbreak Biz," *Esquire* (July 1974), pp. 67-73, 155-158, and "The Four Horsemen of the Nightly News," *More* (March 1978), pp. 27-29.

The debate over the effects and "logic" of advertising includes the following. See the relevant chapters on advertising in Joward Kahane, *Logic and Contemporary Rhetoric* (Wadsworth, 1980) and Stuart Chase, *Guides to Straight Thinking* (Harper, 1956) for critiques of advertising themes. Varda Langhoz Leymore, *Hidden Myth: Structure and Symbolism in Advertising* (Basic Books, 1975) uses structural analysis of advertising. The effects debate is now focused on children. See Marie Winn, *The Plug-In Drug* (Bantam, 1977); Seymour Banks, "Public Policy on Ads to Children," *Advertising and the Public Interest* (American Marketing Assn., 1975); Pat and Richard Burr, "Television Advertising to Children: What Parents Are Saying About Government Control," *Journal of Advertising Research* (1975); Wolf Feldman, "What's Wrong with Children's Commercials," *Journal of Advertising Research* (February 1974); James Frideres, "Advertising, Buying Patterns, and Children," *Journal of Advertising Research* (February 1973); Gorn Goldberg, "Some Unintended Consequences of TV Advertising to Children," *Journal of Consumer Research* (June 1978), and "TV Messages for Snack and Breakfast Foods: Do They Influence Children's Preferences?", *Journal of Consumer Research* (September 1978); "What TV Does to Kids," *Newsweek,* February 21, 1977.

One of the best researched and most spectacular political propaganda efforts was in Nazi Germany. See works such as Z.A.B. Zeman, *Nazi Propaganda* (Oxford University P., 1973); Viktor Reimann, *Goebbels* (Doubleday, 1976); Jay W. Baird, *The Mythical World of Nazi War Propaganda* (University of California P., 1975).

A study of the origins of USIA propaganda themes is discussed in Leo Bogart, *Premises for Propaganda* (Free Press, 1976). Some popular culture articles that discuss cases relevant here include Jerome L. Rodnitzky, "The Evolution of the American Protest Song," *Journal of Popular Culture,* Vol. III (Summer 1969), pp. 35-45; Peter C. Rollins, "Victory at Sea: Cold War Epic," *Journal of Popular Culture,* Vol. VI (Spring 1973), pp. 463-482; Arthur Frank Wertheim, "Relieving Social Tensions: Radio Comedy and the Great Depression," *Journal of Popular Culture,* Vol. X (Winter 1976), pp. 501-519; Louis F. Helbig, "The Myth of the 'Other' America in East German Popular Consciousness," *Journal of Popular Culture,* Vol. X (Spring 1977), pp. 797-807; J. Fred MacDonald, "Government Propaganda in Commercial Radio: The Case of Treasury Star Parade, 1942-1943," *Journal of Popular Culture,* Vol. XII (Fall 1978), pp. 285-304; Lester J. Keyser, "Three Faces of Evil: Fascism in Recent Movies," *Journal of Popular Film/TV,* Vol. IV (1975), pp. 21-31; Michael T. Isenberg, "An Ambiguous Pacifism: A Retrospective on World War I Films 1930-1938," *Journal of Popular Film/TV,* Vol. IV (1975), pp. 98-115; and Ina Rae Hark, "The Visual Politics of The Adventures of Robin Hood," *Journal of Popular Film/TV,* Vol. V (1976), pp. 3-18.

We have already noted some of the works that concern themselves with political campaign propaganda. See also works such as Dan Nimmo and Robert L. Savage, *Candidates and Their Images* (Goodyear, 1976); Murray B. Levin, *Kennedy Campaigning* (Beacon, 1966); James D. Barber, et. al., *Race for the Presidency: The Media and the Nominating Process* (Prentice-Hall, 1978); Thomas E. Patterson and Robert D. McClure, *The Unseeing Eye* (Putnam's, 1976); Kenneth G. Shienkopf, et. al., "The Functions of Political Advertising for Campaign Organizations," *Journal of Marketing Research,* Vol. 9 (November 1971); Allen Winkler, The Politics of Propaganda (Yale University P., 1978); "Political Advertising: Making It Look Like News," *Congressional Quarterly,* Vol. 30 (November 4, 1972), pp. 2900-2903; Walt Anderson, *Campaigns: Cases in Political Conflict* (Goodyear, 1970).

A unique study of "official information" is David Altheide and John Johnson, *Bureaucratic Propaganda* (Allyn and Bacon, 1980).

Some recent articles on propaganda the reader might find useful are G.H. Mond, "Mass Media: Mouthpiece of the Soviet Foreign Policy Between Peaceful Coexistence and Ideological Struggle," *Southern Atlantic Quarterly,* Vol. 72 (June 1973), pp. 374-385; G. Handberg, "Propaganda and Information: The Case of U.S. Broadcasts to Eastern Europe," Vol. 8 (January 1975), pp. 391-412; V.S. Bunham, "Uses of Stalinist Literary Debris," *Slavic Review,* Vol. 32 (Winter, 1973), pp. 115-128; D.D. Smith, "Some Effects of Radio Moscow's North American Broadcast," *Public Opinion Quarterly,* Vol. 34 (Winter 1970-1971), pp. 531-551; symposium, "Socialization," *Studies in Comparative Communism,* Vol. 10 (Autumn, 1977), pp. 235-342; M. Schleifer, "Moral Education and Indoctrination," *Ethics,* Vol. 86 (January 1976), pp. 154-163; Lucian W. Pye, "Communication and Chinese Political Culture," *Asian Survey,* Vol. 18 (March 1978), pp. 221-246; R. Navazio, "Experimental Approach to Bandwagon Research," *Public Opinion Quarterly,* Vol. 41 (Summer 1977) pp. 217-225

Chapter Eight
SHOWBIZ: Show Business and Politics

"There's no business like show business," goes the song, and apparently a great many Americans agree. American love of entertainment has made the industries that create popular fare multi-billion dollar parts of our economy. We seem to never tire of interest in new songs, plays, movies, television shows, and indeed in new popular figures themselves. Popular media industries cater to our thirst for play-dramas, trying to anticipate new desires and moods on the part of the consuming public. The entertainment industry has become established — movie companies, record companies, television networks — to the point that they have become symbolic of glamour, wealth, and fame: "Hollywood," "Nashville," "Tin Pan Alley," "Broadway," "Las Vegas." America has become the world center of popular culture, and most popular culture establishments legitimate and important parts of American culture. It was inevitable then, that something that people valued so much and became so powerful, show biz, was to become involved in politics.

Show biz and learning

Show business creates for us a dramatic world of play. We want to be entertained — diverted from the mundane barriers of our existence and transported to worlds of illusion and fantasy, worlds of adventure, mystery, romance, nightmare horror.[1] Even something as simple as a rock song creates for us a dramatic world of play from which we learn. More complex popular creations, such as a movie, offer us a dramatic world that may have deep and long-term impact on our attitude toward the real world. Our voluntary participation in show business means that we are drawn to play-worlds because we want to get something out of them. Thus, the

121

experience is *vicarious,* in which we learn through imaginative play with the dramatic stories and roles of the show biz world. If, then, we value the vicarious experiences created for us by popular culture, it should not surprise us that we learn political messages from that play-world, and indeed not think it odd that figures from that play-world should become involved in the real world of politics. For we experience both worlds vicariously. Both politics and show biz are for us worlds beyond our immediate experience, glamorous, exciting worlds which we only know through their dramatization in the mass media. What we learn from our vicarious play with show biz may have important consequences for our expectations about politics.

Show biz and cultural mythology

We have already pointed out the extent to which popular culture treats the American Dream, and show biz is of course central to that treatment. The stories and roles that popular culture creates involve material and moral ideals. But there are other factors we should point to here. To a large degree, the success of show business organizations and personalities are "proof" to many of the salience of the American Dream, both positively and negatively. Let us take the example of Hollywood.[2] Positively, one can argue that the success of Hollywood is a demonstration of the truth of the materialistic myth. Many movie magnates and stars were unknown and unlettered, but built studios and careers which show that wealth and fame can be acquired through hard work and capitalist enterprise. Making movies and creating "stars" gave people something they wanted, and thus made the magnates, the industry, and the stars wealthy. Negatively, one can argue that the material acquisition was done through the cynical exploitation of base mass desires — sex, violence, fantasy, and so on. By pandering to people's vicarious desires, Hollywood debased their morality. But not only the stories were debasing. So too was the elevation of actors into stars, so that their private lives were expected to be public property, something sold for its vicarious gossip value. Their lives of glamor, wealth, and debauchery undermined the morals of the populace who looked up to stars as ideals, and learned from their behavior.

In any case, the Hollywood star is an example of the phenomenon of *celebrity.*[3] A celebrity may be said to be in the prestige business, since he or she is someone who is successful if famous. One can become a celebrity in various ways, but in all cases the fame stems from the vicarious relationship that segments of a mass audience develop with the public personage celebrated. Their fame-seeking is motivated by our fame-consuming. A celebrity symbolizes something about the material and moral world for us, and we love or hate them (but follow the careers of all of them) because they are "symbolic leaders."[4] Our attitude toward celebrities is much shaped by our own values and desires, and what they represent with respect to ourselves. We may envy or despise their material and moral lifestyle as it is publicly dramatized, but in both cases they are public objects with which we vicariously play. If they get involved in politics, this adds another element to our attitude toward them, since they come to be famous representations of political values we like or dislike.

The celebritization of politics

It is frequently said nowadays that "all politics is becoming show biz." There is a sense in which politics, especially in societies with means of mass communication, has always had an "entertainment" aspect. Politicians are celebrities, and we are as much interested in their private lives, and see them as popular representatives of material and moral values, as we do movie stars. But in an entertainment society, the extent to which politicians have become celebrities, and politics connected with the entertainment industry, has become much more complex. For the confluence of the world of politics and show biz signals the collapse of some social categories. The entrance of show biz values, techniques, and personalities into politics means the celebritization of politics.

In the past, politics and show biz were separate worlds. Show biz — vaudeville, circus, theater, and the like — were thought to be not quite respectable. Actors, for example, were thought to lead disreputable lives, and a woman of the stage little better than a prostitute. Politics might be sometimes corrupt, but respectable politicians did represent an ideal of material and moral probity. Certainly the idea of, say, an actor becoming President would have been unthinkable. Even today many people feel that the dignity and authority of government has been debased by the introduction of show biz into it.

But our love of show biz probably made it inevitable. We like glamour, hoopla, tinsel, beautiful people, a good show. Since politics has become increasingly a "media act," politicians have turned to show biz advisors to help them be good actors and put on good shows. It is no accident that the post-World War II emergency of campaign management firms, media advisers, and entertainers running for office began in California. President Eisenhower hired an actor, Robert Montgomery, as a television coach, and the 1956 Republican convention was "produced" by actor George Murphy, who went on later to win a Senate seat from California. Candidates began to display their friendship of and support of show biz figures. John Kennedy's sister was married to actor Peter Lawford, and he lined up the support of Hollywood figures. After this, the process took off, and the confluence has become even more intermeshed.

If it is true that we learn from popular culture about the world, let us consider this notion of confluence. When we are asked, "Who in the world do you admire the most?", we tend to make up lists of politicians and show biz celebrities. When children are asked, they will typically include the President and First Lady along with singers, kiddie show stars, and athletes. (In one poll, gradeschoolers admired actor Lee Majors, "The Bionic Man," more than President Carter, and his wife Farrah Fawcett more than Mrs. Carter!) When we read celebrity magazines such as *People* or *The National Enquirer,* we expect to see gossipy stories about both show biz stars and political stars. When we see mimics do imitations of the famous, we expect Rich Little or whomever to do imitations of both show biz personalities and political personalities. The confluence, then, has become a mass expectation.

We expect, for example, that political campaigns for President will be replete with show biz. The campaign — primaries, convention, fall race — will be conducted with attention to show biz values. People expect a good show, a lot of hoopla, entertainment that will hold their interest, and the campaign organization will import show biz "production values" to entertain their mass audiences. People now expect that show biz techniques to prevail — conventions, for instance, will be "choreographed," speeches will have snappy one-liners and jokes like a stand-up comic, the convention show will go off without a snag. Finally, people expect that show biz personalities will be associated with the candidate, since the candidate and the show biz figures belong to the same world of stars. They exist for us in a world of fame, glamour, and opulence that we can only imagine. Politicians and show biz celebrities are play-figures for us, and we expect them to exist in the same world, as personages who get out of limousines and are whisked through the acclaim of crowds into **guarded** settings where they are idolized by cheering audiences. **Both** political and show biz celebrities are different than **you and me**; they have more fame.

Celebrities represent for us some aspect of the American Dream. Show biz celebrities celebrate in their personage and usually in the roles they play something that makes us identify with them because we want to believe it, too. In some cases, it may simply be that they are talented, rich, famous, and successful, and we are taken with their realization of the material Dream. In others, it may be that they represent some "moral" for we would like ourselves to enjoy or the entire country: a swinging movie star symbolizes moral freedom, an actor who plays, both on and off screen, a "man of integrity" is admired for representing moral tradition. We may dislike (and secretly envy) those stars who symbolize activities we don't approve of (and maybe yearn for). But play-figures from the world of show biz certainly mean something to us.

So too do political celebrities. They dramatize, in their public and private lives (at least, as much as we know about them), as communicated to us through the media, the fulfillment, or the perversion, of the Dream. If a President leads an opulent life, we may think him either living out the material Dream he deserves because of his success, or that he symbolizes the immorality of material inequality. Political celebrities are play-figures for us no less than movie stars, and our expectations about them stem from the same vicarious participation in their lives as non-political celebrities. Politicians recognize this, and it draws them closer to the world of show biz.

Celebrity participation in politics

Celebrities, like most people, have their own ideas about what should be done in politics. But because they are famous, it becomes easier for them to air their views. Indeed, politicians invite their participation, because of the show biz factor we have mentioned. To be associated with glamourous celebrities from the world of show biz seems to be important to the public. It used to be important to be endorsed for President by labor leaders, leading politicians, and newspapers; now it seems as important to be endorsed by movie and television stars and other celebrities. Political association with show biz figures is key to building a contemporary political coalition, and politicians attempt to recruit show biz figures. Politicians reason that such associations make the glamour of show biz rub off on them, and assures the mass public that they are "acceptable" in the play-world of show biz.

This is most obvious in contemporary presidential campaigns, and the association is more than for purposes of glitter. Since 1976, entertainment has become a major source of fund-raising for campaigns. Federal election laws limit the amount of money that individuals can contribute to campaigns, but they do not limit the "services" that one can render free for a campaign. For most volunteers, this means licking stamps and handing out leaflets. But for celebrities, this means that they can appear at a fund-raising event and perform for free, and the candidate can charge guests. So a dinner, concert, or other event for large audiences can raise a great deal of money for the candidate, and the appearance of show biz celebrities can enhance the gathering. Thus, the recruitment of stars is quite competitive. In 1980, for example, presidential hopefuls wooed a variety of stars. Senator Edward Kennedy visited and successfully recruited Barbra Streisand. Ronald Reagan utilized his friends from Beverly Hills, older stars such as James Stewart, Bob Hope, and Frank Sinatra. Jimmy Carter relied upon Willie Nelson, Charlie Daniels, and Cheryl Ladd. But the most celebrated help given a candidate was singer Linda Ronstadt for her "good friend" Governor Jerry Brown of California. The relationship between the governor and the star was already celebrated in the popular press, especially when they went off on a safari to Africa together. But Ronstadt recruited other stars in the pop music world — Helen Reddy, *Chicago, The Eagles,* and so on — who appeared at concerts, and also hosted a $1,000 a couple dinner party for Brown at her Malibu beachfront home, altogether pumping more than $400,000 into Brown's presidential campaign. She and a contingent of other stars, such as Cindy Williams of television's "Laverne and Shirley" and director Francis Ford Coppola, appeared for Brown in primaries in New Hampshire and Wisconsin.

Hollywood has been politically active in recent years, and splits down liberal-conservative lines. Ever since the Hollywood Ten case (wherein Reagan got his political start), the ideological split in Tinseltown has been quite dramatic.[5] The politically-conscious stars lend their presence to a variety of races and causes. In California politics, participation is heavy: when Carey Peck (the son of star Gregory Peck) ran against an incumbent Republican Congressman in southern California, the stars turned out on both sides. Peck lined up the help of Charlton Heston, Warren Beatty, and Liza Minnelli, while Congressman Dornan had the help of Bob Hope, Pat Boone, Lucille Ball, and Danny Thomas.

But perhaps most famous are the star activists for causes such as environmentalism and anti-nuclear power. Robert Redford and Paul Newman helped form an anti-oil company lobby called *Energy*

Action. Jane Fonda is a controversial figure who uses her stardom to push several causes, including husband Tom Hayden's *Campaign for Economic Democracy.* She has a flair for show biz techniques, using, for example, the crippled nuclear plant at Three Mile Island as a backdrop for a press conference on nuclear dangers. Her movies, such as *The China Syndrome* and *Nine to Five,* use entertainment to deliver political messages. But her activism doesn't seem to hurt her at the box office, although she does arouse intense hatreds among conservatives, who tend to think her a hypocrite for attacking the materialistic Dream even though she is a benefactor of it. But she is significant as to how show biz stars have become the leading spokespersons for political causes associated with moralistic issues, much more so than leaders drawn from the lower classes and labor. The difference is that she is famous, and indeed much admired: in a woman's magazine national poll of the "Ten Most Admired Women," she was included (along with Pat Nixon and Anita Bryant)!

The celebritization of politics and California culture

Many observers of American popular culture have argued that we are progressively being "Californiaized" or "Losangelized," meaning that social trends — lifestyles, values, fads, politics — begin in California and spread all over the country. California gave us motels, cookouts, franchise foods, the 1960's counter-culture, cults, and most of all, show business. If it is the case that American politics does bow more and more to celebrity, perhaps this is because the style of California politics has "gone national." California politics became the first place in which show business made great inroads. California was the state that witnessed the influx of media technology and publicity into campaigns and government, the rise of "symbolic politics" (e.g., issues such as "communism"), and the entry of show biz directly into politics. The state has also given us presidential politicians — Nixon, Reagan, and Brown — all of whom utilized the show biz connection heavily. If all of America is becoming like California, then it may also be that American politics is becoming like California, too.

The national celebritization of politics augurs many things. For one thing, we may see candidates for public office drawn more and more from popular culture. We already have athletes, radio commentators, television celebrities, astronauts, POWs, and so forth in the Congress. It was rumored that John Anderson wanted Walter Cronkite to run with him in his bid for the presidency in 1980.

The politics of glamour is evident in places other than California: the governor of Kentucky is married to CBS sports figure Phyllis George, and the Senator from Virginia to actress Elizabeth Taylor. In the future, we may see many more celebrity figures offer themselves for public office on the basis of their well-knownness. They will bring their show biz skills and personage into the play-world of politics.

We also noted that California pioneered symbolic politics, by which we mean a politics based on appearances, the dramatization of symbols by political actors for mass audiences. Because we have conflicting and changing ideas of what politics should do to realize the American Dream, politicians can and do manipulate symbols in order to give us the illusion that they are doing something about it. If the future of American politics contains a great deal of symbolic dramatization, then it may be that those schooled in the conduct of symbolic politics and in show biz as a way of life may possess the skills to succeed in politics. What we have called symbolic in California is often termed "hype," a term from the entertainment business referring to the dramatization of appearance to project an image for a mass audience. Movie stars are in the business of hype, and perhaps we should have expected that it would be part of the business of politics. If California politics is based upon rapid changes and confusions about the politics of material and moral worth, then it may be that the same hypes about the American Dream will exist at the national level.[6]

Perhaps all this is so because California itself is a popular symbol for the realization of the American Dream, and the show business which is centered there the most glamorous popular example of the Dream. The California myth was that of a plentiful Golden Country of easy living and good luck. Hollywood became the modern popular manifestation of the California myth, in which any kid could become a star through hype and luck, and then live the high life of instant wealth and moral freedom. California and Hollywood both exist in the American consciousness as symbols of the extremes of the American Dream — getting something for nothing on the one hand, and getting something with hustle and hype on the other. California drew people who looked for the wide variety of versions of the American Dream, and it is no wonder their politics and culture invites extremes. In the popular mind, California experiments with both high morality (political causes, a vast educational system) and low morality (surfer culture, homosexuals), as well as high materialism (Marin County, Beverly

Hills) and low materialism ("back to nature," the simple life of ecotopia). California in a sense is the culmination of the Dream, and Hollywood is its reflection in popular culture. That representatives espousing different aspects of the Dream should be drawn from both California and Hollywood is to be expected.

Ronald Reagan

Ronald Reagan is the most spectacular example of the confluence of show biz and politics, as well as representing a version of the Dream for the rest of the country. Here we are not so much interested in his politics as with his connection to the West, California, and most of all, show biz. The fact that voters in 1980 showed no reticence in voting for him even though he was a product of the Dream Factory of Hollywood suggests that the play-world of show biz is now a completely legitimate place from which to recruit Presidents.

It is fitting that the country that pioneered show biz should elect the first show biz President. We should understand this as not only a new source of political recruitment, but also of political socialization. In other words, to what extent are Reagan's political views shaped by his show biz experience? It does seem to be the case that he believes in some measure in the Western myth. This was shaped in part by childhood experience: he recounts seeing silent Westerns back home in Illinois, wherein robbers decide not to rob the government train because "you don't monkey around with Uncle Sam."[7] But he also migrated West, and adopted Western values, including to some degree the myth that America is a frontierland of unrestrained liberty and opportunity, which could be realized everywhere on the lines of the California promise. Certainly his success in becoming wealthy as a show biz personage and real estate investor confirmed for him the reality of the material Dream.

We may also ask as to what extent actually playing a certain type of character in his movies, and later on television, affected his political perspective. Certainly his familiar public style was shaped in the movies. Very early on, Reagan developed a movie style in the manner of other male actors of the 1930s and 1940s, what we may call the "Aw, shucks" style — low-key, self-deprecating, guileless, amiable, someone who succeeds simply because he is a nice guy who couldn't do bad things. This public manner he was to bring to politics: he could say tough things, but he didn't seem mean or warlike, just a nice fellow with honest convictions that sounded good. We may wonder as to what extent playing roles that called for such a character and the values that that kind of character would hold became a part of Reagan's political character and values.

When he entered politics, he cast himself (with the help of a California campaign management firm) as a "citizen politician." That is, he was an amateur, a common man, someone just like us who was not part of any political Establishment. His "Aw, shucks" manner couched the political rhetoric of his conservative version of the American Dream in pleasing language. The character made the values less threatening and even appealing beyond right-wing ideologies. The material and moral myths he espoused seemed to flow from his public personage, a nostalgic embodiment of "the way we were." Reagan's screen roles cast him oftentimes (as in *King's Row*) in small towns of the pre-industrial and -urban age, and his acting style seemed to fit our myth of such a moral community of traditional virtue. In his Western roles (as in *Cattle Queen of Montana*), he participated in the Western myth of moral resolution through direct action and violence. Some have contended that as Governor of California and President, he seemed to personify the lone marshal taking on those who had "looted" the public treasury.

So it may be that case that both Reagan's political values and, more certainly, his political acting were affected by his show biz experience. Like any politician, we may ask whether he believes what he says or whether it is show biz hype. For example, many occasions on which he has advocated military intervention may suggest that he believes in the Western myth of quick and violent solutions to international problems, but it might also be hype for his frustrated right-wing followers. If he believes we should return to small town virtues and simple values, did he acquire that belief from his childhood in Illinois or from the roles and plots of some of his movies? If he does not, is he simply hyping his conservative audiences, who desperately want us to return to better and more "moral" days?

In any event, Reagan came to be the political symbol of the American yearning to "return to greatness," in terms of both the materialistic and moralistic myth. We may also ask how much of that appeal stemmed from people's perception of him as a celebrity who epitomized, not only in his political rhetoric but also in his show biz depictions, desired aspects of the American Dream. If we wanted "hardline" solutions to international conflicts, perhaps it made sense to recruit a President from a world in which such solutions worked. If we desired a return to small town America of yore, perhaps it was sensible to find a star who had depicted it. For his followers — many from the "World War II" generation — there was no war hero such as Eisenhower to return us to a mythical past, and Reagan was the only political celebrity who could mobilize their feelings.

Reagan, then, represents the logical culmination of the celebritization of politics. We may only wonder if others from the world of show biz will join him in running for political office. Perhaps in the future we will more and more evaluate political candidates by their "stardom," the fame they bring to politics and their ability to entertain us in the play-world of politics. But we should remind ourselves that the world of show biz, while glamorous and entertaining, is a controlled environment. It is true that the play-world of politics is for many of us something experienced, like show biz, through the mass media. But it is more difficult to control the environment of politics, and no amount of glamour or histrionic skill can exercise power over stubborn political realities. Show biz is entirely a world of make-believe, but politics is only partly so. Show biz hype can dramatize the Dream for people, but whether those from the world of make-believe can make the Dream come true in the real world for people is quite another thing.[8]

Conclusion

Show business is an American institution. It is a large, rich, multivarious industry. It created a new social type, the celebrity, identifiable public characters with whom we vicariously play and from whom we learn. Both the unknown captains of the show biz industry and the known celebrities have access to power, and are courted by politicians. Since both politics and show biz are for many of us play-worlds, then the celebritization of politics is a logical consequence of the confluence of the worlds. Show biz fame has given celebrities direct access to politics as the representatives of different interpretations of American mythology. With the election of Reagan, we may see in the future the drama of politics increasingly conducted by those experienced in and known from the play-world of show biz.

The American Dream represented by show biz, both in the values it depicts and in its celebrity personages, will continue to shape and reflect our attitudes toward it in the future. The fate of the California myth will be a key popular indicator of the future of the American Dream. If California popular culture is indeed a national trendsetter, then we should observe political and popular life there closely to glean what the American future is to be. One interpretation already maintains that Reagan and Brown, as governors, have denied aspects of "California dreamin' ": Reagan attacked the myth of the soft life, getting something for nothing, and Brown attacked the myth of plenty and consumption. In different ways, both called for a renunciation of what California has come to symbolize for Americans.[9] If the politicians of California attack the mythic aura of California itself, then the redefinitions may augur different popular and political representations of the Dream. Perhaps, following Reagan and Brown, it will be a myth of simplicity, thrift, and hard work, closer to the Calvinist ethic than that of the surfers at Malibu. In any event, show biz will reflect the popular and political tides.

In particular, show biz will mirror the fate of entertainment values themselves. Show biz, many observers have argued, helped to create a society — again symbolized by California — that is a "leisure state," a "culture of narcissism" in an "age of sensation" in which we seek both entertainment and learning from show biz.[10] Many of us are imbued with "fun morality," in which we absorb ourselves in an intense and even desperate search for play.[11] We spend less time and interest on work, and more on playing. The consumer economy more and more provides services (such as show biz entertainment) which attempts to satisfy our insatiable demand for fun. But if there is a social tide which denies the mythic value of entertainment, then this may work against not only our desire for constant entertainment, but also our willingness to recruit political heroes from the world of show biz. We shall see.

If not, then we may see more and more show biz figures — with entertainment values and skills — lead us in politics. The politics of glamour may be enough, satisfying our desire for political entertainment. It is said that the Roman emperors of old ruled the teeming and restless masses of Rome with "bread and circuses." In the latter case, they turned out the multitudes for Roman holidays, triumphant parades, gladiatorial matches, and so on — the show biz of their day. Perhaps in the American present, figures from show biz can provide us with political circuses that will keep us entertained and quiescent. The question may be, however, whether they can provide us with bread.[12]

Notes

[1]Harold Mendelsohn, *Mass Entertainment* (College and University Press, 1966); Heinz Dietrich Fischer and Stephen R. Melnik (eds.), *Entertainment* (Hastings House, 1978); Myron

Matlaw (ed.), *American Popular Entertainment* (Greenwood Press, 1979); several of the essays in M. Thomas Inge (ed.), *Handbook of American Popular Culture,* Vol. I and II (Greenwood Press, 1979 and 1980), such as "Stage Entertainments"; Don B. Wilmeth, *The Language of American Popular Entertainment* (Greenwood Press, 1981); several of the essays in Peter Davidson, et. al., *Literary Taste, Culture & Mass Communication* (Somerset House, 1979), fourteen volumes; David Altheide and Robert P. Snow, "Media Entertainment," Chapter Two in *Media Logic* (Sage, 1979), pp. 18-60.

[2]Both the sociology and psychology of the Hollywood Dream Factory has been much studied. See, variously, Phillip French, *The Movie Moguls* (H. Regenry, 1969); Hugo Munsterberg, *The Film: A Psychological Study* (Dover, 1969); Garth Jowett, *Film: The Democratic Art* (Little, Brown, 1976); Marjorie Rosen, *Popcorn Venus: Women, Movies, and the American Dream* (Avon, 1973); Robert Sklar, *Movie-Made America: A Cultural History of the American Movies*; I.C. Jarvie, *Movies and Society* (Basic Books, 1970); Hortense Powdermaker, *Hollywood: The Dream Factory* (Little, Brown, 1950); Martha Wolfenstein and Nathan Leites, *Movies: A Psychological Study* (Atheneum, 1970); Michael Wood, *America in the Movies* (Basic Books, 1975).

[3]See Daniel Boorstin, "From Hero to Celebrity: The Human Pseudo-Event," in *The Image* (Harper Colophon, 1964), pp. 45-76; and James Monaco (ed.), *Celebrity: The Media as Image Makers* (Delta, 1978).

[4]Orrin E. Klapp, *Symbolic Leaders: Public Dramas and Public Men* (Minerva, 1964).

[5]Accounts of the great Hollywood political trauma include Cedric Belfrage, *The American Inquisition* (Bobbs-Merrill, 1973) and Jessica Mitford, *A Fine Old Conflict* (Knopf, 1977); but perhaps the best account is Corinth Film's documentary, "Hollywood on Trial," 1976.

[6]J.D. Lorenz, "An Insider's View of Jerry Brown," *Esquire* (February 1978), p. 132.

[7]The complete quote is cited in Chapter Three, footnote 12. Reagan has also been interpreted as a popular representation of "the All-American boy," a solid Midwestern smalltown boy. Positively, such a "common man" image connotes for people traditional and trusted virtues. For others, negatively, such an image represents babbittry and stupidity. One interpreter, for instance, concludes that Reagan was only cast brilliantly in a role once: "It was when he was cast in the role of the citizen politician. There his liabilities as a performer — his lack of imagination and his inability to project a state of thoughtfulness or compassion — were turned into assets. Regardless of what unknown directors are guiding that performance, it makes him a terrifying, distorted image of the common man." Mitch Tuchman, "Ladies and Gentlemen, the Next President of the United States," *Film Comment* (July 1980), p. 58.

[8]On Reagan, see Joel Kotkin and Paul Grabowicz, "Dutch Reagan, All-American" *Esquire* (August 1980), pp. 25-35; Gary Wills, "Ron and Destiny," *ibid.*, pp. 36-37; Mitch Tuchman, "Ladies and Gentlemen, the next President of the United States . . ." *Film Comment* (July 1980), pp. 49-58; Jules Witcover and Richard M. Cohen, "Where's the Rest of Ronald Reagan?", *Esquire* (March 1976), pp. 90-93, 150-153; Larry May, "A Leading Part for Hollywood," Chicago *Tribune*, January 24, 1981; Films, "Ronald Reagan Bloopers," available from Bob Mizell, Mizell Films, Pasadena, California, consisting of outakes of Reagan goofs and swearing; United Artists Entertainment, 729 Seventh Avenue, New York, New York 10019 has the most complete selection of Reagan films, although not exclusively; in an uncomplimentary column, Mike Royko referred to Reagan as the "Ted Baxter of American politics"! "Why Not the Worst? Failure Triumphs," Chicago *Sun-Times,* November 6, 1980, p. 2.

[9]Neil J. Smelser, "Collective Myths and Fantasies," plenary address, meeting of the American Psychoanalytic Association, May 3, 1980.

[10]See Lewis H. Lapham, Fortune's Child (Doubleday, 1980), from which we draw the term "leisure state"; Christopher Lasch, *The Culture of Narcissism* (Norton, 1979); Herbert Hendin, *The Age of Sensation* (Norton, 1975); John Shelton Lawrence, " 'Entertainment': The Ritual Center of American Culture," delivered at the 1978 Ministers' Seminar at Morningside College, April 3-5, 1978.

[11]Martha Wolfenstein, "The Emergence of Fun Morality," *Journal of Social Issues,* Vol. 7 (1951).

[12]Along with the works cited above, the reader desiring more knowledge of entertainment and show business can draw upon the following works. Still a classic treatment of aspects of leisure is Eric Larrabee and Rolf Meyerson (eds.), *Mass Leisure* (Free Press, 1958). One of the best analyses of celebrity is Richard Schickel, *His Picture in the Papers: A Speculation on Celebrity in America Based on the Life of Douglas Fairbanks, Sr.* (Charterhouse, 1973). See too such works as Ronald Barthes, *Mythologies* (Hill & Wang, 1972); Alexander Walker, *Stardom* (Stein & Day, 1970); and the chapter on "Celebrities" in C. Wright Mills, *The Power Elite* (Oxford University P., 1956).

There is much work on different show biz establishments. On television, see Gaye Tuchman (ed.), *The TV Establishment* (Prentice-Hall, 1974); many of the articles in Barry G. Cole (ed.), *Television* (Free Press, 1970); Richard Adler and Douglass Cater (eds.), *Television as a Social Force* (Praeger, 1976) and *Television as a Cultural Force* (Praeger, 1976); Eric Barnouw, *Tube of Plenty: The Evolution of American Television* (Oxford University P., 1975); Martin Mayer, *About Television* (Harper & Row, 1972). On the popular music business, see such works as R. Serge Denisoff, *Sold Gold: The Popular Record Industry* (Nelson-Hall, 1975); Steve Chapple and Reebee Garofalo, *Rock 'N' Roll is Here to Pay: The History and Politics of the Music Industry* (Nelson-Hall, 1977); Paul Hemphill, *The Nashville Sound: Bright Lights and Country Music* (Simon & Schuster, 1970); Bill C. Malone, *Country Music, U.S.A.: A Fifty-Year History* (University of Texas P., 1968); Greil Marcus, *Mystery Train: Images of America in Rock 'n Roll Music* (Dutton, 1975). On Hollywood, see also the account of the Fatty Arbuckle case, David Yallop, *The Day the Laughter Stopped* (St. Martin's, 1976); Richard S. Randall, *Censorship of the Movies* (University of Wisconsin P., 1968); Murray Schumach, *The Face on the Cutting Room Floor* (Morrow, 1964); Raymond Moley, *The Hays Office* (Bobbs-Merrill, 1945); Tino Balio (ed.), *The American Film Industry* (University of Wisconsin P., 1976); Leo Rosten, *The Movie Colony, The Movie Makers* (Harcourt Brace, 1941). For radio, see J. Fred MacDonald, *Don't Touch That Dial: Radio Programming in American Life from 1920 to 1960* (Nelson-Hall, 1980). Other popular industries — sports, religion, advertising, etc. — we have treated in other chapters. See too the discussions of pop figures in Ray Browne, et. al., *Heroes of Popular Culture* (Bowling Green Popular Press, 1970) and Ray Browne and Marshall Fishwick, *Icons of America* (Bowling Green Popular Press, 1977). *The Journal of Popular Culture* often has "In-depth" issues dealing with some popular entertainment industry, such as *Radio,* Vol. XII:2 and *Musical Theater,* XII:3. An earlier actor in politics is dealt with by Thomas H. Arthur, "An Actor in Politics: Melvyn Douglas and the New Deal," *Journal of Popular Culture,* Vol. XIV:2 (Fall 1980), pp. 196-211. See too Peter W. Kaplan, "On the Road with Bob Hope," *New Times,* August 7, 1978, pp. 37-45. A glance through the *Reader's Guide to Periodical Literature* will reveal many profiles of the popular and political celebrities of the moment. Indeed, Leo Lowenthal's study over time of "Biographies in Popular Magazines," in P. Lazarfeld and F. Stanton (eds.), *Radio Research, 1942-1943* and reprinted in B. Berelson and M. Janowitz (eds.) *Reader in Public Opinion and Communication* (The Free Press, 1953), pp. 289-298, notes changes in what kind of popular figures are profiled. Literature on Reagan, California culture, and aspects of entertainment can be obtained from the same bibliographic source.

Chapter Nine
SUPERPOP: International Popular Culture and Politics

American mass media have made our popular culture the most "popular" in the world. Popular culture proliferated in the United States because people love to play with the popular dramas created for them by the various pop industries. But even though there are vast cultural differences between the United States and other countries, they enjoy American pop culture as much as us. The proliferation of popular culture into the international world is not, however, without consequences. Here we will evaluate some of the political consequences that result from this world-wide diffusion of popular culture.

Cultural diffusion and international learning
The technology of American mass media in recent decades has made the spread of our popular culture abroad feasible. America produces vast amounts of television, movies, music, and so on that goes into the international market and plays abroad in an astounding range of places. It is natural for capitalist industries to try to expand their market areas, but popular culture has effects that marketing American steel and computers don't have. For popular culture includes the diffusion of ideas and images which may have long-term consequences as to what people think, and subsequently act. Indeed, the play-dramas of American popular culture may have an impact on the world, for good or ill, far more important than any other American product or activity, including the military. Popular culture attracts the attention of mass audiences abroad, and what they learn from it about us and the world has a broader and deeper effect than other American exports.

The spread of American popular culture is an example of

cultural diffusion, wherein aspects of one culture are used and even adopted by another.[1] An "emerging nation," for example, may adopt industrial techniques, political organization, and ideology from Western practices. And it may also import popular culture — dress, styles, dance, music, movies, and so forth. All of these have their impact in changing the lives of people in that country. Popular culture is probably the least assessed of these, but also the least assessable. One can see how industrialization or military rule affects the lives of people. But what access to popular culture does is less obvious.

American popular culture diffuses learning. People overseas play with popular culture for the same reasons we do, and like us, they learn from it. They gain ideas and images about the world, which affects their behavior. For example, access to popular culture that depicts an American world of affluence, sexual freedom, and constant fun may affect the *expectations* people have. If a youth in an Eastern European country gains access to rock 'n roll, *Playboy,* and designer jeans, this may suggest to him that life does not have to be like it is for him here and now. If people in a Third World country gain access to American advertising, with its promise of affluence and pleasure, they may conclude that economic development and individual wealth are good things, and wonder why they don't have those things now. Clearly, such learning may have subversive consequences for a government by creating expectations among people. American pop culture brings people fantasy worlds beyond their immediate existence, and by doing so may give people the notion that fantasy should become reality. That this can have explosive political results is clear enough.

The American Dream abroad

International learning through the diffusion of popular culture gives people ideas and images of what America is like. Since most people will only experience American culture through popular culture, what popular culture says about us shapes the way people think of us. And since popular culture deals with aspects of the American Dream, people overseas learn things about the American material and moral condition.[2]

The materialistic myth has "been abroad" for a long time. One of the lures of immigration to people in foreign countries was the widespread belief in America as a "land of opportunity." American advertising, television, and other media still give people the idea that we are a culture of material wealth and opulence. If people in

Hong Kong, Kenya, or Argentina watch *Dallas,* they may well be impressed with the opulent, hedonistic lifestyle and vast wealth of Americans, and may even generalize that "this is what America is like." But that is not to say that they will necessarily conclude that such materialism is a good thing. If they believe in another Dream — a traditional religion or revolutionary Marxism — they may think that such a depiction illustrates the degradation and decadence of American material culture.

Similarly, the depiction of the moralistic myth in American popular culture may give people overseas conflicting views of the state of the American moral condition. If they watch only crime shows, like American users of television, people overseas might think America is extremely violent and crime-ridden. On the other hand, if they get a steady diet of Christian television, they might get the notion that Americans are highly moral and consumed with religiosity. In any case, since they do not have direct access to the complexities of American culture, they may come to conflicting — and probably oversimplified — conclusions about us.

That popular culture might project a "negative" image about America has long worried politicians and official propagandists. A United States Information Agency (the government overseas propaganda agency) study in 1954 discussed ways in which to project a positive image of American life overseas, but noted that some Hollywood films present a distorted picture of our country. In particular, the study said that gangster films and other types of movies might give people the impression that all Americans are millionaires, women are golddiggers, and other dramatic role stereotypes. The propagandist, of course, is interested in depicting the positive aspects of the Dream.[3]

This can be illustrated by Soviet reactions to our popular culture. The American government and American films exhibit aspects of American life at Soviet trade fairs and cultural events. At a 1979 trade exhibit, Russian citizens gawked at American produced household gadgets, cosmetics, blue jeans, and so on. The motive for the exhibit, of course, was to show the Soviets the material manifestations and promises of the material Dream, but even then some were skeptical, since many Russians assumed that only the monied upper class could afford Estee Lauder, electric can openers, and designer jeans. Others thought the display evidence of Western decadence and excessive materialism, demonstrating the corrupting influence of capitalism. Too, some Soviet travelers to the United States wrote a piece on American movies and television for a

Soviet magazine which came to the same conclusion. American television, they argued, glossed over such problems as the subordination of blacks, glorified the cold war through the depiction of "secret agents," and supported fascism through crimestopper shows. Game shows, they thought, taught us greed and acquisition, television dramas degraded our tastes, and advertising manipulated our desires.[4] For them, imbued with another Dream, the American Dream is a nightmare, reflected in popular culture. Overall, it is likely that many Russians have ambivalent feelings about America, learning both positive and negative messages about us.

Pop imperialism

The extent of the proliferation of American popular culture around the world is greater than most of us think. Some facts will illustrate this astounding outflux and consumption. *The Reader's Digest* is the most popular magazine in many countries around the world, more so than native magazines. Thirty-five countries import more than thirty percent of their television programs, mostly from the United States; thirty-five percent of the movies shown in the fifty-four largest countries are American. The world's two most popular television shows are *Dallas* and *The Muppet Show*. It is estimated that *Dallas* has around 300 million viewers in fifty-seven countries! Over a third of the British population watched the *Dallas* episode in which J.R. was shot. Among the most popular programs in Australia are American soap operas. Mickey Mouse and Donald Duck are recognizable to over half the human race.[5]

The ubiquity of American popular culture has given rise to charges of "pop imperialism" that American cultural dominance has detrimental effects on local culture and perhaps eventually on political stability. For that reason, many countries have tried to ban or control American pop imports. Countries such as India and Egypt attempt to protect their fledgling film industry by banning or refusing import licenses for American movies, but people still mob and even bribe their way into the movies that are shown. The Communist countries of Eastern Europe have fought unsuccessfully against the influx of "youth culture" influences from the West, such as rock 'n roll, blue jeans, and *Playboy*, and still such items sell for exorbitant prices on the black market. Since pop play involves learning, such influences appear to affect behavior. Young toughs from Djakarta to Prague seem to find role models in Hollywood gangster and youth gang mythology.

As foreign countries develop the means (television, radio, movie theaters, etc.) to absorb American popular culture, the question they must ponder is to what extent the massive importation of it is good for them. If they attempt to control it, they face the creation of a black market or discontent because people can't gain access to it. If they allow it, they may face the "culture shock" of how it changes things, not always for the better. In this regard, one country that will be interesting to watch in the future is China. With the political changes in China in the 1970s, the decision was made to import technology from the United States to aid in their "four modernizations." American corporations began to import products, including popular culture. Chinese television began to run "Laverne and Shirley," "Sesame Street," and showed movies such as *Patton* and *Gone with the Wind.* Coca-cola, Sheraton Hotels, skateboards, and cosmetics began to appear. But the government did resist the influx of disco and rock, arguing that it was morally polluting. (We may recall that the Ayatollah Khomeini, when he banned rock music from Iranian radio, argued that such music, like opium, "stupefies persons listening to it and makes their brain inactive and frivolous.") In any event, China is especially interesting because it is an ancient and proud culture intermingled with Maoist ideology. It has been relatively untouched by the West, and how it is affected by the lure of Western popular play will be a major case of the diffusion and effects of popular culture.[6]

Thus, the outflux of American popular culture is bound to have not only impact, but also political backlash. For if the play-creations of popular culture dramatize dreams which are alien to a culture, and thought dangerous by the authorities, it is likely that they will resist this influence. They sense the power of popular culture to shape people, and thus the potential threat to political stability. But they may be overwhelmed by the desire of people to play. If that is the case, then for good or ill American influence in the world has gained a powerful force. American political and military power may not be able to change communism in Eastern Europe, but Western popular culture might through its own peculiar power to affect learning and create expectations and desires. As far as China goes, one may ask — to paraphrase the old tune — how are you going to keep them down on the (collective) farm after they've seen TV?

Political controversies over popular creations

The internationalization of popular culture has brought

political controversies over particular popular creations. Because of the power of popular culture to dramatize an event, personage, or symbol, something over which a country or faction is sensitive can generate much political heat. Such play-dramas have the power to inspire real political dramas.

In 1979, one such controversy developed in Germany over an NBC-TV production entitled "Holocaust." Originally serialized as a "docu-drama" in the United States in 1978, it was a dramatization of the Nazi "Final Solution," in which millions of Jews and other prisoners were systematically killed in concentration camps. In 1979, West German regional stations ran the show, and somewhat to their surprise, gained a large and growing audience, competing with network competition. More importantly, even though the show was criticized for "soap opera" elements about such a cataclysmic event, it broke something of the unspoken taboo in Germany over open discussion of the Nazis and the Final Solution. German young people, who had had only minimal exposure in school and family to the Nazi past, were particularly affected. The debate became quite emotional, with some Germans arguing the series was overdrawn and opened old wounds needlessly, and others believing that it was a welcome airing of what should never be forgotten. The controversy reached the German *Bundestag,* where Chancellor Helmut Schmidt defended the program as encouraging "critical reflection." The program's effect was directly felt when the *Bundestag* took up the debate on whether to extend the statute of limitations for prosecuting capital offenses committed by Germans during World War II. In the emotional climate created by the program, the German parliament extended the statute.[7]

Another politically explosive episode occurred over a television docu-drama aired first in Britain and then in the United States in 1980 entitled "Death of a Princess." The story was about a Saudi Arabian princess and her commoner lover who were publicly executed for adultery. When it was shown in England, the Saudi government expelled the British ambassador and hinted they would review trade agreements with England. The British government apologized for any offense the show might cause, but could not stop the show. And, as is usual when a play-drama becomes notorious, it was immediately in demand by television stations and audiences in twenty other nations. In the United States, public broadcasting stations showed it, much to the consternation of the State Department and Mobil Oil Company, which does large business with the Saudis. Both pressured PBS not to run it, but again more publicity generated more audience interest and more determination on the part of PBS to run it.[8]

These incidents illustrate the extent to which popular culture creations can become embroiled in political controversy if they depict something upsetting to some political interest. And since popular culture now occurs in an international setting, it is easy for the controversy to involve international interests.

Further, they show that the diffusion of popular dramas can have unintended political effects which are quite immediate. Both docu-dramas became the "trigger" for politically-charged tempests which "blew over" quickly, although not without effect. Popular culture can stir people's emotions, and sometimes these emotions can become politically focused. Popular play is transformed into political play.

The diffusion of foreign popular culture into the United States

The growth of popular culture industries in foreign countries means that they can now not only import and consume popular artifacts, they can also produce and export them abroad, including to us. We are all so used to the eclectic economy and society of America we forget that the huge volume of foreign imports is a relatively recent thing. Increasingly, we are influenced in our popular fads and fashions by foreign imports. After all, what could be more American than pizza, gyros, wok cooking, and enchiladas? Or for that matter, bikinis, miniskirts, Mao jackets, and Japanese sandals! We are no more immune from the "internationalization" of popular culture than anyone else, and indeed, given our propensity to consume popular culture, are more likely than many other countries to absorb pop artifacts from abroad. Producers abroad often target what they want to sell at us, knowing that Americans are the world's most prolific consumers of popular culture.

A moment's reflection will make us aware of the extent of this phenomenon. American films are now often bankrolled by foreign money; many movies are shot overseas, star international casts, and count on multinational audiences. British television produces a wide variety of high quality videoplays, with the big American market very much in mind. Rock 'n roll is an international industry that pervades a variety of cultures, and Americans in particular are familiar with rock groups from other countries marketed here — British rock groups, the Swedish group *Abba*, the Japanese group *Pink Lady*. Foreign countries hire American advertising agencies to shore up their national image here in the United States. In a word, popular culture is now highly cosmopolitan, seeking and finding audiences in many countries.

The internationalization of popular culture dramatizes the extent to which cultural creations diffuse and "permeate" other cultures. It also reflects how much the economies of the world are intertwined. What is of interest to us here, however, is the potential social and political consequences of such a trend. In other words, what may we learn through playing with an increasingly cosmopolitan popular culture?

It has been speculated that the proliferation of mass media and popular culture may turn the world into a "global village."[9] A spreading world culture created by the communications revolution would create identities and interests among the people of the world that transcends local ideology and culture.[10] They would be able to communicate because they hold certain things in common. Popular culture is one of these things. The international "youth culture," for example, can "talk" to each other because they share popular interests which permit them to identify with each other beyond the barriers of language and culture. They share a common dress, know and admire the same rock groups, like the same popular writers and movies, and so on. Since these youths often are the educated and traveled class in their society, it is probable they will wind up being the economic and political elite there in later life. Will these youthful contacts and commonalities promote international understanding and peace when these people come to power? If so, then there is something to the "global village" thesis. The world that plays together stays together! Popular culture then gives us a mode of international learning, a "common language" which transcends local biases and national stereotypes. If young Americans, Russians, and Chinese all wear similar fashions, listen to the same music, and read the same novels, they will have things in common which previous generations of young elites-to-be in their countries did not! It remains to be seen whether popular culture in the long run does have such a beneficial social and political effect.

Political elites in many countries are very much aware of the potential effects of popular culture, and often attempt to control or discourage its use. Perhaps they sense its power to overcome ideology and local culture, to create identities across cultures and nationalities, and even to undermine social and political values. It is no wonder, then, that political elites in various countries worry not only about the "Americanization" of their culture but also about the long-term consequences of the introduction of popular culture. Since the young are to be the "carriers" of the culture, including the political culture, alien popular culture and the obvious identifications with foreign ideas and habits it brings among the young poses a threat. Political elites may perceive the threat to be not only decadence, but also the introduction of identifications with things other than "what we believe in." The parents of many young Americans have trouble enough with their offspring's use of popular culture, so it is not difficult to imagine how troubling foreign popular culture is to Eastern European communist commissars or Islamic mullahs.

In the future, we may expect attempts to control the diffusion of popular culture in many quarters through political means. The lure of popular culture is, however, great. Like alcohol or drugs, banning it makes it all the more alluring. The ingenuity of people in getting hold of it in places where it is now banned is astounding. So it is likely that in the future, international popular culture will continue to diffuse, and will become an increasingly important source of social and political learning. A spreading world popular culture is not only technologically feasible now, it is fast becoming a reality with which more and more countries will have to cope. A world popular culture would certainly be a unique innovation in human history. What kind of world it will help create we can only guess. In particular, what political consequences it will have many of the younger readers of this book may well live to see.

Conclusion

The American Dream is abroad in the world, carried by popular culture. Ideas and images of the myth diffuse to the far corners of the Earth. We may expect that popular culture will evoke both positive and negative reactions to America. In any case, international popular culture will play a role in shaping and reflecting the attitudes of people overseas toward us. Further, the internationalization of popular culture suggests that we may see the worldwide diffusion of popular artifacts which are played with by people from a wide variety of cultures. This points up not only the universality of the desire to play, but also the possibility that learning from popular culture may take place all over the world. The universal spread of popular culture, creating common popular habits, could have long-range unifying effects with political consequences. If, as we have argued, popular culture teaches us myths, then it may be that an international popular culture, not particularly tied to one national mythology or another, may create something quite new in the world. An international mythology carried by a popular culture might create identities antithetical to specific ideological and political interests. That would mean a new and widely diffused popular Dream will be loose in the world, the nature of which we can only imagine.

Finally, the diffusion of popular culture through international mass media may have an unintended — and ultimate — consequence. Scientists now believe that television signals from earth satellites beam into outer space, announcing the presence of Earth civilization to whomever (or whatever) is watching Out There! Although radio waves travel about one light-year a year, in time intelligent life with the technical means could pick up broadcasts of *I Love Lucy, The Beverley Hillbillies,* and *Let's Make a Deal!* In other words, popular culture may alert aliens from space as to the presence of life on Earth, but what they may think of us by observing our popular culture is another matter.[11] What does American popular culture tell the beings out at Alpha Centauri about us? Perhaps the ultimate political consequence of popular culture will be to prompt an invasion of Earth from beyond.[12]

Notes

[1]On diffusion and innovation, see Everett M. Rogers, *Diffusion of Innovation* (Free Press of Glencoe, 1962); H.G. Barnett, *Innovation: The Basis of Cultural Change* (McGraw-Hill, 1953); Dennis Gabor, *Innovations: Scientific, Technological, and Social* (Oxford University P., 1970).

[2]Two works that detail aspects of American popular proliferation are C.W.E. Bigsby (ed.), *Superculture: American Popular Culture and Europe* (Bowling Green University Popular Press, 1975); and Jeremy Tunstall, *The Media are American* (Columbia University P., 1977).

[3]Leo Bogart, *Premises for Propaganda* (The Free Press, 1976); also his "Projecting America," *Society,* Vol. 12 (September 1975), pp. 57-61.

[4]Jim Gallagher, "Soviets Yearn for the Frills — Especially Ours," Chicago *Tribune,* July 8, 1979, sec. 2, p. 12; David K. Willis, "Soviets Get Muddy View of United States Through Films, TV," *Christian Science Monitor,* February 15, 1978, p. 3.

[5]See Tunstall, *op. cit.;* Richard Reeves, "Media: TV Imperialism," *Esquire,* October 1979, pp. 20, 36-37; Richard Critchfield, "What's POP culture doing in a place like this?", *Christian Science Monitor,* July 26, 1979, pp. B4-B5, B9.

[6]Richard Reeves, "China Beams Abroad," *Esquire,* January 30, 1979, pp. 9-10; Timothy McNulty, "A Class-Struggle Hit, Zorro smashes Box Office Records across China," Chicago *Tribune,* February 17, 1980; James P. Sterba, "China Prepares a New Course: 'Sesame Street,'" New York *Times,* January 24, 1981; Timothy McNulty, "Chinese Officials Fighting Rock, Disco Craze," Chicago *Tribune,* August 3, 1980, pp. 1, 6. In the last article, a Shanghai newspaper is quoted as editorializing about the effects of Western dances: "It is moral pollution . . . The youths are done up in an evil way and dance and swing, singing strange tunes while rocking themselves up and down. The spectacle causes one to vomit."

[7]Alice Siegert, " 'Holocaust' Backlash: Germans Decry Postwar Killings," Chicago *Tribune,* July 8, 1979, sec. 3, p. 14; Arthur H. Samuelson notes in *The Nation,* November 3, 1979, that during a Congressional debate on arms sales to Saudi Arabia, a lobbying organization called the American Israel Public Affairs Committee distributed copies of Gerald Green's book *Holocaust* (culled from the script of the show) to members of Congress, with a letter urging a no vote on the arms sale (p. 421).

[8]William Mullen, "Saudis Fume, But Can't Stop Spread of 'Shameful' Movie," *Chicago Tribune,* May 4, 1980, sec. 3, pp. 5-6; Associated Press, "PBS pressured on Saudi movie, May 9, 1980; Richard M. Harley, " 'Death of a Princess' Gave Flawed View of Arab Society, Islamic Law," *Christian Science Monitor,* May 15, 1980, p. 6; M. Cherif Bassiouni, "The Princess and Islamic Law," *Chicago Tribune,* May 15, 1980, sec. 3, p. 3; J.B. Kelly, "Saudi Censors," *New Republic,* May 17, 1980, pp. 14-16, advertisement for Mobil Oil, "A New Fairy Tale," *Chicago Tribune,* May 9, 1980, p. 7.

9. Marshall McLuhan, *Understanding Media: The Extensions of Man* (Signet, 1966), p. 20.

[10]The idea of a "spreading world culture" was given great impetus by Arnold Toynbee's lectures, *The World and the West* (Oxford University P., 1953), especially the chapter "The Psychology of Encounters," pp. 66-84.

[11]Walter Sullivan, "TV Signals may Alert Aliens to Earth," *Chicago Tribune,* February 25, 1978, sec. 1, p. 12.

[12]The reader wishing to pursue helpful works that treat aspects of culture, diffusion of technology and other innovations, and the growth of international communication should consult the following: On the spread of technology, see Victor Basiuk, *Technology, World Politics and American Policy* (New York: Columbia University P., 1977); Lester B. Laye, *Technological Change: Its Conception and Measurement* (Englewood Cliffs: Prentice-Hall, 1966); Gayl D. Ness, *The Sociology of Economic Development* (New York: Harper & Row, 1970); Ali Al Amin Mazrui, *Cultural Engineering and Nation-building in East Africa* (Evanston: Northwestern University P., 1972); Richard S. Rosenbloom, *Technology and Information Transfer* (Boston: Division of Research, Graduate School of Business Administration, Harvard University, 1970); H.C. Greisman, "Marketing the Millenium: Ideology, Mass Culture, and Industrial Society," *Political Science Quarterly,* No. 4, pp. 511-524; A. Vafa and M. Drobyshev, "Technological Progress and Spiritual Culture in the Countries of the Third World," *Asian Survey,* Vol. 14, pp. 207-219 (March 1974); J.G. Ruggie and E.B. Haas, "International Responses to Technology," *International Organization* (Summer 1975), Vol. 29, pp. 557-920; C. Horner, "Redistributing Technology," *Commentary* (January 1979), Vol. 67, pp. 52-54; N.H. Leff, "Technology Transfer and U.S. Foreign Policy: the Developing Countries," *Orbis* (Spring 1979), Vol. 23, pp. 145-165; E.B. Parker, "Implications of New Information Technology," *Public Opinion Quarterly* (Winter 1973-1974), Vol. 37, pp. 590-600; G.G. Hamilton, "Chinese Consumption of Foreign Commodities: a Comparative Perspective," *American Sociology Review* (December 1977), Vol. 42, pp. 877-891; K.P. Sauvant, "Multinational Enterprises and the Transmission of Culture," *Journal of Peace Resolution* (1976), Vol. 13, No. 1, pp. 49-65; M. Wilkins, "Role of Private Business in the International Diffusion of Technology," *Journal of Economic History* (March 1974), Vol. 34, pp. 166-188, 189-193; R.S. Fortner, "Strategies for Self-immolation: the Third World and the Transfer of Advanced Technologies," *Inter-American Economic Affairs* (Summer 1977), Vol. 31, pp. 25-50; L.M. Lance and E.E. McKenna, "Analysis of Cases Pertaining to the Impact of Western Technology on the Non-Western World," *Human Organization* (Spring 1975), Vol. 34, pp. 87-94; "Importing Technology into a Third World Nation," *Futurist* (April 1977), Vol. 11, p. 77; J.P. Martino, "Adopting New Ideas," *Futurist* (April 1974), Vol. 8, pp. 88-89; R. Braibanti, "American Experience in Diffusing Administrative Technology," *Annals of American Academy of Political and Social Science* (November 1976), Vol. 428, pp. 65-76; C.A. Salter and A.I. Teger, "Change in Attitudes Toward Other Nations as a Function of the Type of International Contact," *Sociometry* (June 1975), Vol. 38, pp. 213-222; N. Katzman, "Impact of Communication Technology: Some Theoretical Premises and their Implications," *Ekistics* (August 1974), Vol. 38, pp. 125-130.

For works on the spread of communication in particular see, Kaarle and Herbert I. Schiller (eds.), *National Sovereignty and International Communication* (Ablex, 1978); Molefi K. Asante, et. al., *The Handbook of Intercultural Communication* (Sage, 1980); Glen Fisher, *American Communication in a Global Society* (Ablex, 1979); N. Lin and R.S. Burt, "Differential Effects of Information Channels in the Process of Innovation Diffusion," *Social Forces* (Spring 1975), Vol. 54, pp. 256-274; John B. Robinson, "Mass Communication and Information Diffusion," in M. Janowitz and P. Hirsch (eds.), *Reader in Public Opinion and Mass Communication* (The Free Press, 1981), pp. 348-362.

Works dealing with the impact of diffusion on culture include Robert Tarbell Oliver, *Culture and Communication: the Problem of Penetrating National and Cultural Boundaries* (Springfield, Illinois: Thomas, 1962); UNESCO, *Freedom and Culture* (Freeport, New York: Books for Libraries, 1971); Edmund Ronald Leach, *Culture and Communication: the Logic by Which Symbols are Connected* (New York: Cambridge University P., 1976); Margaret Mead (ed.), *Cultural Patterns and Technical Change* (World Federation for Mental Health) (Paris: UNESCO,

1953); Harry Gordon Johnson, *Technology and Economic Interdependence* (London: Macmillan, 1975); Melvin Kransberg, *Technology and Culture: an Anthology* (New York: Schocken Books, 1972); Louise S. Spindler, *Cultural Change and Modernization: Mini-models and Case Studies* (New York: Holt, Rinehart, Winston, 1977); J. Goldthorpe, *The Sociology of the Third World: Disparity and Involvement* (New York: Cambridge University P., 1975); Wilton S. Dillon (ed.), *The Cultural Drama: Modern Identities and Social Ferment* (Washington: Smithsonian Institution P., 1974); A.E. Hippler, "Some Alternative Viewpoints of the Negative Results of Euro-American Contact with Non-Western Group," *American Anthropology* (June 1974), Vol. 76, pp. 334-337.

Four interesting articles which treat directly the impact of popular culture abroad are J. Loboda, "Diffusion of Television in Poland," *Economic Geography* (January 1974), Vol. 50, pp. 70-82; D.E. Payne and C.A. Peake, "Cultural Diffusion: The Role of U.S. TV in Iceland," *Journalism Quarterly* (Autumn 1977), Vol. 54, pp. 523-531; A. Sisson, "American Fads — German Fads," *Journal of Popular Culture* (Spring 1974), Vol. 7, pp. 812-815; U.K. Pak, "Impact of Technology on the Youth of Developing Countries," *Impact of Science on Society* (October 1975), Vol. 25, pp. 307-311.

Chapter Ten
FUTUREPOP: The Vision of the Political Future in Popular Culture

One of the biggest roles of science fiction is to prepare people to accept the future without pain and to encourage a flexibility of mind. Politicians should read science fiction, not Westerns and detective stories.
Arthur C. Clarke[1]

American popular culture is now "deep" in our culture, and is also now "wide" in the world. More than this, it has also extended into the future. This is because we all are interested in the future, in what will happen to us and the world the day after tomorrow. Popular culture therefore has created for us fantasy worlds about the future, through which we can vicariously imagine what is in store for us and mankind. "Futurepop" — science fiction, fantasy literature, superhero tales — uses the future to help us deal with the present. Since the present is always the preface for the future, anticipating what the world may be like helps us to deal with what may come. Politics is always an activity which aims at gaining control over the future. The political future is as problematic and unknown as any other future. We try to imagine what the political future, and indeed alternative political futures, might be like. Futurepop helps us to "flesh out" the political future. In this chapter, we want to point to recurrent popular themes in science fiction that may give us clues to the political alternatives of our futures.

Futurepop and political learning

Futurepop, then, is a major modern form of popular play-learning. We are all much aware that we live in a world of great change, wherein our world and lives may be much affected by the great technological changes of our time. If we are anxious about what we and the world will be like in the wake of those changes, science fiction provides us with dramatic play-stories about what we may expect. Futurepop in general has given shape to what we may be and how we may have to act in alternative futures. For the attraction of science fiction (and indeed fantasy and superhero stories) is that it lets us play with the possibilities that may be in store for us. This includes, and often highlights, dramatic scenarios of possible political futures.

Much of our interest in science fiction is because it gives us futuristic looks at how technology will affect our lives. This stems from our present awareness of living in a world of advanced technology and technological innovation. Whatever the storyline of science fiction, it takes an attitude toward technology. Some of the heroic fantasies and anti-technological, transporting us to ancient, often Gothic, worlds of chivalric conflicts and primitive technology. But science fiction is typically highly technological, and whatever moral or material conflicts emerge revolve around technology. The story may think technology bad, but envision an alternative technology; or it may think technology good, at least in the hands of the right beings. In any case, it is technology that fascinates us, and gives much of science fiction its compelling interest for us. We want to know what our technological future will be like.

Science fiction and the fate of the Dream

In particular, we are interested in the fate of the American Dream. Our uncertainty as to how the American story will turn out directs our attention to science fiction tales which dramatize the future of the Dream. Will technology realize, extend, undermine, or pervert the Dream? For science fiction projects our present anxieties about the fate of the Dream into mythical future settings with which we may play. Such *technofables* speak to both our desires and doubts about the future of the Dream. If we think on the great corpus of sci-fi, we see different endings: the Dream is realized in a moral and material Utopia through technological perfection, which either creates universal abundance and social goodness, or minimizes scarcity and human conflict. Alternatively, we see negative Utopias, called Dystopias, in which the Dream turns into a nightmare: the commitment to material abundance leads to eventual depletion, or material abundance leads to moral decadence; in either case, the result is *chaos*. The other kind of dystopia is one of *control,* in which technology creates a future which perverts the Dream through manipulation of behavior.

These themes run through a variety of sci-fi technofables. The variations of mythic themes of interest to Americans are too numerous to detail here, but let us mention a few which have political overtones. The *Frankenstein* technofable is a tradition in popular culture which appeals to our fear that technology may bring chaos. In this story line, science uses technology to create something which becomes a monster let loose on us. The monster — be it a man revived by electricity, or rabbits and lizards grown to enormous size by nuclear fallout, or a nuclear power plant suddenly out of control — lurks out there because of the Faustian sin of science, "fooling around with Mother Nature" and creating something evil.[2] The technofable of *benevolent empire* reassures us that our use of military and space technology is for moral purposes in the tradition of manifest destiny. *Star Trek,* for example, projects us into "the final frontier" in which American good will plus technology extends the umbrella of the empire.[3] The negative vision of *malevolent empire* fleshes out a world of technological power used for evil purposes. The *Star Wars* series tells of a fascist empire which uses malevolent technology (the "Death Star").[4] Although not directly political, we also see in sci-fi a theme of *transcendant adventure,* in which cosmic theological truths are discovered through advanced technology, as in the movies *2001* and *Close Encounters of the Third Kind.*[5]

It is with themes of Utopia and Dystopia, however, that we see most directly the political dimensions of the American Dream dramatized in science fiction. In Utopias, the Dream comes true because of the good use of technology. In Dystopias, the Dream is destroyed by the bad use of technology. In these technofables, the fate of the Dream depends on political technique directly.

The Utopian technofable

There are many variants of the Utopian technofable, but we may point to two major versions which relate to the Dream. First, there is the *high-tech* conception, which realizes aspects of the Dream through benevolent technology. Such conceptions often include a technocratic elite which utilizes rational planning and technical expertise to achieve material and moral purposes. NASA and the astronauts are often pointed to as a model of such benevolent rule. Disney's "City of Tomorrow" in Florida is touted as a showcase of what high-tech communities, guided by corporate technology, will look like in the future. Utopians since Edward Bellamy and H.G. Wells have envisioned future Utopias in which marvelous technology and rational elites have realized the ultimate fruition of the Dream — eternal abundance in an atmosphere of moral equality and achievement.

But doubts about the use of technology to exploit the environment and "moral engineering" have led to *low-tech* visions of the future. Such visions fantasize about a benevolent Utopia which uses "alternative" technologies which respect nature and human freedom. Their futuristic image of the American Dream involves a cooperative rather than competitive material community and an egalitarian and libertarian moral community. Rather than the high-consumptive, big-organization, and "dinosaur-technology" society imagined above, they see an ecologically-balanced, scaled-down, and humane-technologized society in balance with ecological and humane values. This imaginary future has emerged in the wake of environmental problems, huge organizational complexes remote from the individual, and massive, threatening technologies such as nuclear power plants.[6] Clearly there are divergent views of what Utopia should be, centering around the role of technology in creating the good community.

The Dystopian Technofable

The Dystopian technofable sees future man, armed with advanced technology, destroying the Dream through politically-sanctioned disasters. Governments of the future will either create a dystopia of chaos through war, environmental pollution, or other disasters, or they will create a future hell by technological control over human behavior.

In the first case, science fiction has envisioned future *wars,* either on earth or in the stars. In either instance, they have imagined the possibility of cataclysmic results, such as the breakdown of civilization, the disappearance of knowledge, and even the demise of human life. The technology of war, in this vision, brings images of vast destruction that plunges us into unending horror that even taxes the imagination of sci-fi fantasists — uninhabitable lands; crop production and human fertility disrupted by radioactivity and germs; vast starvation because of the loss of grains; mutuated and lethal strains of virus and bacteria; mutant populations roaming deserted cities; weather modification and a depleted ozone layer. Star wars involve solar systems and galaxies allied against each other, and uncanny technologies arrayed in wars across millions of miles.[7]

In the latter case, science fiction has imagined dystopias of nearly absolute *control,* states in which the technology of surveillance and manipulation has reached its logical result. The government elite that does the controlling may believe itself to be quite benevolent, but the effect is the same. The techniques imagined are varied and ingenious — prenatal conditioning, sleep-teaching the young, propagandizing by suggestion, mind alteration through drugs and operations, thought control and re-education, eugenics, and so on.[8]

One of the most famous and enduring of such popular technofables is Aldous Huxley's *Brave New World* (written in 1931).[9] In this fantasy, a benevolent elite uses the most advanced technology to create a world of uniformity and order in which everyone, except for a few misfits, believes that they are happy. They believe so because they have been psychologically conditioned since birth. Society is ordered into a functional class system, where everyone is scientifically assigned to a place in the scheme of things. Drugs are widely used to suppress pain, stimulate pleasure, and avoid thought. Eugenics are used to produce the requisite human types manipulable by society's managers. Sexual promiscuity is widely permitted in controlled situations, but family life and parental attachment to children are forbidden. Children are reared by the community. Social control is exercised without recourse to power or direct suppression, depending rather on scientific techniques of persuasion, suggestion, and organization. Huxley's tale is still powerful, since it reminds us of the possibility of a totalitarianism that deludes itself in believing it is benevolent and "scientific," using science to control us for our own good. It scares us because it conjures up a future dystopia that is clean, efficient, scientific, and orderly, but is also inhuman. The technological *ethos* will be used to make us into automatons who are no less obedient, efficient, and predictable than the machines that rule us.

The appeal of both kinds of sci-fi fantasies stems from the fact that we can see seeds of both cataclysmic war and totalitarian controls in the present. In a more imaginative way that the social-scientific "futurists," science fiction writers sketch out for us our deepest anxieties about the political future that may befall us. We read of the latest advances in military and space technology, and of the technology of psychological and social conditioning. Science fiction gives flesh to our deepest political fears: that the future may be a nightmare, either of chaos or control.

1984

Since we are fast approaching that now symbolic year, perhaps we should remind ourselves of some of the features of George Orwell's popular political fantasy, *1984*.[10] It still may be the most malevolent prospect for the human race ever envisioned, a future State of absolute control exercised by an elite that is thoroughly scientific but has no illusions about being benign. Orwell sees a future ruled by a totalitarian superstate committed to nothing less than absolute control over human thought and personality. Like the other great works of science fiction, *1984* could not be a believable technofable unless we are aware of certain aspects of our century which makes such a nightmare world possible.

Orwell was much aware, as we are, of the modern rise of *totalitarianism* as a political reality. Soviet Russia and Nazi Germany were to take on political features virtually unknown in the past. Unlike the autocratic states and despotisms of old, totalitarian states are more ambitious. Armed with an absolute ideology transformed into doctrine, they believe they can transform man and the world into something new. They utilize technique — socialization, propaganda, coercion, organization, etc. — to create a "new order." Although the elite of such a State may see themselves as benevolent, totalitarianism takes on a life of its own. The leader becomes god-like; the State intrudes into every area of life; every aspect of society is coordinated and controlled; orthodoxy is enforced in thought and deed; power is concentrated at the top in the State bureaucracy. Power becomes an end in itself, and the individual becomes the object of its extreme application. Power over individual life is "total."[11]

We are also aware that the *technology* of such absolute controls now exists and is becoming more sophisticated. Even in democratic countries with traditions of civil liberties like the United States, the technology of control is increasingly available and used. The government uses propaganda to sell programs and Presidents. The police and government agencies keep massive files on millions of citizens. The technology of surveillance and "bugging" is now fantastically sophisticated. As social stresses increase, governments justify more and more the exercise of supervision and control over their own citizens. Such thinking may mean that democratic governments will evolve into totalitarian ones with no restraints on the use of technological and political power.

All this may come about because of certain historical *trends* which help to intensify social stress and therefore the justification of increased State power. Here we may see the interplay of chaos and control. Chaotic trends — population growth and the threat of foreign migration, environmental depletion and scarcities of food, water, and fuel, economic spasms of inflation and depression, and war — may convince governmental elites that they have to increase controls over restless populations. Necessity would then be exalted into an ideology, and totalitarian controls justified as a survival tactic. One futurist claims that the societies that survive in the future will be those that blend "a 'religious' orientation with a 'military' discipline." Totalitarian states can provide in such circumstances the ideology that gives us a political religion, and the enforcement power to regiment us into a disciplined and militaristic order.

Orwell's fantasy has all of these features. The "Oceania" of 1984 is a totalitarian Superstate that takes such orders to their logical conclusion. It possesses an advanced technology of control. And it is apparently a product of war and scarcity. More importantly, it fleshes out in popular form what individual life comes to be like in such a future political order.

The life of the protagonist of the novel, Winston Smith, is one of unending repression and fear. Every act, even every thought, is suspect, and one constantly has to suppress ideas, feelings, and expressions. For surveillance is everywhere — "telescreens" in one's apartment, worksite, and streets, the "Thought Police" undercover everywhere, and everyone, even members of one's own family, willing to turn you in for "thoughtcrime." The ordinary person is placed in the horrible position of being able to trust no one, including himself. One's internal motivation is fear, one's external expression obedience and controlled manifestations of hate.

The society of 1984 is organized in a vast bureaucracy: the "Ministry of Plenty" administers scarcity; the "Ministry of Love" administers hate; and the "Ministry of Truth" administers lies. The last, where Winston works, controls reality through propaganda. There is no such thing as objective truth, an unchangeable past, or fixed meanings to words. Thought control is exercised by rewriting the past, altering facts to fit State needs, and changing language ("Newspeak") to eliminate certain ideas, such as "freedom." Nobody even knows for sure whether Oceania is really at war, and indeed during a speech, who the State is at war with is changed, and people accept it! The State is led by a mythical figure called "Big Brother," a kind of composite personality who symbolically presides over Oceania, is thought to be benevolent, and is "watching you."

Oceania is a totalitarian society based on external suppression and internal repression, including sexual repression. One's energies are supposed to be directed toward work and serving Big Brother, and sexual love is a threat to that. Thus, sex is discouraged, and young women are organized into the "Junior Anti-Sex League." The family is to be eliminated, as are emotional ties between men and women, and adults and children. Sexual drives are to be eradicated through conditioning, and even the physical orgasm somehow eliminated. The idea that sex is satisfying and love is possible is denied and made a crime.

1984 is a picture of a future State in which government becomes the obsessive and pervasive play-drama of ordinary life, in which people have to deny their independent human existence. People are mobilized into a never-ending drama of production and war, show trials and the hunt for enemies, persecution, and victimage. The goal of the State is not a materialistic or moralistic Utopia based on some positive political value, but rather simply the aggrandizement of power into more and more complete control over human nature and social reality. "If you want a picture of the future," says the Inner Party member to Winston, "imagine a boot stamping on a human face — forever."

1984 is a technofable of the political future that could not be more malignant and bleak. But something like it is not entirely impossible. The age of Orwell is upon us, and post-1984 America might have some potential for becoming like the "Oceania" of the novel. Armed with technological power, a coalition of government, corporate, and military elites might face awesome historical trends and the social stresses they produce by imposing what would evolve into a totalitarian order. And the "logic" of that order would impel it closer and closer to the 1984 model. In our case, the all-powerful State will convince us that the American Dream is still real, even though material prosperity will dissipate and political democracy and social morality will be abandoned. Perhaps the ultimate horror of Orwell's fantasy is that people accept the gap between official reality and the actual reality of their lives. If the generation of students in school now live to see something like what Orwell predicted come true in America, it will be in part because they will believe what they are told since they are afraid to believe anything else, are afraid of critical thinking and doubt, and "will to believe" desperately in the wake of disconfirming facts. In that case, they will not notice the contradiction between what they are told is true and what is true.[12]

Perhaps popular culture is teaching us to become the subjects of the post-1984 world. If popular culture is preparing us for a world ruled by technology, convinces us we have to sacrifice democratic and civil concerns because of "necessity," makes us believe that the dream world of popular fare is more real, and more pleasant, than our own lives, then it may play an important role in conditioning us to fit into the world we have described above. But science fiction such as Orwell's 1984 is a play-fantasy that is a warning: all those habits, including popular culture, which contribute to us accepting such a world are evil, and all those ideas and creations, political or popular cultural, which glorify or justify such a world are demonic.

Conclusion

Futurepop, then, gives fictional shape to our present feelings about technology, and how that technology might be used to create alternative futures. For Americans, technofables about the future give us a glimpse of the fate of the Dream in different forms. Our anxieties about the future leads us to play with it in the present through popular culture. But science fiction since Jules Verne has had a recurring habit of turning into science-fact. One generation's play-fantasy becomes another's reality. The polar choices in today's sci-fi are paradise or nightmare, and it is likely that the younger readers of this book will live to see which technofable the future approximates. In whatever case, popular culture will have provided us with alternative maps of the future which we will recognize when we get there, like it or not.[13]

Notes

[1]Arthur C. Clarke, quoted in Jerome Agel (ed.), *The Making of Kubrick's 2001* (Signet, 1970), p. 300.

[2]James Combs and Dan Nimmo, "The Return of Frankenstein: The Popular Media Aesthetic of Three Mile Island Coverage by ABC Evening News," *Studies in Popular Culture,* Vol. IV (Spring 1981), pp. 38-48.

[3]William Blake Tyrell, "Star Trek as Myth and TV as Mythmaker," *Journal of Popular Culture,* Vol. 10 (1977), pp. 711-719.

[4]Robert Jewett and John Shelton Lawrence, " 'Pop Fascism' in 'Star Wars' — or Vision of a Better World?", Des Moines *Register,* 1977, undated.

[5]Ronald J. Sommer, "Religious Themes in Science Fiction," *The Cresset* (October 1978), pp. 21-25.

[6]The best Utopian fantasy in this vein is Ernest Callenbach's *Ecotopia* (Bantam, 1977); a work that tries to calculate what this would mean for the American Dream is Rufus E. Miles, Jr., *Awakening From the American Dream: The Social and Political Limits to Growth* (Universe Books, 1976).

[7]The futurist and sci-fi literature on future wars is vast. Perhaps the most sophisticated, and best place to start, is Walter M. Miller, Jr., *A Canticle for Leibowitz* (Bantam, 1976).

[8]The vision of control is many-formed, but a classic treatment is Kurt Vonnegut, Jr., *Player Piano* (Delta Books, n.d.).

[9]Aldous Huxley, *Brave New World* (Bantam, 1946). See also his *Brave New World Revisited*

(Perennial Library, 1965).

[10]See Orwell's *Nineteen Eighty-Four: Text, Sources, Criticism* (Harcourt, Brace, Jovanovich, 1963), Irving Howe, ed.

[11]On totalitarianism, see Hannah Arendt, *The Origins of Totalitarianism* (Harcourt, Brace & World, 1951); Stephen J. Whitfield, *Into the Dark: Hannah Arendt and Totalitarianism* (Temple University P., 1980); Carl J. Friedrich and Zbigniew K. Brzezinski, *Totalitarian Dictatorship and Autocracy* (Praeger, 1961); Alex Inkeles, "The Totalitarian Mystique," in Carl J. Friedrich (ed.), *Totalitarianism* (Harvard University P., 1954), pp. 87-107; Bernard Crick, "The Elementary Types of Government," *Government and Opposition*, Vol. 3 (Winter 1968), pp. 3-20; and Arthur Koestler's novel, *Darkness at Noon* (Macmillan, 1941).

[12]Two pioneering essays which point to such a State are Harold D. Lasswell, "The Garrison State," *American Journal of Sociology*, Vol. XLVI (January 1941), pp. 455-468, and Bertram M. Gross, "Friendly Fascism: A Model for America," *Social Policy* (November/December 1970), pp. 1-9. See also Gross's expansion on the original theme in his book, *Friendly Fascism* (M. Evans, 1980). Robert Heilbroner, in his pessimistic *Inquiry into the Human Prospect* (Norton, 1980) envisions the kind of State that might be able to survive in a future rent by chaotic changes:

"The order that comes to my mind as most likely to satisfy these requirements is one that blends a 'religious' orientation with a 'military' discipline. Such a monastic organization of society may be repugnant to us, but I suspect it offers the greatest promise of making those enormous transformations needed to reach a new stable socio-economic basis." (pp. 172-173).

[13]The "futurist" literature tends toward the pessimistic. See, for instance, Roberto Vacca, *The Coming Dark Age* (Doubleday Anchor, 1974); L.S. Stavrianos, *The Promise of the Coming Dark Age* (W.H. Freeman, 1976); Richard J. Barnet, *The Lean Years* (W.H. Freeman, 1977). But others envision a Utopian future of some kind: Gerald Feinberg, *The Prometheus Project* (Doubleday, 1969); Herman Kahn and Anthony J. Weiner, *Year Two Thousand* (Viking, 1970); Robert Theobald, *The Economics of Abundance* (Pitman, 1970). A low-tech classic is E.F. Schumacher, *Small is Beautiful* (Harper & Row, 1973). See also Bernard Gendron, *Technology and the Human Condition* (St. Martin's Press, 1977). The reader might also want to examine the brief of *The Global 2000 Report to the President: Entering the Twenty-First Century*, Vol. 1 (U.S. Government Printing Office, n.d.).

The bibliographic sources on science fiction include Marshall B. Tymn, "Science Fiction," in M. Thomas Inge (ed.), *Handbook of American Popular Culture*, Vol. 1 (Greenwood Press, 1979); Donald H. Tuck, *The Encyclopedia of Science Fiction and Fantasy Through 1968* (Advent, 1974); Marshall B. Tymn, *A Research Guide to Science Fiction Studies* (Garland, 1977); and Thomas Clareson, *Science Fiction Criticism: An Annotated Checklist* (Kent State University P., 1972).

Histories of sci-fi literature include Paul A. Carter, *The Creation of Tomorrow: Fifty Years of Magazine Science Fiction* (Columbia University P., 1977); Robert M. Philmus, *Into the Unknown: the Evolution of Science Fiction from Francis Bodwin to H.G. Wells* (Berkeley: University of California Press, 1970); Brian Wilson Aldiss, *Billion Year Spree: the True History of Science Fiction* (Garden City, N.Y.: Doubleday, 1973); Howard Bruce Franklin, *Future Perfect: American Science Fiction of the Nineteenth Century* (New York: Oxford University P., 1968); Samuel Moskowitz, *Explorers of the Infinite: Shapers of Science Fiction* (Westport, Conn.: Hyperion Press, 1974); James E. Gunn, *Alternate Worlds: the Illustrated History of Science Fiction* (Englewood Cliffs, N.J.: Prentice-Hall, 1975); Leslie Fiedler, *In Dreams Awake: a Historical Critical Anthology of Science Fiction* (New York: Dell, 1975).

The many critical studies of sci-fi will give the student an idea of the concerns and depth of the genre. See Thomas B. Clareson, *Voice for the Future: Essays on Major Science Fiction Writers*, Vols. I & II (Bowling Green University Popular Press, 1976 and 1978); Darko Suvin, *Metamorphoses of Science Fiction* (Yale University P., 1979); *Science Fiction: History, Science, Vision* (New York: Oxford University P., 1977); Richard Stanley Allen, Science Fiction: the Future (New York: Harcourt, Brace, Jovanovich, 1971); Robert E. Scholes, *Structural Fabulation: an Essay on Fiction of the Future* (University of Notre Dame P., 1975); Mark Rose (ed.), *Science Fiction: a Collection of Critical Essays* (Englewood Cliffs, N.J.: Prentice-Hall, 1976); Neil Barron (ed.), *Anatomy of Wonder: Science Fiction* (New York: R.R. Bowker Co., 1976); Damon F. Knight, *In Search of Wonder: Essays on Modern Science Fiction* (Chicago: Advent Publishers, 1967); Peter Nicholls, *Science Fiction at Large: a Collection of Essays by Various Hands about the Interface Between Science Fiction and Reality* (New York: Harper & Row, 1976); Thomas Clareson (ed.), *Many Futures, Many Worlds: Theme and Form in Science Fiction* (Kent State University P., 1977); Lois Rose, *The Shattered Ring; Science Fiction and the Quest for Making* (Richmond, Va.: John Knox Press, 1970); Thomas D. Clareson (comp.), *Science Fiction: The Other*

Side of Realism: Essays on Modern Fantasy and Science Fiction (Bowling Green University Popular Press, 1971); Reginald Bretnor, *Science Fiction: Today and Tomorrow; a Discursive Symposium by Ben Bova and Others* (New York: Harper and Row, 1974); Nicholas P. Smith, *Thought Probes: an Introduction to Philosophy Thru Science Fiction* (Nelson-Hall, n.d.), Damon Knight (ed.), *Turning Points: Essays on the Art of Science Fiction* (New York, 1977).

But the study we wish to single out as most relevant to our theme in this chapter is Harold L. Berger, *Science Fiction and the New Dark Age* (Bowling Green University Popular Press, 1976), which touches on the dystopian themes we have discussed.

The reader might also want to read the collection of short stories gathered by Martin Harry Greenberg and Patricia S. Warrick (eds.), *Political Science Fiction: An Introductory Reader* (Prentice-Hall, 1974).

Conclusion
Popular Culture and the American Political Future

On March 30th, 1981, a young man named John Warnock Hinckley, Jr., shot President Reagan and three other people. This incident dramatized many of the things we have talked about in this book. The young man was a Westerner, and deeply involved with the gun culture. Apparently he was motivated by a pathological attachment to actress Jodie Foster, and reportedly wrote love letters to her, including the line, "If you don't love me, I'm going to kill the President." In a bizarre mimicry of one of Ms. Foster's movies, *Taxi Driver,* in which Robert DeNiro buys guns, stalks a political figure, and kills people connected with Foster, Hinckley apparently tried to act out something of the plot. The President, himself a figure from the world of popular culture, acted with the aplomb we associate with the Western sheriff who is wounded but unruffled. The news media carried the incident in continuing coverage to a large popular audience used to mass-mediated violence, and indeed much mass reaction seemed to include a kind of resignation about the recurrence of American violence. Popular events such as the NCAA basketball final and Hollywood's Academy Awards gala were affected by the shooting. Popular religious figures such as Jerry Falwell announced they were leading prayer vigils for the President. Popular editorial writers once again attacked the widespread depiction of violence in popular culture, which they claimed contributes to such violent attacks in real life. Propagandists went to work assuring everyone that the government still functioned. News of the shooting was immediately transmitted around the world by the media. The site of the shooting became an attraction for tourists. In a diversity of ways, popular culture was involved in a major political incident.[1]

This incident raised again the complex question of the importance of popular culture for political thinking and acting. Although most of us do not attempt to assassinate Presidents, nevertheless we should reflect on the fact that we are not all that different from Hinckley, and like him, we get a lot of what we know about politics from popular culture. That is what this book has been about. It is now up to the reader to try to use this knowledge for self-knowledge, i.e., how he or she is affected in their political views and actions by the popular culture which pervades our everyday lives.

The Reagan shooting also reminds us of the extent to which politics *is* popular culture, an activity that occurs in the mosaic of a popular society. Politics is a creature of popular culture. Most of us probably do not separate the play-worlds of popular culture and politics all that sharply in our minds. Politicians themselves are creatures of popular culture, and they bring to politics conceptions drawn from popular culture. Politics bends to the necessities — the "popular logic" — of our popular culture. By the end of this century, when today's students will be the politicians, the "popculture-ization" of politics will be complete. What that historical process augurs for American politics, we can only guess. But let us try.

The future of the Dream

This book has tried to stick to a theme: that popular culture both shapes and reflects the American Dream, and that the Dream, in its contradictions and tensions, is central to American politics. The story of America is a story of the quest for the completion of that Dream, and our political conflicts are conflicts over what the Dream means. The play of both popular culture and politics involves symbolic realities wherein we can see the Dream enacted. As times change, so too does the popular and political treatment of the Dream. Yet it endures as the central cultural and political myth which binds and divides us as a people.

But the furious pace of contemporary history suggests that the Dream will go through transformations in the future. As the science-fiction writers know, the future will be different from our past and present. In our lifetimes, we can expect vast technological, cultural, and political change. The futurists now speak of America as a "post-industrial" society, characterized by high technology, intense consumption, widespread leisure and permissiveness, fluid family structure, and of course the proliferation of popular culture. As things change, the American Dream is put to the test. For example, if we are in for a future of material scarcity, then the materialistic aspect of the myth brings new tensions. In 1980, voters rejected Carter's pessimistic and moral call for energy conservation for Reagan's more upbeat and optimistic picture of the energy future. Certainly too, the television picture of material affluence and the commercial call for us to consume reinforces our material faith. But if the reality of the future "disconfirms" the myth, then we can expect both popular and political tensions.

Too, our moral future will be a subject of treatment in both popular culture and popular politics. Certainly the distribution of material wealth and privilege in an age of scarcity will activate treatment of the morality of inequality. But if our future popular culture includes widespread activities which moralists find objectionable, then we can expect political conflicts over mass tastes and pleasures. Popular culture will continue to be controversial as to its effect on the American moral character, and moralists will attempt to control or ban popular activities. But the popular culture of a free society is difficult to stop. Nevertheless, since the Dream includes a moral vision, how popular culture treats that vision, and how it affects those of us who use it, will continue to generate political conflicts.

We may also expect that popular culture will be an increasingly important factor in political learning. The America of the future may be a period when the influence of family and school as sources of political socialization may decline in importance. If we will spend more time playing with popular culture, and also value what is communicated by popular culture more than family or school, then it is likely that we will learn more about politics through it. For many of us, of course, family and school will still be important, but popular culture will become a more important "validator" of what we want to believe. It may well be that there will be an increase in the number of Americans who will learn the bulk of what they know and value about politics through popular culture. These people's expectations and evaluations of politics will be a function of their popular experience. In that case, we are left with the question as to whether they are imagining a mythical or a real world. For these people, the symbolic realities of popular culture and politics have converged.

How American politics will adjust to this will be important. Politicians who understand the popularization of politics will attempt, no doubt, to use the popular fads, fashions, and language of the moment for political purposes. More importantly, they will try to "read" popular trends to get some idea of the mood of the time. For popular culture will remain a repository of the popular consciousness, and politicians would be wise to interpret and exploit its rhythms. Perhaps too we can expect politicians to be increasingly recruited from popular culture — Hollywood, sports, religion, news, or whatever popular activity that can create celebrity. Celebrities may become for us more adequate bearers of the Dream, play-figures who represent in a play-world values we want to see played.

If popular culture makes us different people in the future, then, we may expect that politics will be different. This is not to say that it will be better or worse. Since America is the first society with a universal and virtually unfettered popular culture, we have no precedents to tell us what the historical outcome might be. But we do think now that popular culture is not without effect, and for some it is not harmless. We do believe the impact of popular culture in the future will be greater. But as to how it will affect the politics of 2001, we will just have to wait and see.

The future search for identity

Since the Dream is unfinished, we are unfinished. In the future, we will all grapple with the unending quest for an American identity, the personal component of the Dream. Popular culture will play a large role in our self-definition, including our political identity. If the world of the future changes as rapidly as many experts predict, then we will all probably experience confusions, ambivalences, and doubts about who we are and what we should do. It is likely that popular culture will both shape and reflect these identity crises. Popular culture will continue to be popular because it will treat, or sometimes be an escape from, our anxieties about ourselves and the world. If politics change as much as the rest of the world, and it is likely to, then we may seek in popular culture learning about who we are politically and what the political world is like.

We will seek those cues because we will be marginal people caught between two ages. As the world we have inherited wanes, and the world of tomorrow waxes, we can expect that we will be uncertain as to who we are and what is going on. As Huizinga understood with the "waning of the Middle Ages," living in such an era sends people to play to attempt to redefine who they are.[2] So it should not surprise us that we now play alternatively with themes of death and decay (in, for example, movies about disaster, possession and horror, evil at the top), and themes of life, vitality, and innocence (sex, youth, family movies). As science fiction suggests, we sense the future to be both a threat and a promise. Our marginality will mean that many of us will cling to old myths — the Dream — treated in new popular creations that place them in our new reality, but that some of us will seek new myths in cults, ideologies, and leaders. Some others of us, unable to come to grips with change, will experience the disintegration of identity in drugs, insanity, and anomie. One may wonder if John Hinckley is one of those — a young person unable to come to grips with himself and the world, so he retreats into a play-fantasy with an actress, and decides to "impress" her by play-acting assassin.

If we are marginal men and women caught in a world of change, then our identities may be said to be *Protean*.[3] Like the god Proteus who could change shapes at will, we sense the uncertainty of our identity and search for roots, values, permanent relationships. We feel historically dislocated, part of a world we never made which changes with increasing rapidity. We feel "sensory overload," flooded with ideas and imagery which are overwhelming and confusing. Indeed, popular culture plays a central role in these feelings, with its emphasis on the new and now, and with its massive presence in our lives. Too, the popularization of politics contributes to those feelings. We tire of Presidents as quickly as we do of television programs; we find it difficult to commit ourselves to a party of ideology; we feel cut off from political roots; we are deeply uncertain about the fate of ourselves and the Dream. Our political identity is Protean. We are no longer sure of our political selves and our relationship to the Dream.

Popular culture is often accused of being the chief cause of these changes in us. Our infatuation with popular culture, it is argued, has deteriorated our ability to read, write, and think critically; has shortened our attention span; makes us impatient with deferred gratification; orients us toward immediate, hedonistic gratification; makes us insensitive to suffering and horror; makes us expect to be constantly entertained; and so on. If these are widespread traits in us now, then popular culture may indeed have detrimental effects. There are, of course, many other forces at work. But certainly all of these traits represent the confusion that Protean people would feel, and popular culture may contribute to those feelings. Surely popular culture does at least reflect the frustration and fragmentation many of us feel. If contemporary popular culture includes the outrageous, bizarre, antisocial, nostalgic, violent, sensational, and so forth, this is because a lot of people play with those feelings.

The will to believe

If it is true that we are having a political identity crisis, then we may suggest that it will not last. People want to believe; they cannot drift forever anxiety-ridden and valueless. We want to replace our ambivalence with certainty. The myth of the Dream is still imbedded deep in our consciousness, and we would like to see political vindication of it. But since we are caught between two ages, we want to go back but we want to go forward, too. Popular culture reflects our tension: we have deep nostalgia for the past, but are also deeply fascinated by the prospect of the future. We want the world restored, but also transformed. We play with popular culture to orient ourselves both toward a mythical past and a mythical future. We play with popular politicians who promise us restoration *and* transformation, that the Dream works both in our past and in our future. We want to both recreate and create a political reality and identity to our liking.

But the objective facts of contemporary historical process may widen the gap between the American myth and political reality. This may not lessen, but rather will intensify, our will to believe.[4] We will seek both popular culture and politics that will offer us political identity. Both popular culture and politics offer us heroes who act for us in a heroic quest to realize the Dream. If both of these areas are becoming play-worlds for us, perhaps in the future we will identify with and follow popular heroes who promise us restoration and transformation. We may seek a popular culture and a politics that offers us certainty and prophecy, restoring the American Dream in both the past and the future. If we are all now creatures of popular culture, maybe we won't let the chilly facts of recalcitrant political reality interfere with our enjoyment of the political show, simply because we want to believe so much.

American popular culture has been hitherto a product of a free society. Thus, its treatment of the American Dream and politics has been both positive and negative, dealing with the complexities of what America is all about. But perhaps our contemporary malaise will make us demand a popular culture and a politics that is all positive, that avoids the conflicts and failures of the Dream. Perhaps we will seek and find a popular political hero who will enforce the Dream in both popular culture and politics, reassuring us in the face of disconfirming reality that the Dream still lives. In that case, we will not be very far from the totalitarian logic of 1984.

The demonic temptation

The collective will to believe can lead to "true belief," fanatical devotion to mythic reaffirmation.[5] The frustrations and fears created by historical trends impels people to seek desperately simple and "total" solutions. They become intolerant of the gap between myth and reality, and those that deny the promise of the myth. They seek to create the moral and material community by enforcement, denying all messages that are not affirming. In such a way, the Dream is symbolically realized, satisfying belief and suppressing doubt.

Such a heroic quest, however, is *demonic*.[6] Heroes come to represent for people leadership in realizing the Dream, and their desperation frees the hero from moderation, compromise, and ethics. He or she comes to be "beyond good and evil" because of the magnitude of the quest. A demonic redeemer is a charismatic figure who personifies the fanatical will to believe. He augurs a political drama of high mythic import, beyond the ordinary quibbles of mainstream politics. Neither he nor his followers of course think of him and their quest as demonic. It is demonic in the sense that they bring evil fruits. By abandoning democratic values and civility, they have invoked a power over other people that is evil. They have asserted the power of a political genius to magically realize for them the Dream. In that sense they are "possessed" with an "evil spirit." They have invoked what the Old Testament Hebrews called "the lawless." They have turned to the evil use of power in order to save the American Dream. They have burned the American village in order to save it.

The heroic quest of a demonic redeemer is epic in scope. His charismatic "gift of grace" is invoked to justify personal rule as the personification of the epic quest. The epic drama is more than symbolic. It follows a familiar pattern. First, the redeemer figure calls for communal *integration*. The community is urged to unify, to integrate everyone who is a "true" American into a solidified and reaffirming tribe. The call for demonic integration leads to the *identification* of enemies — those different, critical, or sinful. Because of their guilt in denying the Dream, they must be punished. The integrated community through the redeemer-figure calls for *victimage*. The victim is always guilty, and therefore must suffer. The victim is a scapegoat which the community must sacrifice to *purge* itself of its alien elements and collective guilt. Purgation perfects the community. The leader's heroism has thus brought communal *redemption* through a retributive quest. The *salvation* of the community is assured.[7] The Dream is now to be realized.

Such a quest is drenched in blood. And the quest is never really completed. The intoxication of power that it creates is turned on itself. Demonic redemption, like revolution, devours its own children. The redeemer cannot return to ordinary politics. Nor can he relinquish the power concentrated in him, since he believes himself to be the representation of a higher truth. His demonic power is thus visited on those that created him. Armed with the rightness of the cultural quest, and with the technological and organizational power of a now totalitarian State, the conditions for an Orwellian world of 1984 have been created. Absolute power has corrupted absolutely. Power has become the demon that the will to believe has conjured up out of Hell, and is used to create a Hell in the name of a Heaven.

We are familiar with precedents of the drama of demonic redemption. The quests of Hitler, Stalin, and Mao are the most obvious political examples. Such quests are also common to myth, fairy tale, and literature. One thinks of Dostovsky's "Grand Inquisitor," Melville's Captain Ahab, Conrad's Kurtz, O'Neill's Emperor Jones, Camus's Caligula. In recent times, we have been horrified and fascinated by such figures as Charles Manson, Jim Jones, and "Cinque" of the Symbionese Liberation Army.

The demonic temptation stems from the popular fascination with power. The eternal popular fascination with Hitler is an example of this. The popular literature and movies about Hitler is endless, to the point of fantasizing about clone-children (*The Boys from Brazil*) being created to carry on his demonic quest.[8] This fascination with evil power suggests that we play with the idea of creating it here in America and becoming part of it. It relieves us of responsibility, makes us part of a grand drama, lets us vent our emotional wrath on those we hate and fear, satisfies our mythic anxieties. The spectacle is so exhilarating that we will risk destruction to see it. In our heart of hearts, do we *want* 1984?

This is a large speculation, but it should remind us that the demonic is a large theme in our popular culture. We have cheered the demonic quest of vigilante figures who take lawless vengeance on those that torment them. We have been fascinated by fictional demonic figures — Ming the Merciless, Fu Manchu, Ernst Stavro Blofeld of the James Bond novels, Don Vito Corleone. We played with demonic figures straight from Hell itself — Rosemary's baby, a child fathered by Satan; a girl possessed by a devil in *The Exorcist;* and the baby of *The Omen,* who is no less than the AntiChrist. If we were not tempted by the demonic alternative, then why the popular fascination?

It is as if we were no longer satisfied with nice political Dr. Jeckylls and seek instead a more elemental and violent Mr. Hyde. The demonic temptation augurs an ensuing struggle for the American soul. A recent report by a national public-opinion firm concluded that "our society is at a transition point and that the public may be willing, under almost imperceptible influences, to throw its entire weight behind a leader who strikes the correct 'moral' or 'reaffirming' tone . . . [T]his suggests the opportunity for a truly visionary leader, or a dangerous demagogue, who, by striking the appropriate religious-moral notes, could be swept into a position of awesome power."[9] Whether Americans will succumb to the demonic temptation remains to be seen. Perhaps our popular culture, by glorifying the role of the demonic redeemer, will aid the public temptation. On the other hand, if our popular culture dramatizes the evil fruits of demonic power, perhaps it will aid us in resisting such a destructive temptation.

Self-knowledge and political competence

This book has been a study of public opinion, concerned with one major source of our political knowledge. We have argued that the play-world of popular culture is an important agency of political socialization. It affects our identity as an individual and political being. We argued that the American Dream is the central myth in popular culture, and that the learning we get from it affects our attitude toward the Dream. This play-learning has political consequences. Popular culture helps us to think and act as we do in politics.

The reader now has gained knowledge about one of the major cultural forces that affect his or her life. Such self-knowledge should make us more aware of this cultural influence, and therefore more "rational." If it is true that we all seek to become more socially and politically competent, then the knowledge gained here should make us all more intelligent and critical. For we should never forget that popular culture is, after all, a world of play, and the play world is not the real world. We may experience popular culture and politics as play, but that is a mythic and mediated play-world and not the real-world that exists "out there" in actuality. Thus, knowledge gained from popular culture about politics will not make us politically competent. We must always remind ourselves that beyond the world of fantasy is the world of fact, which is difficult to know, disconfirms our myths, and is vast and frightening. The real world of politics does not inherently conform to our ideas and images about it. We are reminded of the enduring figure of Niccolo Machiavelli, who understood the extent to which we are prisoners of our illusions. It is the beginning of political wisdom, and competence, for us to face hard political facts, and thereby achieve that level of self-knowledge which is the essence of education and citizenship. Once we realize that much of what we know about politics is illusory, we can never see the sources of those illusions in quite the same way. Popular culture takes on a very different aspect for us when we realize that it is teaching and shaping us. Politics doesn't seem the same to us when we realize that it is not the same as our illusions about it. Such self-knowledge leads us to Socratic doubt, but that condition is a preface not only to political competence but also to political maturity.

Notes

[1]Robert Jewett and John Shelton Lawrence, "Hinckley's 'Werther Effect' Fantasy," Des Moines *Register,* April 3, 1981.

[2]Johann Huizinga, *The Waning of the Middle Ages* (London, 1924).

[3]Robert Jay Lifton, "Protean Man" in Michael Weinstein (ed.), *The Political Experience* (St. Martin's Press, 1972), pp. 68-79.

[4]William James, "The Will to Believe," in *Essays in Pragmatism* (Hafner, 1969), pp. 88-109.

[5]Eric Hoffer, *The True Believer* (Perennial Library, 1966); Erich Fromm, *Escape from Freedom* (Avon, 1965).

[6]Ernest Becker, "Bunuel and the Demonic," in *Angel in Armor* (George Braziller, 1969), pp. 101-118; Robert Jewett and John Shelton Lawrence, *The American Monomyth* (Anchor Doubleday, 1977), pp. 210-216; James Combs and Dan Nimmo, *Subliminal Politics* (Prentice-Hall, 1980), pp. 242-243; Lionel Rubinoff, *The Pornography of Power* (Ballantine, 1969).

[7]This is a variation of Kenneth Burke's dramatism. See Hugh D. Duncan, *Symbols in Society* (Oxford University P., 1968); Jerry Washington, "The Politics of Cowboy Culture: An Inquiry," paper delivered at the 9th annual convention of the Popular Culture Association, April 25-28, 1979, pp. 23-28; see too Ernest Becker, "The Nature of Social Evil," in *Escape from Evil* (The Free Press, 1975), pp. 96-127.

[8]Donald M. McKale, "Hitler's Children: A Study of Postwar Mythology," paper delivered at the 10th annual convention of the Popular Culture Association, 1980, forthcoming in the *Journal of American Culture,* 1981; for a study of the demonic drama of Hitler, see Bill Kinser and Neil Kleinman, *The Dream That Was No More a Dream: A Search for Aesthetic Reality in Germany, 1880-1945* (Harper Colophon, 1969).

[9]National opinion poll report, *Research and Forecasts, Inc.,* for Connecticut Mutual Life Insurance Company, quoted by David S. Broder, "America's Values: Religious Minority Reshaping Opinion" reprinted in *TODAY* (April 17, 1981) (King's Court Communications, Inc.), p. 11.

Appendix

Studying popular culture is both easy and hard. It is easy because the available data literally surrounds us daily. It is hard because it requires careful interpretation as to what it means. Nevertheless, the instructor or interested student can use popular culture as a mode of analysis. Here we just want to make some suggestions as to the best and most fruitful way to analyze popular culture.

First, perish the thought that studying popular culture is *frivolous*. If there is any idea we have tried to hammer home in this book, it is that popular culture is meaningful, and thus studying television shows, rock lyrics, or demolition derbies tells us something about the way Americans play and therefore something about how they think and act. The trick is to interpret popular culture correctly to find out what is significant about it. For that reason, the wise student will have read widely in the literature of popular culture for insights into how good research is done.

Second, the popular researcher has to select a *perspective*. This means that one has to be aware of theories and concepts available, and select the ones that seem to make the most sense to use in interpretation. Here we have tried to interpret popular culture as politically meaningful because people learn from it mythic messages about the status of the American Dream. But that is not the only way to interpret popular culture, as familiarity with the literature will reveal. The "approaches" are varied — Freudian, Jungian, aesthetic and critical, sociological, historical, Marxist, institutional, comparative, and so on. There is no one "right" way to interpret popular culture, and likely will never be. So the researcher is on his own, although the precedents of perspectives that seem insightful and "work" are the best guideline.

Thirdly, research is more than just gathering data, so one has to be *methodical*. Again, familiarity with previous work will give ideas about the choices of methods. Methods can range from simply selecting a case and gathering information about it through library research to sophisticated quantitative methods. Case studies are fine, but be aware that one case may illustrate and not validate a point. It is often wise to compare cases, since they offer evidence that one may contrast. Comparing, say, themes and images of a type of movie made in the 1930s and the 1980s offers a way to see continuities and contrasts which reveal something about the popular "mood" of those two decades. One of the most useful quantitative methods, relatively easy to grasp and use, is content analysis. Armed with a video tape or cassette recorder, the researcher can then study television ads, dramas, news, game shows, soaps, and movies.

It is also essential that the popular research define the *focus* of the topic well. Is it macrocosmic or microcosmic? What is to be studied? Values, climate of opinion, social roots, history and development, and just what? What is it that you are observing? If you decide to study soap operas, what do you hope to find? In a sense, what you can observe in the popular world around you is infinite. Thus, you have to select what it is that you want to observe. The soap, for example, can be observed for the clash of values, socio-economic status, sexual depictions, how minorities are portrayed, aesthetic quality (or lack of it), and so on. The wise researcher is clear about what she is studying, how much and how long it will be studied, and what can be done with what is observed. You can't study everything, so select what you can study with care.

Most of the best popular studies demonstrate considerable *ingenuity*. Use your imagination. Study your friends. If you're interested in celebrity, give them a questionnaire about who they admire. Study children about what they learn from popular culture. Study the popular habits of your family. Is television viewing a ritual? Why? If you dare, study yourself. A self-study as to what you have learned from popular culture is educative. Write a "pop biography" about yourself. How much are you a product of popular culture? Why are your popular tastes the way they are? Keep a notebook of observations and thoughts about the popular culture you see in everyday life.

One wise strategy in studying popular culture is to study what's *available*. Your library, school, or whatever may not have certain things, but may have others. Browse, ask, discover. If, say, you discover that the library has a good collection of women's magazines, a complete set of Horatio Alger novels, a library of films, a donated set of books on food, or whatever, you're in business. Your roommate's father may have a vast collection of political campaign memorabilia. The guy down the hall may be a sci-fi freak. Seek, and ye shall find.

Studying popular culture does involve *risks*. Once you start looking at it critically, you probably can never look at it the way you once did. It takes on a new aspect. Every movie, television show, record, and so forth acquire a new meaning and significance for you. You become self-conscious of the fact that it affects you and those around you. You begin to see the covert cultural messages inbedded in it. You acquire the ability to discriminate good and bad popular culture. You are aware of its cultural and institutional roots. It becomes a little more scary, but also more understandable. But then, all education involves such risks.

We should also mention that the Big Questions about popular culture have in no sense been answered. This book has taken a position, but not everyone agrees with it, and can provide good reasons not to. Does popular culture really have the power that we have attributed to it? Or is it really harmless diversion? Does it rot the brain, or does it just go in one ear and out the other? Does it keep us quiescent and alienated, diverting us from understanding ourselves and our society? How distorted or ambiguous is the mirror that popular culture holds up to society? Are we "overinterpreting" popular culture? Perhaps among the readers of this book are those who in the future will tackle again, and even give better answers for, the question of popular culture.

Additional Bibliography

In studying popular culture, look at classic studies, such as some of the ones we have used above. The following also deserve attention: A.L. Kroeber, "On the Principle of Order in Civilization as Exemplified by Changes in Fashion," *American Anthropologist,* Vol. 13 (1919), pp. 235-263; Bernard Wolfe, "Uncle Remus and the Malevolent Rabbit," *Commentary* (July 1949), pp. 31-41; Paul M. Mirsch, "Processing Fads and Fashion: An Organization-set Analysis of Cultural Industry Systems," *American Journal of Sociology* (January 1972), pp. 639-659. A classic comparative piece is Donald V. McGranahan and Ivor Wayne, "German and American Traits Reflected in Popular Drama," *Human Relations,* Vol. I (1948), pp. 429-455. Classic interpretations of film are Hugo Munsterberg, *The Film: A Psychological Study* (Dover, 1969) and Siegfried Kracauer, *From Caligari to Hitler: A Psychological History of the German Film* (Princeton University P., 1947). See too Kracauer's "National Types as Hollywood Presents Them," *Public Opinion Quarterly,* Vol. 13 (1949), pp. 53-72. An excellent interpretation of everybody's favorite movie is by Umberto Eco, "Casablanca: The Archetypes Hold a Reunion," *Decade,* premier issue (1978), pp. 19-21. The essays of Tom Wolfe gave great impetus to pop culture studies. See especially his *The Kandy-Kolored Tangerine-Flake Streamline Baby* (Pocket Books, 1966). A collection that has some good sociological pieces on popular culture is Marcello Truzzi (ed.), *Sociology and Everyday Life* (Prentice-Hall, 1968).

A bibliography useful for popular culture studies is James R. Nesteby, "Theories and Methodologies in American Studies and Popular Culture: A Bibliography," available from Bowling Green State University's Popular Culture Center.

Two useful books on content analysis are William Adams and Fay Schreibman (eds.), *Television Network News: Issues in Content Research* (School of Public and International Affairs, George Washington University 1978), and Bernard S. Greenberg, *Life on Television: Content Analyses of U.S. TV Drama* (Ablex, 1980).

A fruitful concept that could inspire popular culture studies in the future is the concept of fantasy. The idea is that people in groups, exposed to a "rhetorical vision" which they share, jointly participate in a "symbolic drama" conjured up by the group. Popular culture is a major source of such shared visions, and so it might behoove popular culture analysts to utilize this approach in studying how people come to share and use the dramas of popular culture. See John F. Cragan and Donald C. Shields, *Applied Communication Research: A Dramatistic Approach* (Waveland Press, 1981); Ernest G. Bormann, "Fantasy and Rhetorical Vision: The Rhetorical Criticism of Social Reality," *Quarterly Journal of Speech,* Vol. 58 (1972), pp. 396-407.

A work that includes popular culture in its purview is Ken Baynes, *Art in Society* (Overlook Press, 1975). Two recent books on the movies worth examining are Charles Eidsvik, *Cineliteracy* (Random House, 1978), and George Wead and George Lellis, *Film: Form and Function* (Houghton Mifflin, 1981). A good example of what you can do with Freudian analysis of popular culture is Harvey R. Greenberg, *The Movies on Your Mind* (E.P. Dutton, 1975).

The best argument that popular culture is beneficial, or at worst, harmless, is made by Herbert Gans, *Popular Culture and High Culture* (Basic Books, 1974).

There is surprisingly little analysis by futurists on the future of popular culture. Two that do include such speculation are Alvin Toffler, *Future Shock* (Random House, 1970), and Louis B. Lundberg, *Future Without Shock* (Norton, 1975). See also Thomas M. Kando, *Leisure and Popular Culture in Transition* (C.V. Mosby, 1975). An interesting set of essays on the present and future of television is collected in "Television in America," *Wilson Quarterly,* Vol. 5 (Winter 1981), pp. 52-101.

We will conclude the bibliography by mentioning some works which either came to my attention after the manuscript was typed or are incomplete, but which might be of use to the interested reader pursuing various popular culture topics. Dan Nimmo and William Rivers' *Watching American Politics* (Longman, 1981) includes many insights in the popular dimensions of American politics. Two books on stereotyping in the movies are Joan Mellen, *Big Bad Wolves* (Pantheon, 1977) and M. Joyce Baker, *Images of Women in Film, The War Years, 1941-1945* (UMI Research Press). A new book on rock is Geoffrey Stokes, *Star-Making Machinery: Inside the Business of Rock and Roll* (Vintage Books). A history of sci-fi is Lester del Rey, *The World of Science Fiction: 1926-1976, The History of a Subculture* (A Del Rey Book). Two popular critiques of television are Frank Mankiewicz and Joel Swerdlow, *Remote Control: Television and the Manipulation of American Life* (Ballantine) and Rose K. Goldsen, *The Show and Tell Machine: How Television Works and Works You Over* (Delta, 1977). A history of popular newspapers is Michael Schudson, *Discovering the News: A Social History of American Newspapers* (Basic Books, 1978). A new study of cultural diffusion is Armand Mattelart, Multinational Corporations and the *Control of Culture: The Ideological Apparatus of Imperialism* (Harvester Press, 1979). A study of news as storytelling is Robert Darnton, "Writing News and Telling Stories," *Daedalus*, Vol. 104, no. 2 (Spring 1975). See too the study of the depiction of the New Left in the press, Todd Gitlin, *The Whole World is Watching: Mass Media in the Making and Unmaking of the New Left* (University of California Press, 1980). Edward W. Said's *Covering Islam* (Pantheon, 1981) critiques Western press coverage of "Death of a Princess" and the Iranian crisis. More general about the image of the Arab in American popular culture is Edmund Ghareeb (ed.), *Split Vision: Arab Portrayal in the American Media* (Washington: Institute of Middle Eastern and North African Affairs, 1977).

Some useful pieces on popular heroism that have come to my attention are B.A. Rosenberg, "Kennedy in Camelot: The Arthurian Legend in America," *Western Folklore*, Vol. 35 (January 1976), pp. 52-59; S. Mondello, "Spider-Man: Superhero in the Liberal Tradition," *Journal of Popular Culture*, Vol. 10 (Summer 1976), pp. 232-238; A.S. Horton, "Ken Kesey, John Updike, and the Lone Ranger," *Journal of Popular Culture*, Vol. 8 (Winter 1974), pp. 570-578; Richard C. Carpenter, "007 and the Myth of the Hero," *Journal of Popular Culture*, Vol. 1, no. 2 (Fall 1967), pp. 80-89; T.A. Zaniello, "Popular Hero in Contemporary China," *Journal of Popular Culture*, Vol. 1 (Spring 1977) pp. 903-909; P. Zweig, "Hero in Literature," *Saturday Review*, Vol. 5 (December 1978), p. 30; M. Mannes, "What Your Choice of Heroes Reveals about You," *Today's Health*, Vol. 51 (September 1973), pp. 16-19; E.M.R. Ditmas, "Way Legends Grow," *Folklore*, Vol. 85 (Winter 1974), pp. 244-253; J. Wise, "Tugging on Superman's Cape: the Making of a College Legend," *Western Folklore*, Vol. 36 (July 1977), pp. 227-238; J. Olney, "Of Griots and Heroes," *Studies in Black Literature*, Vol. 6 (Spring 1975), pp. 14-17; L.W. Rosefield, "August 9, 1974: the Victimage of Richard Nixon," *Communication Quarterly*, Vol. 24 (Fall 1976), pp. 19-23; N.R. Jones, "Sweetback: the Black Hero and Universal Myth," CLA Journal, Vol. 19, (June 1976), pp. 559-565; S. Edwards, "Political Heroes and Political Education," *North American Review*, Vol. 264 (Spring 1979), pp. 8-13; D. Sirota, "Electronic Minstrel: Toward a New Folklore and Hero," *ETC*, Vol. 35 (September 1978), pp. 302-309; J.W. Sattel, "Heroes on the Right," *Journal of Popular Culture*, Vol. 11 (Summer 1977), pp. 110-125.

An important new volume that touches on various themes is Sam Girgus, *The American Self: Myth, Popular Culture, and the American Ideology* (Albuquerque: University of New Mexico P., 1980). Many other titles in popular culture may be obtained from the leading commercial and university presses that emphasize such works. The leading university press in this field is the University of Illinois Press, but others, such as the University of Indiana Press and University of Oklahoma Press, are active also. The commercial presses one should write for catalogs also are Ablex, Beacon Press, Macmillan, Methuen, Nelson Hall, Vintage and Ballantine Books, Greenwood Press, and of course Bowling Green's Popular Press, with its wide assortment of titles. The Popular Culture Center at Bowling Green State University has a wide collection of popular materials students of popular culture can use, and the department offers graduate programs in popular culture. Membership in the Popular Culture Association will put one in touch with other scholars and bibliography. There are many conferences and conventions which touch on popular subjects. The niversity of Wyoming American Studies Conferences, held annually, deal with the merican West. The Humanities Department at Michigan State University hosts an annual International Conference on Television Drama. There are many associations and journals which specialize in the study of sports, religion, the media, and so on.